T0295849

Meritocracy, Growth, and Lessons from Italy's Economic Decline

Meritocracy, Growth, and Lessons from Italy's Economic Decline

Lobbies (and Ideologies) Against Competition and Talent

Lorenzo Codogno
Giampaolo Galli

OXFORD
UNIVERSITY PRESS

OXFORD
UNIVERSITY PRESS

Great Clarendon Street, Oxford, OX2 6DP,
United Kingdom

Oxford University Press is a department of the University of Oxford.
It furthers the University's objective of excellence in research, scholarship,
and education by publishing worldwide. Oxford is a registered trade mark of
Oxford University Press in the UK and in certain other countries

© Lorenzo Codogno and Giampaolo Galli 2022

The moral rights of the authors have been asserted

Impression: 1

Published in the United States of America by Oxford University Press
198 Madison Avenue, New York, NY 10016, United States of America

British Library Cataloguing in Publication Data
Data available

Library of Congress Control Number: 2022933182

ISBN 978–0–19–286680–6

DOI: 10.1093/oso/9780192866806.001.0001

Printed and bound by
CPI Group (UK) Ltd, Croydon, CR0 4YY

Preface

Looking at the table of contents, this book appears more ambitious than it actually is. True, the book scans many aspects of Italian political, social, and economic life, and the reader might find some of the topics of interest for their own sake. But our intention was not to write an encyclopaedia of Italy or of the Italian economy. We wanted to convey some fundamental messages. The key one concerns the importance of merit and meritocracy for economic growth, especially in today's international scenario. Related messages are that GDP growth is essential, despite burgeoning literature against it, and that merit has important moral dimensions. A society based on connections, nepotism, and patronage—the opposite of merit—cannot be a 'free society'. In any case, it is far away from any reasonable notion of equality of opportunity. The moral standards of institutions are typically high when hirings and promotions are based on merit. When people perceive that they are based on patronage, inside or—worse—outside the institution, moral standards are bound to collapse. The sense of identification of employees with their institution and its very efficiency are equally bound to suffer.

These are the concepts that we have touched on many times in our professional life and want to convey to our sons and daughters, our students, and their peers. The hope is that the book will help them build a better country than the one that our generation has left them.

Since this is not an encyclopaedia and we are aware of our limitations, in every chapter in the book we tell the reader what to read in order to expand her/his learning. There are many books on Italy or various aspects of Italy, written in English. But here, we want to cite just two. One is the *Oxford Handbook of the Italian Economy since Unification*, edited by Gianni Toniolo and published in 2013. The opening article by the editor ("An Overview of Italy's Growth") goes a long way to explain the historical roots of today's Italian problems. With Gianni Toniolo and several of his co-authors, we have shared ideas and experiences for many decades; so the reader should not be surprised to find several similarities between the two books.

The other book is *Good Italy, Bad Italy* by Bill Emmott (2013) which recognised the lack of meritocracy as one of Italy's key problems:

The greatest asset of Italy, it is often said, is the Italians themselves, with their spirit of initiative, of inventiveness, of building relationships with one another. That asset, however, doesn't just develop on its own. Training, education and technology all build it and provide it with opportunities to flourish. Most of all, however, what has been lacking has been a spirit and practice of meritocracy: ability and top-class performance have neither been valued nor rewarded, especially in the universities.

We couldn't agree more. We are glad that a very acute non-Italian observer sees the same problems that we see. However, our book is different from Emmott's. It is perhaps less easy to read, and a bit more engaging. We have tried to illustrate our statements with analytical tools, more than through anecdotes. In addition, we have tried to draw out some general lessons about the merits of meritocracy.

Some early readers of our manuscript have encouraged us to be more explicit about what we think about the much-debated issue of market versus state. It is a theme that is treated in a somewhat fragmented way in the book. Putting the pieces together, we say that "As it has developed in almost all European countries in recent decades, the welfare state is an achievement of civilisation." However, the very concept of meritocracy is inextricably linked with the notion of open competition in the market. Merit can and should also be applied in public administration, but it has its historical roots in market competition; merit has been the bread and butter of western prosperity. Meritocratic values can prosper only if there are free markets. All attempts to introduce merit and competition in planned economies have failed as was the case, for instance, for what was called 'socialist emulation', introduced in the USSR soon after the October Revolution. In line with these general ideas, we dare to write a few clear lines.

Failure to deliver on growth and prosperity can happen when, for some reason, a large number of actors in a relatively affluent society are no longer willing to go through the efforts and the sacrifices that have made it possible to achieve well-being. Instead, they look for other supposedly easier means to reach further prosperity. The demand for more state subsidies, privileges, and protection from competition, which is the main role of lobbies, tends to substitute hard work, ingenuity, entrepreneurship, risk-taking; in a single word, merit.

We also add that in Italy, 'ideas and practices have spread, especially since the 1970s, which have frustrated competition between companies and people in the name of a misunderstood concept of egalitarianism. Italy has moved from the right idea that there should be solidarity to a practice that ends up punishing rather than rewarding the merit and creativity of individuals and communities'.

Finally, we do say in the book that so-called neoliberal policies were never a reality in Italy, despite much literature condemning the timid—and quite useful—liberalisation of the 1990s. As we say in Chapter 2,

> [L]iberalisation [of the 1990s] was only partial, and the labour market was still very rigid. . . . To have a Tony Blair requires to have had a Margaret Thatcher. Italy had neither a Thatcher nor a Blair, although several centre-left leaders sympathised with the latter. Some literature and narrative argue that liberalisation went too far, and in the UK, workers' rights were compressed too much. Perhaps this is what happened in that country, but for sure, not in Italy.
>
> L.C. and G.G.

Acknowledgements

To Paola, *per tutto*; to Silvia, Gabriele, Michele, and Elisabetta (G.G.),
to Alessandro, Vittorio, and Gloria (L.C.)
for whom we have undertaken this endeavour
with the hope that it can help them to build
a better Italy than the one that our thoughtless
generation has left to them.

Many people have contributed to the development of this book. We thank Silvia for having stimulated us to find proofs and make our statements less subjective, though not as rigorous as those she is used to in astrophysics. We are grateful to Gabriele and Michele for having given us the type of useful comments that we can expect from managers who know the economy but are not professional economists. We thank Alessandro and Vittorio for having carved some time from their studies for reading it, and Gloria, for having provided a fresh non-economic viewpoint.

We want to convey our gratitude to the friends who have read, and sometimes harshly criticised, preliminary versions of the various chapters. In particular, we want to thank Iain Begg, Sabino Cassese, Stefan Collignon, Carlo Cottarelli, Natale D'Amico, Paul De Grauwe, Jørgen Elmeskov, Kevin Featherstone, Andrea Gavosto, Daniel Gros, Stefano Micossi, Alberto Mingardi, Carlos Martinez Mongay, Paola Parascandolo, Stefano Scarpetta, Paolo Sestito, Philipp Steinberg, Zeno Tentella, and Paul van den Noord for useful exchanges of views.

We also want to thank Luca Brugnara, Luca Favero, Luca Gerotto, Giulio Gottardo, Salvatore Liaci, Ivo Maes, Giorgio Musso, and Giacomo Ricciardi for having carefully read and commented on specific chapters.

Obviously, any remaining mistakes are exclusively our responsibility. We very much hope that the need to summarise and simplify many complex themes has not come at the expense of technical precision and proper balance.

This work builds on our lifetime experience in Italy and abroad, as well as our writings on Italy's problems through several decades. This means that we owe much to many persons with whom we have interacted.

G.G. would like to express gratitude to his economics teachers, in particular Franco Modigliani and Rudi Dornbusch, whom he greatly misses, and Robert Solow; to many colleagues and senior managers at the Bank of Italy, who have been the most careful observers and critics of Italian developments throughout several decades; to the many colleagues and managers of Ania and Confindustria for having broadened his horizons from the standpoint of the various facets of the private sector. Enrico Letta and Pierluigi Bersani deserve mention for the rather bold decision to bet on an independent, non-partisan economist in a highly challenging political environment. This book owes much to Carlo Cottarelli and his indefatigable work at the Observatory of Italian Public Accounts, a research team at the Università Cattolica del Sacro Cuore.

L.C. would like to thank the many friends and former colleagues at Bank of America, and the Ministry of Economy and Finance, with whom he has interacted regularly and exchanged treasured views on Italy and other countries over many years. A special thanks to the various Ministers of Economy and Finance. Also, gratitude goes to colleagues from the Economic and Financial Committee, and more broadly from the Ecofin network of economists from EU ministries of finance, the European Commission, and OECD for the exchange of views and peer discussions on many themes related to EU countries, economic growth, and structural reforms. He would also like to thank colleagues at the London School of Economics, and more recently, the College of Europe, for having allowed him to be part of a stimulating and competent group of thinkers, researchers, and opinion leaders.

The authors are very grateful to Adam Swallow, editor of Oxford University Press, for having believed in the project and given them some valuable clues on how to submit and defend their proposal. Several anonymous referees have also provided much appreciated and insightful comments.

Contents

List of Figures

List of Tables

Introduction

Why a book in English on Italy's decline?

> *Unfortunately, now I realise that I live in a very different country from the one I was dreaming of in my youth. So lately I have started to use the expression: the slaughter of illusions.*[1]
>
> **Carlo Azeglio Ciampi**

This book is a reflection on Italy's economic decline, written by two economists who share the same sentiment of deep disillusionment expressed in this sentence by Carlo Azeglio Ciampi, President of the Italian Republic from 1999 to 2006, but who also have some hopes.

A hint about the origin of the decline was given to us by Franco Modigliani, a former Professor at the Massachusetts Institute of Technology (MIT) and 1985 Nobel Prize winner in Economics and a friend of Ciampi. Modigliani had left Italy in 1939 to escape the racial laws of Mussolini. In his memoirs, he wrote:

> In 1955, I returned to Italy as a lecturer. My negative impression was very strong. I had forgotten how deep were the differences between the education system in the US and Italy. The Italian system was a structure with three castes, in which very few, usually old, professors occupied the top caste and were immediately under God; a large group of hopeful and servile assistants were the intermediate caste; finally, the students, of whom nobody cared, were the base of the pyramid. This is the deep origin of the Italian crisis because a leadership that has been selected on the basis of its ability to accept humiliation and forgo self-respect cannot rule Italy.[2]

We believe that Modigliani was essentially right. Many things have changed since 1955. However, what he said is still valid to a large extent and is at the origin of the present Italian disease: too often and in many different sectors of society, leadership is not selected based on merit but is co-opted based on loyalty to some powerful person, be it a boss, a university baron, a banker, an entrepreneur, or a politician. This mechanism nourishes and is defended

---

[1] Ciampi-Orioli (2011); authors' translation.
[2] Modigliani-Peluffo (1999).

Meritocracy, Growth, and Lessons from Italy's Economic Decline. Lorenzo Codogno and Giampaolo Galli, Oxford University Press. © Lorenzo Codogno and Giampaolo Galli (2022). DOI: 10.1093/oso/9780192866806.003.0001

by vested interests and lobbies in many different corners of society and the economy.

The book is written in English because studying Italy's case might be helpful to many other countries. Italy was the country of the economic miracle after World War II (WWII), and it is still an advanced economy and a member of the G7 club. According to the International Monetary Fund (IMF), it is the eighth largest economy in the world. Until the 1960s, it seemed destined to catch up with the best-performing countries.[3] Until the mid-1990s, it managed to grow like its peers. Then, the growth engine stopped.

The failure to deliver on economic growth over the past decades is spectacular by any country's standards. In 2019, before the Covid-19 crisis, Italy's real GDP per capita was about the same as in 1999; no growth in twenty years. Relative to 1995, it was only 8 per cent higher; this compares with the United States (US) at +45 per cent, the United Kingdom (UK) at +42, Spain at +41, Germany at +36, France at +30. Even in Greece, despite an unprecedented and dramatic underperformance over the past decade, real GDP per capita has grown by 19 per cent, much more than in Italy. Japan, which used to be considered the sick country of the world, has increased by 22 per cent.

Italy's dismal growth has become critical at the global level in light of the pandemic crisis and the related potential global financial instability issues. As a percentage of GDP, Italy has one of the largest public debts globally. With its open economy and financial linkages, an economically weakened Italy may endanger the very survival of the Eurozone as well as global economic stability.

Failure to deliver on growth and prosperity can happen when, for some reason, a large number of actors in a relatively affluent society are no longer willing to go through the efforts and the sacrifices that have made it possible to achieve well-being. Instead, they look for other supposedly easier means to reach further prosperity. The demand for more state subsidies, privileges, and protection from competition, which is the primary role of lobbies, tends to substitute for hard work, ingenuity, entrepreneurship, risk-taking; in a single word, merit.

To be sure, a modern society needs solidarity. As it has developed in almost all European countries in recent decades, the welfare state is an achievement of civilisation. Some of the achievements of the welfare state—school, health,

---

[3] With regard to the English language literature, this optimistic view was forcefully argued by Hildebrand (1965); Vera Lutz (1963) expressed an opposite and quite pessimistic view, based on her studies on the North–South divide.

and social security—are essential to promoting merit and competitiveness because they create equality of opportunity and avoid waste of human capital.

However, especially since the 1970s, ideas and practices have spread that have frustrated competition between companies and people in the name of a misunderstood concept of egalitarianism. As a result, Italy has moved from the right idea that there should be solidarity, to a practice that ends up punishing rather than rewarding the merit and creativity of individuals and communities.

The semi-feudal system so effectively chastised by Modigliani probably has its roots in a long history in which Italy was seldom an independent nation and lobbies were often seen as self-defence of parts of the population. The extreme case is the mafia, which was perceived for a long time as a legitimate power against the northerners' dominated Kingdom of Italy.

Such a system found a sort of unexpected partner in the egalitarian ideas that had prevailed since the late 1960s because it gave excellent justification to the top caste for its disregard of merit. In turn, such egalitarian ideas were more relevant in Italy than in other countries probably because of the crucial political and social role of catholic and communist parties in post-WWII Italy and the virtual disappearance of market-oriented liberal parties and ideas.

To be sure, Italy has many other problems with deep roots in its troubled history. They are discussed in this book: mass tax evasion, corruption, the North–South divide, gerontocracy, inefficient bureaucracy, slow justice, and lack of trust in all sorts of institutions.

All these problems became evident when Italy could no longer grow through low wages and imitation of foreign innovation, as it did until the 1960s, or through devaluation and accumulation of public debt, as it did until the 1980s. In the 1990s, as many other nations, Italy had to face the challenges of an international environment characterised by open competition due to the creation of the euro and the rise of China and Eastern Europe. Thus, knowledge became an essential input for economic growth. Except for a few hundred manufacturing companies, the bulk of Italian firms and Italy's institutions did not withstand the challenges of the new era. An open knowledge-based economy requires a structure of incentives that rewards individual effort and top-level research. This was missing in Italy.

We know well that some criticise merit, or rather the arrogance of merit, but we believe it is always helpful to remember three things.[4]

---

[4] Such criticisms will be discussed in Chapter 1.

First, the only known alternative to merit is co-optation, either by inheritance or loyalty to some powerful person. In essence, the alternative to meritocracy as a criterion for social promotion is some variant of a feudal society: in this context, the term lobby may sound like a euphemism.

Second, the caste at the top of a feudal system typically ends up disregarding the law. Why should someone close to God—as Modigliani said—be a good law-abiding citizen? The victim of this system is a fundamental concept of liberal democracy: the rule of law.

Third, economic growth requires effort, creativity, the appetite to take risks, and the ability to implement projects. In a word, it requires merit.

Can meritocracy, as shaped by market forces, lead to excessive inequalities and does this require a rebalancing role for the state? Our answer is yes, sometimes, and within limits.

This book is based on a large body of research done in Italy and elsewhere on the role of institutions and social norms to explain economic growth. However, we should honestly tell the reader that the idea of putting merit at centre stage is in part inspired by our personal experiences in Italy and abroad, mainly in the USA and the UK.

We both completed our graduate studies in US universities, and we were struck by many more aspects than those cited by Franco Modigliani. As all persons that went through this same experience, we were impressed by how serious and meritocratic is the selection for admission; by how teachers, no matter how famous, find it necessary to be available for their students; by how researchers, no matter how young or old, struggle to always be up to date with new developments in the discipline; by how tough is the peer review process for publishing in top journals. It does not matter whether you are a young graduate student or a Nobel Prize winner, the review process is the same, and it is always demanding. In Italian schools and universities, cheating is, of course, forbidden, but it is almost a must because a good student is supposed to help others; in US or UK universities, cheating is considered immoral or, in any case, wrong.

We were also struck by how serious, competitive, and indeed meritocratic, is the selection at the end of a university course, in the labour market. In the US and UK, graduates ask for letters of recommendation; in Italy, despite the change in recent years, they still ask for *raccomandazioni*. The latter is not the Italian translation of the former. In Italy, *raccomandazioni* are informal and hidden words that a powerful man or woman uses to help a person, which is often done in exchange for personal loyalty. The letters of recommendation in the US and UK are part of the normal selection procedures (for admission in universities, graduate studies, and the academic job market). Professors do not write one unless they are convinced that a person really deserves it. They carefully calibrate the words they use because they know that their own credibility is at stake in the process.

The result of all these differences is the relatively low quality of Italian universities and researchers—with obvious and deserving exceptions—as is certified by their low positions in most international rankings.[5] We have struggled all our life to understand why such large differences exist and to see how the gaps could be closed. We thought that our generation could bring about change by being exposed to international experiences. But such change did not happen or was much too slow, as is documented in Chapter 5 on Education.

One could say that the gap is in terms of moral attitude, and there is probably more than a grain of truth in this, as will be argued in Chapter 3 on Social Capital. In this case, it is perhaps more compelling to say that merit is not rewarded simply because competition is absent from the Italian educational system. The career of a professor, like that of all public employees, depends very much on her/his connections and belonging to a particular lobby. Once promoted to full professor, the salary is fixed. It does not depend on how well her/his university ranks in terms of research and teaching. The collective lobby of university professors has managed to keep evaluation and merit outside the door of universities. This has led to a surprisingly large number of scandals and judicial inquiries into so-called *concorsopoli*, i.e. selections that have been manipulated so as to favour a candidate loyal to a particular professor rather than the most deserving.[6]

Another important piece of personal experience is with the Bank of Italy.[7] The Bank of Italy is not perfect but it is one of the few meritocratic institutions in Italy. It is widely recognised that hiring and promotions do not depend on connections but on merit. The results of this system are visible in terms of prestige, quality, and legitimacy of the people coming from this institution, both in Italy and internationally.[8] This is a different case from that of universities because the Bank of Italy is not competing with other banks. Over the decades before and after WWII, several highly inspired leaders have created a favourable climate with highly motivated staff, a strong sense of belonging, and high moral standards: merit is the word that encapsulates all

---

[5] See Chapter 5.

[6] For instance, on 8 February 2017, the former rector and several other professors of the University of Messina were condemned in the third degree (Cassazione) to between 2 and 4 years in gaol for manipulation of a university hiring selection process.

[7] One of the authors worked there for 16 years, the other had close relations with the bank, especially when he was chief economist of the Italian Treasury.

[8] See, among others, Padoa-Schioppa (2007) and Codogno (2021).

these dimensions of a well-functioning institution. The case of the Bank of Italy demonstrates that in Italy things can also be done in the right way. It is an example of how public administration (including the education system and the judiciary) could function. The case of the Bank of Italy also convinced us that when merit is appropriately recognised and rewarded, the moral standards and the efficiency of an institution are highly enhanced.

We have been in touch with (or have worked for) several other international institutions, and we have found fairly high moral standards and meritocratic criteria, despite some exceptions. Most importantly, we have direct knowledge of the private sector (industry, banking, insurance, consultancy, etc.) in various countries. Although in the Anglo-Saxon world there have been major scandals (from Enron to subprime mortgages, Libor, and exchange rate manipulation), we find that merit is more highly regarded than in Italy.

In Italy, we know what every Italian knows from direct experience: often, one needs a *raccomandazione* to find a job, even in the private sector. As soon as they look out for a job, young Italians learn that sending around excellent CVs is of little help. According to official statistics,[9] more than 80 per cent—the highest number in Western Europe—of those who search for a job do so by asking relatives, friends, and acquaintances, in any case persons considered influential like the local parson, the mayor, or a trades union leader. This is why a large and growing number of brilliant Italian graduates go abroad to find employers who can appreciate their knowledge and abilities; the brain drain problem has become as severe as in many less developed countries.

Merit has disappeared from public administrations—or perhaps it has never existed. In the vast majority of cases, promotions occur by seniority. In the judicial system, it is almost impossible to reward those magistrates who manage to prosecute within a reasonable time frame. The most surprising thing is that merit plays a secondary role even in the private labour market and even in the choice of managers. There is clear evidence that families who own the vast majority of Italian companies generally prefer loyal rather than capable managers. Therefore, except for the few hundred manufacturing companies that export and have successfully managed to withstand the challenges of international competition, it is hard to get a compelling message about the need to reward merit even from the business world.

Two of the most odious consequences of this state of affairs, which we analyse in this book, are the gender gap and gerontocracy. Italy is one of the countries in the world with the highest gender gap in the employment rate. Though this is not the only factor at play, if merit were a careful consideration

---

[9] Eurostat database: methods used for seeking work. See Chapter 8.

in the hiring decisions of companies, the gender gap would be closer to that of most advanced countries. Italy is also one of the countries in which young people have the lowest employment rate and, when they find a job, their pay is often quite low and improves very slowly with seniority, rather than with merit. The message is that the young can wait no matter how talented. Then, of course, those who can—often the most brilliant—leave the country.

Some may say that Italy has changed over the years, and we are still looking in the rear-view mirror or not seeing the country's positive aspects. Not so; in this book, we will account for the positive aspects, as well as for the negative ones. However, we feel obliged to contrast many common convictions of large numbers of Italians.

Another reason we wrote this book, and wrote it in English, is that it is helpful for many to understand how Italy has fallen into a terrible trap, from which it is indeed difficult to escape. The majority of Italians, and with them the politicians who represent them, do not seem to realise the extent of the disease and the dangers associated with it. All lobbies and vested interests—bureaucrats, magistrates, teachers, bankers, notaries, etc.—defend their positions and privileges tooth and nail.

The result is that the reforms needed to return to growth are viewed as the cause of the problems rather than the solutions. The European Commission (EC), the OECD, and the IMF have been proposing such reforms for many years. They are mainly reforms to increase competition in the goods market, make the labour market less rigid, and most importantly, increase the efficiency of the public administration and judiciary systems. In addition, all these organisations have been telling Italy that it must gradually address its public debt problem.

Populist parties exploit fear of reform of some of the population and accuse the establishment—well represented by the three international organisations mentioned above—of causing the problems. In their view, Italy's decline is proof of the evil of globalisation, the failure of so-called neoliberal ideology, the damage of fiscal austerity and liberalisation, or even the counterproductive effects of Italy's participation in monetary union.

Simplifying somewhat, the problem with Italy's reforms is that they were half reforms or were undone by the governments that followed. Therefore, many people felt the threat, but reform advantages in terms of higher growth for the entire population were not seen.

In April 2021, the government chaired by Mario Draghi indicated the necessary reforms in Italy's National Recovery and Resilience Plan. We know that everyone will be on the side of Draghi and the EU as long as it means spending. However, when it comes to delivering structural reforms, resistance will become daunting and wrapped in pseudo-noble arguments about the speci-ficities of Italy, its extraordinary history, culture, and heritage, to hide the special interests and protectionism that fuel it.

Our wish is that the evidence provided in this book, which encompasses different countries on all continents, helps clarify that many nations have achieved much better results than Italy. And there is no reason why Italy cannot attain them as well.

The novelty of this book is not only the attempt to summarise the key findings of a large body of literature on 'Italy's decline' but also delve into behavioural, social, and political aspects. In light of our own experience in the public and private sectors, it digs deeper into why there is a failure and the levers to use for possible redemption.

The book puts together the comparative evidence of about 300 indicators of 167 countries in the world. Such indicators go beyond purely economic variables and provide insight into such key dimensions as social capital, gov-ernance, corporate practices, education, the rule of law, organised crime, and corruption. On many dimensions of civicness and prosperity, not only of competitiveness, Italy's comparative scores are abysmal.

The book is organised as follows. Part I (Meritocracy and Decline) summarises the basic arguments of the book: Chapter 1 (In a nut-shell) presents the links between merit and growth. Chapter 2 (Italy's decline: stylised facts) tells a brief story of the Italian economy over the last half century, sets out the basic facts about the present crisis, and presents the methodology for the book's empirical research. In Part II (Comparative Evidence: Society), we look at cross-country data on such basic fields of civil life as social capital (Chapter 3), governance, including that of the judiciary (Chapter 4), and education (Chapter 5). In Part III (Compara-tive Evidence: Economy), we look at data on the fundamental indicators of economic performance including the gender gap, the North–South divide, inequality, and social mobility (Chapter 6); we then inquire into why it is dif-ficult to do business in Italy and into the issue of competitiveness (Chapter 7); into the malfunctioning of the labour market (Chapter 8); into why compa-nies remain small (Chapter 9). Finally, in Part IV (Summing Up and Lessons), we draw out lessons, or suggestions, on Italy (Chapter 10) and the role of merit for economic development (Chapter 11).

PART I
MERITOCRACY AND DECLINE

1

In a nutshell

What is meritocracy?—Meritocracy and equality of opportunity—The ene-mies of meritocracy: vested interests and lobbies—Meritocracy and moral standards—Why did growth stall in Italy?—Meritocracy versus connections and lobbies—Historical legacies and social capital—The interplay of social capital and meritocracy—Egalitarianism and the 'long '68'—The 1975 wage indexation accord, inflation, and debt

1.1 What is meritocracy?

Meritocracy is such an intuitive concept that defining it feels redundant. However, strange as it may seem to most readers throughout the world, there is a flurry of publications against meritocracy in the US and the UK. This obliges us to be rather precise in defining what we mean by meritocracy.

Meritocracy is the idea that social and economic success should reflect talent, effort, and achievement. Would anyone be happy to know that her/his cardiologist was not selected according to merit and is, therefore, at best, a mediocre doctor? Would anyone want the engineer who completes projects for our homes, roads, bridges, and aeroplanes to be mediocre? And why should merit be less important for such critical functions as those of the teachers to whom we entrust the education of our children, or those of the judges who have the power to limit our personal freedoms? And why should the same not apply to all civil servants, to whom we entrust many critical functions, such as internal and external security, and regulation to protect children, consumers, workers, the environment, the competitiveness of enterprises, etc.? And of course, everybody pretends that corporate managers are highly competent, deserving their handsome salaries and making their companies a success for all employees and stakeholders.

Merit is almost a synonym of competition, but it is a broader concept because it can also be applied to public institutions, such as ministries, which are not in competition with anyone. All liberal democracies promote

Meritocracy, Growth, and Lessons from Italy's Economic Decline. Lorenzo Codogno and Giampaolo Galli, Oxford University Press. © Lorenzo Codogno and Giampaolo Galli (2022). DOI: 10.1093/oso/9780192866806.003.0002

competition and try to keep monopolies in check, on the basis of the principle that competition is the way to reward merit, that is to say, the most deserving companies; likewise, merit is promoted in the public sector by requiring that civil servants be selected through transparent and competitive procedures. As is convincingly argued in Wooldridge (2021), merit and competition have been the bread and butter of western prosperity, and meritocratic values can prosper only if there are free markets. On the contrary, attempts to introduce merit and competition into planned economies—for instance, through what was called 'socialist emulation', a concept introduced in the USSR soon after the October Revolution—have failed.

According to Michael Sandel, a philosopher at Harvard Law School, we must beware of what he calls the 'tyranny of merit', the idea that those at the top of the social ladder can forget about the rest.[1] The dark side of meritocracy arises when some people fail and appear to have little merit. This, in turn, creates a loss of self-esteem in those groups of the population that are seen to have failed in the meritocratic contest. Populism can be an understandable reaction to the arrogance of the most fortunate.

We understand this preoccupation. In France, President Emmanuel Macron has announced that he wants to abolish the École Nationale d'Administration (ENA), the top graduate school that has formed much of the French ruling class, in both the public and private sectors. It will be replaced by a public management school with wider responsibilities. Populist resentment, such as that of the *gilets jaunes*, against the presumed arrogance of so-called ENArques, was at the heart of the decision.

Sandel also argues that merit is often only a way to hide what, in fact, are privileges due to connections or wealth. Suppose Ivy League universities in the US were attended by the wealthy and not by those with merit. In that case, having a degree from such universities would be just a way of legitimising a position in society that has been obtained for other reasons. However, this is not really a criticism of merit but rather of the effective lack of meritocracy.

Radical criticism of meritocracy comes from a professor of the Yale Law School, Daniel Markovits.[2] His book, titled *The Meritocracy Trap*, starts with the following sentence: 'Meritocracy is a sham'. That is to say that it is a farce, in the sense that 'Merit itself is not a genuine excellence, but rather—like the false virtues that aristocrats trumpeted in the *ancien régime*—a pretence, constructed to rationalise an unjust distribution of advantage'. The basic claim is

---

[1] Sandel (2020). Some of the criticisms of meritocracy were already present in Arrow et al. (2000).
[2] Markovits (2019).

that only privileged children can go to the best schools and then to the best colleges and graduate schools. So that Ivy League (plus MIT, Chicago, Stanford, and Caltech) universities are constructed so as to justify an increase in the share of income and wealth of the top 1 per cent of the population. An even stronger claim, which is somewhat at odds with the idea of 'sham', is that the very existence of elite universities is a cause, if not the only cause, of the increasing wealth of the top 1 per cent. Markovits argues that meritocracy is also a trap for the elite because it transforms life into a competition that creates anxiety and depression.[3] Interestingly, he argues that the wealth of the rich does not depend on the possession of capital goods, as in Marx or Piketty, but on the possession of high skills, what is commonly known as human capital. But such human capital is productive only if people win a highly competitive contest and work very long hours. The key figure displayed in his book shows that, for most low-paid workers (bottom 60 per cent of the distribution), working hours have decreased by about 20 per cent (from almost 50 hours per week to about 40 hours) since the 1940s. This is in sharp contrast with what happened to the top 1 per cent: they used to work about 45 hours in the 1940s, and now they work about 52 hours per week.

As economists, we feel uncomfortable with the idea that universities shape the class structure of a society. If Ivy-League-plus universities did not exist, would the top 1 per cent be less rich? We doubt it. It seems to us that the class structure of society is determined mainly by other factors, such as technology and international trade, as well as social policies. Indeed, we have not been able to find scholarly papers written by economists arguing that the enrichment of the top 1 per cent is due to top universities' structure and admission policies.[4] We also note the sharp contrast between the radical critique and the low intensity of the proposed remedy: the key proposal is to oblige universities to admit at least one-third of students from the bottom half of the population in terms of income or wealth. It is hard to believe that this proposal would solve problems of inequality in the US or elsewhere.[5] Still, it is almost certain that it would reduce the quality of the top universities' admission process. Such top universities would look a little more like the hundreds of decent but not top universities that exist in the US and elsewhere.

---

[3] For a sharp critique of this statement see Menand (2019) on the New Yorker.

[4] There may of course be distortion, misbehaviour, and misconduct also on the part of universities, but that is the exception rather than the rule.

[5] There are many examples of 'affirmative action' policies aimed at 'positive discrimination' intended to promote the opportunities of a defined minority group within society to give this group equal access to those of the privileged majority of the population. The policy of providing special opportunities for and favouring members of a disadvantaged group who suffer from discrimination may also extend to economically disadvantaged students, regardless of merit. Within limits, these policies do not contradict our main tenet.

1.2 Meritocracy and equality of opportunity

There is a message in Markovits's book that should be taken seriously. It has to do with the problem of equality of opportunity, an issue that has been treated very extensively by John Roemer, an economist and political scientist at Yale, in his groundbreaking book titled *Equality of Opportunity*.[6] There is hardly any doubt that the offspring of rich or well-educated families have a better chance not only in top universities, but in life.

Here we must declare our own views so that the reader can judge from the very beginning if she/he is likely to agree with us or not.

The first point is that we believe that inequality of opportunity is not determined by the school or university system. If there were no selective universities, selection would be in the job market and favour the rich and well-educated even more than happens today.

The second point is that we do not share the view that the elite in the US or UK is a cast that excludes everybody else. For instance, top universities admit large numbers of students from foreign countries who have no previous connections whatsoever with the institutions and are often financed through scholarships or through waiving of tuition fees.

The third point is that equality of opportunity is not and should not become equality of results. We say this because sometimes it is argued that to create equality of opportunity, the government should intervene so much during the lifespan of individuals as to create something similar to equality of results.

However, how much should the government intervene to eliminate or attenuate inequality in the initial condition of children born in different social contexts? Our view is that the state must intervene as it does in most European countries, but absolute equality of opportunity is an impossible and dangerous utopia.[7]

Absolute equality of opportunity is impossible. Even if one could imagine a 100 per cent effective inheritance tax, children from well-educated house-holds would have an advantage relative to the rest in terms of the human capital transmitted to them by their parents and the environment. Such utopia is also dangerous because it implies experiments in social engineering such as those advocated by early anarcho-communists (e.g. children taken away from their families to be re-educated) and resonates with the ideological roots of immense tragedies such as the Chinese Cultural Revolution initiated in 1966 by Mao Zedong. The 'new man' that was supposed to be created by

---

[6] Roemer (1998).

[7] The link between inequality and opportunity is what Allan Krueger (2012) labelled 'the Great Gatsby Curve', a concept developed empirically by Corak (2013). Bènabou (2000) had developed a theoretical framework that shows these links, within a major research project on Meritocracy and Inequality; see Arrow et al. (2000).

that dramatic set of events was one in which there would have been no difference between a professor and, say, a farmer. To make that effective, professors were eradicated from their schools and sent to rural labour camps; likewise, educated youth in urban areas were sent to live and work in agrarian areas to be re-educated by the peasantry.

Equality of opportunity is hence a beautiful concept, but it is also a very deceptive one. John Roemer, who defines himself as a Marxist, is not in favour of complete equality of opportunity, although he designs several actions for the government to minimise the initial advantage of lucky children in the birth lottery. In Chapter 12 of his book, he asks: 'Should the equal-opportunity principle be applied to admit a certain number of short players, who try very hard, to [join] professional basketball teams? Being short is, after all, a characteristic beyond one's control, and might well be considered a circumstance.' The answer is that the 'equal-opportunity principle, if applied, would answer [the] question affirmatively. But I would not advocate applying the principle in these cases'.

We also believe that an inheritance tax is appropriate and that the tax currently in place in Italy is too low. According to OECD data (2018), the revenue from this tax is only 0.05 per cent of GDP (820 million euros), much lower than in most other European countries.[8] For example, in France, the revenue is at 0.6 per cent of GDP (14.3 billion euros). Germany with a revenue of 6.8 billion euros, the UK with 5.9 billion euros, Spain with 2.7 billion euros are all around 0.20–0.25 per cent of GDP.

To conclude this brief discussion, we favour public schools, scholarships to help the capable and needy get an education, free health systems for all, public pension schemes, and social security networks to support those who lose their job or fall into poverty. We view these achievements as an essential part of our civilisation. Still, going beyond that would cause many problems and challenge the very foundation of a liberal democratic society.

1.3 The enemies of meritocracy: vested interests and lobbies

Whatever criticism one may raise against meritocracy, one must always be aware that its alternatives are patronage, vested interests, powerful lobbies, and sometimes cronyism, which means essentially a semi-feudal system where societal positions are either inherited or obtained through connections with barons, dukes, bosses, etc.

[8] OECD (2018).

The main enemies of meritocracy are vested interests and the elites that want to preserve their own privileges. They do not like competition and merit because they would endanger their positions in society to the advantage of deserving outsiders. So the critiques to meritocracy are almost always useful means or excuses for the self-preservation of insiders and the many lobbies created over time.[9] They often coincide with part of the old elites.

This is something that a modern liberal democracy cannot accept as a matter of principle. And it cannot take it because, in the absence of merit, leaders in all fields of society would be mediocre, and they would end up losing legitimacy. Lack of legitimacy and low economic growth give some justification to populist movements and create general resentment about the institutions that may undermine the very foundation of the democratic state.

In addition, there is the specific contribution of this book: in a knowledge-based competitive scenario, a society not based on merit is unlikely to display sustained economic growth.

Of course, lobbies per se are not the problem. All democratic countries have organised lobbies. They may provide a useful contribution to the governance of the system. No one would ever think of prohibiting or even putting limits to the activity of lobbying. Trades unions are lobbies, as are organisations representing the interests of certain groups of companies, and they are all perfectly legitimate. The problem arises when lobbies are so powerful, relative to the government, as to be a major determining factor in the rule-making process; or when they impede competition among their members or influence their professional careers or successes. When this happens, vested interests prevail over the innovative forces of society and the economy suffers.

1.4 Meritocracy and moral standards

So far, we have made two arguments in favour of meritocracy. One related to economic efficiency: the economy is efficient when there is competition and reward to merit. The second argument is social justice: elites preserve their social positions by denying opportunities to deserving outsiders.

But there is also an argument about moral standards. In many cases, especially in the public sector, a meritocratic institution produces highly motivated staff, a strong sense of belonging, and high moral standards. On the contrary, when merit is not rewarded, and connections are the key to hiring and promotions, one typically finds a less motivated staff, a weak sense

---

[9] A brilliant account of Italy's many lobbies can be found in Giavazzi (2005). For the lack of competition relative to the rest of Europe see Galli-Pelkmans (2000).

of belonging, and lower moral standards. Only in the former types of institutions does one find true civil servants, i.e. officers who act in full awareness that they are paid with public money to serve citizens efficiently. As we mentioned in the Introduction, in our experience the Bank of Italy is one such institution. When moral standards are low, corruption and other abuses of power are likely to be serious problems.

In the end, there may indeed be arrogance in the meritocratic elites. To those who complain about it, we contrapose the arrogance of the mediocratic elites and their lobbies. This book should convince the reader that the latter is worse.

1.5 Why did growth stall in Italy?

Inefficient bureaucracy, slow justice, weak governments, lack of funding for education and research, crumbling infrastructure, the small size of firms, corruption, mafias, tax evasion, high public debt, clientelism, labour market rigidities: all these explanations for Italian decline have more than a grain of truth.

However, many of these factors were also present in the first few decades after WWII, when Italy was a success story. Also, there does not seem to be any evidence showing that meritocracy has either increased or decreased relative to the post-war period.

What happened then?

As pointed out in much of the existing literature, Italy could grow until the 1990s by imitation when it was far from the efficient frontier of production and was still playing catch-up relative to the then technologically advanced nations.[10] In addition, the following factors played a key role: (a) low wages and compressed workers' rights until the end of the 1960s; (b) continuous depreciation of the external value of the currency in the 1970s and, to a lesser extent, in the 1980s; (c) accumulation of public debt, starting in the 1970s and becoming very large in the 1980s—the second largest as a percentage of GDP among advanced countries after Japan.[11]

Since the mid-1990s, the economy has been suffering from increase in competition stemming from globalisation, the entry of China in the World

---

[10] The key reference is Toniolo (2013b). Phelps et al. (2020) estimate that more than 80 per cent of total innovation was imported in the period 1959–72 and that this imitation was a key factor explaining an average annual growth of 2.47 per cent in total factor productivity. In the period 1972–2012, the sources of innovation were more balanced but potential growth fell almost to zero as did total factor productivity (0.11 per cent per year).

[11] On these points, see Chapter 2 and Signorini-Visco (1997), Galli (2002, Vol. III), Toniolo-Visco (2004), Zamagni (2018), Rossi (2020), and Sestito-Torrini (2020).

Trade Organization (WTO), the European Union enlargement to Eastern Europe, and stabilisation of exchange rates in the run-up to the single currency.

It failed to withstand these challenges, as well as the ICT revolution, because it was not prepared for entry to the new knowledge-based era. A knowledge-based economy requires a structure of incentives that rewards merit, individual effort, and top-level research.

In this new international scenario, a lack of meritocracy at every level of society (schools, public administration, justice, and even private companies) and a structure of privileges acquired mainly (but not only) through political connections becomes the heart of the problem.

Political connections, or connections with high-level bureaucrats or bankers, may be vital for a company that needs to overcome the problems of an inefficient and obscure bureaucracy. Indeed, rather convincing literature shows that politically connected firms have higher revenues and profits than their competitors in the same sector (see Chapter 9). They also tend to have lower productivity, which is a handicap when such companies face international competition.[12]

In a knowledge-based economy, the type of connection a company needs is one with top-level universities and research centres. To win on the international scene, a company needs to be a top performer in its sector; this requires links with universities at the top of their field. As shown in Chapter 5, Italy has few top universities because, in the prevailing egalitarian culture, all universities should be equal. Italy also has few leading companies, mainly because owners place family members in the top positions; they do so because they need managers who are loyal and accept the type of compromises necessary to maintain domestic connections.

Aghion et al. (2021) give a similar explanation to what they call 'the trap of middle-income countries'. Countries must undergo a radical transformation of policies and institutions to switch from imitation-driven growth to frontier innovation. The latter comes above all from high-level basic research and postgraduate education. These authors cite the example of South Korea, a country that successfully managed to make the switch. During the catch-up period

> the government deliberately promoted exports by supporting the growth of large conglomerates, the chaebols. But the decline of the chaebols with the 1998 financial crisis stimulated the entry of new innovative firms, and, at the same time,

[12] See Lippi-Schivardi (2014), Bandiera et al. (2015), Akcigit et al. (2018a), Bugamelli-Lotti (2018), Bugamelli et al. (2018), Baltrunaite et al. (2019), Andretta et al. (2021).

opened a path to structural reforms, which enabled South Korea to return to substantial growth after a brief slowdown.

Italy had several crises, but never managed to switch to a fully liberalised knowledge-based economy. As a result, it is still in the trap.

As the reader will certainly have understood, this book is in the tradition of literature on the role of institutions in the economy; this literature goes beyond the boundaries of a narrow interpretation of standard neoclassical economics to analyse the role of institutions and social norms in shaping economic activity.[13] Following Acemoglu and Robinson (2012) and their previous writings, that literature distinguishes between 'extractive' institutions—aimed at excluding the majority of society from the process of political decision-making and income distribution, and 'inclusive' institutions—aimed at including the widest possible strata of society in economic and political life. We view Italy as an intermediate case. It cannot be said that its institutions are extractive because Italy is a vital western democracy, although with many shortcomings. At the same time, the lack of meritocracy is a powerful means of self-preservation of the elites and their lobbies, as will become apparent when we discuss the education system and corporate nepotism.

Sometimes the word 'extractive' elites is used to evoke corruption or, in any case, some sort of exchange of favours between two parties that makes both rich at taxpayers' expense. We argue in the book that Italy is less corrupt than is suggested by the most popular indexes of corruption.[14] Although corruption is a serious problem, elites should not be characterised as corrupt; they are conservative and actively lobby to avoid change and innovation. They also tend to be rather mediocre because they have not been chosen according to meritocratic criteria.

1.6 Meritocracy versus connections and lobbies

In this book, we document that, although there are exceptions, mediocrity, rather than merit, is the dominant feature of Italian elites. We show, in particular, that this is the case in such a crucial sector of society as education, where teachers and university professors reject being evaluated, and families have virtually no criteria for choosing one school over another (see

[13] The main references in this tradition are Douglass North (1990), Oliver Williamson (2000), Acemoglu-Robinson (2012), Rodrick (2014). However, throughout the book, we make use of the analytical tools of neoclassical growth theory, see Dasgupta (2005).

[14] We hence do not share the view of Capussela (2018) that the problems of Italy are essentially attributable to corruption.

Chapter 5). All schools are equal because this is what the dominant culture wants. For the powerful lobby of teachers, this is an excellent excuse to avoid evaluation and competition.

As has been forcefully argued in Ichino-Terlizzese (2013) and Ichino-Tabellini (2015), more competition and autonomy are needed in the Italian school system. Reform was attempted in 2010, aimed at rewarding the best universities through additional research funding. However, it failed mostly because additional financing was expected to be provided for the worst universities to catch up with the best.

From nursery schools to universities, all teachers have equal salaries at each level of education. No one has the power to reward the best teachers or offer better wages to excellent teachers to attract them to a particular school.

In another reform attempt in 2015, it was proposed to give a modicum of autonomy to school headmasters to choose teachers from predetermined lists at local levels. Teachers' unions brutally rejected this reform. They shouted that schools were not corporations, did not need managers, and that the proposed reform was anti-democratic and unconstitutional. It violated—so they claimed—the article of the Constitution that establishes that 'arts and sciences are free and their teaching is free' as well.[15] A few general strikes of teachers, followed by crowds of protesting students, buried the attempt to reform the system. The result is that school headmasters are bureaucrats with essentially no power except what may stem from their ability to persuade.[16] Teachers' lobbies, typically organised in the form of autonomous trades unions, are indeed powerful.

The OECD has made great efforts to promote the evaluation of educational outcomes and the rewarding of merit in school systems worldwide. This has been pursued by means of the Programme for International Student Assessment (PISA) standardised tests.[17] However, the dominant Italian culture, not just that of teachers' unions, tends to reject these tests, claiming they are Anglo-Saxon trickeries that do not fit the complex reality of Italian society. It also tends to consider it irrelevant that Italy, particularly in the South, ranks very low in these tests. As a result, young Italians start with competitive disadvantage when entering the labour market and being exposed to international competition.

Moreover, school and university careers are still largely dominated by loyalty to powerful professors in a quasi-feudal system. This is confirmed by the colloquial use of the word *baroni*, i.e. barons, to refer to those powerful professors. In international rankings, Italian universities rarely lie in

---

[15] Article 33 of the Italian Constitution.
[16] A good account of this attempt at reform is in Gavosto (2021b).
[17] Available at https://www.oecd.org/pisa/.

the top 100; most likely the best ones are between 100 and 200, and most are in much lower positions.[18] Young Italians with good university diplomas systematically go abroad for their graduate studies, as did both authors of this book. Many of them remain abroad and give rise to a severe—and well-documented—brain drain problem.[19]

Similar stories can be told for public administration at large. Public employees are well organised in trades unions and have managed to boycott any attempt to introduce merit into public administration. All attempts to give top layers of the administration some degree of discretion in hiring or differentiating salaries have failed.

A large part of the responsibility is with political masters at various administration levels (ministers, governors of regions, mayors, etc.). They have rarely cared about improving the quality of administration, reducing the administrative burden, and enhancing or simplifying rules and regulations. Instead, they typically chose the people they needed for their cabinet (often close to them politically) and put their predecessors (especially when there was a change of government) in places where they could not harm them. Therefore, at the top of the administration, many people had moments of glory and high responsibility with one government and then disappeared after an election for years until they were—maybe—rediscovered after one or two legislatures. As a result, the administration is filled with zombies, in many cases excellent civil servants, who wait for their political party to win an election and take them out of the tombs where they had been buried.[20]

The system that produces zombies rather than an efficient administration is self-evident in the public broadcasting company (RAI). At each change of government, hundreds of people are either buried or resuscitated, depending on the success or failure of the political lobby to which they belong. Merit in RAI is optional even though there is some competition with at least two private broadcasting groups (Mediaset and La7).

Many excellent journalists have left RAI because they had the misfortune to be among those who were buried for long periods. In May 2021, Roberto Fico, speaker of the House of Representatives and a leader of the Five Star Movement, candidly admitted that even his political party had participated in decisions about the top positions in RAI. Instead, the board should decide independently,[21] as the same Five Star Movement had indicated in the past, vibrantly criticising the patronage behaviour.

---

[18] See Chapter 5.
[19] See Chapter 6.
[20] This situation is not unique to Italy. In Italy, it is probably more widespread than in many other countries.
[21] La Repubblica, 3 May 2021.

Italy's justice system is a place where the absence of any measure of outcomes and reward to merit is particularly odious because it is one of the causes of the eternal duration of civil and penal trials (see Chapter 4). It is challenging to reward an office that manages to speed up the proceedings or punish or discourage the slower ones.[22] As patently shown by the recent 'Palamara scandal', in which top magistrates promoted colleagues based on their (hidden) political affiliations, judges are often directly connected with political parties.[23] Generally, they are affiliated with magistrates' associations, which are their trades unions or lobbies, and some of them have clear political ties with left- or right-wing parties.

Another example relates to the health care system. That even chief physicians in hospitals are sometimes chosen according to political criteria rather than merit is the most damning indictment of the system of patronage and influence.[24] Generally, this is because the health system is mainly public, governed by regions and their political masters.

Another important field where lack of merit does significant damage is the labour market. In the name of the same misguided egalitarian idea, workers' salaries should be more or less the same and should be protected from the vagaries of the market (see Chapter 8). Unfortunately, the system has not favoured labour participation either. The official employment rate was about 59 per cent before the pandemic, one of the lowest in the world. There is a sharp divide between the relatively few insiders who are meant to be protected and the many outsiders: Italy has record numbers of self-employed and people who work either in temporary jobs or in micro-firms, which are often part of the informal economy.

Only 3 million people out of a working-age population of 39 million are employed in large-size structured companies. For these workers, national labour contracts determine most of the wages, i.e. not just the minimum wage but also the wage for each level of qualification inside the company. Very little room is left for company-level add-ons to national contracts and for rewarding individual productivity and effort. However, kicked out of formal labour relations, merit finds its place in the world of outsiders: the 4 million classified as irregular workers in official statistics; the 5 million self-employed; the temporary workers; the 7 million employed in small and

---

[22] See Barbuto et al. (2020).

[23] Sallusti-Palamara (2021).

[24] For instance, in March 2021, the General Director and other managers of the Hospital of Perugia were sentenced to 3 years in gaol for having manipulated the selection of new doctors. For this scandal, on 20 May 2019 an important politician, President of the Umbria Region, had to resign from office. The problem is so acute that the government has proposed to Parliament a law requiring that holders of top medical positions in hospitals be selected by a committee half of whose members are drawn randomly from a national list; the law also defines rigid criteria for the selection, including the requirement that CVs of all candidates be made public on the web (Art. 18 of decree law 25 November 2021).

micro-companies, where often merit is rewarded with top-ups which are 'out of the envelope' (i.e. undeclared to the tax authorities).

Trades unions have an essential role in a market economy; however, they often behave more like lobbies in that they defend their members to the detriment of the generality of workers. This is also a risk for the associations that represent companies.

Perhaps most surprising is that merit is often not an essential criterion even in the private sector, particularly domestic services. In manufacturing, several hundred companies—the so-called pocket multinationals—compete rather successfully in international markets. For these companies, evaluation and merit are essential ingredients for success. However, this is not the case in other sectors and in the majority of companies. One would normally expect that the owner or majority shareholder of a company would want to pick the best managers and talents found in the market. However, as we mentioned, a vast body of evidence shows that often this is not the case: single-family-controlled companies—the most common type in Italy—tend to put their members (sons and daughters, relatives) in the top posts in the company, not just on the board of directors, but also in executive positions.[25] Even at lower levels, skills and qualifications are not always the most important hiring criteria. Italian companies also tend to remain small for this reason. The family does not want to risk losing control and does not want to invest in human capital. This is also why there are very few listed non-financial private companies in Italy. Market capitalisation of the very few (twenty-five) Italian companies included in the Forbes list of the top 2,000 in the world represents only 15 per cent of Italian GDP, which places Italy after all western countries and many emerging ones.

We go to some length in the book to explain 'corporate nepotism'. There may be some sociological or cultural explanations for it, such as the importance in Italy of family links. However, we find other much more convincing reasons.

The main one has to do with the burden of regulation and the complexity of the laws. Giovanni Giolitti, a prime minister at the turn of the nineteenth century, said that laws should be applied to enemies and interpreted for friends. Since the era of Giolitti, laws have increased enormously in number and complexity.[26] The result is that a firm often needs to have connections to find its way through the intricacies of laws and bureaucracies. Such connections may be with local or national politicians, with public employees, members of the authorities, bankers, and, at times, even magistrates. Sometimes there

[25] See Brandolini-Bugamelli (2009), Giunta-Rossi (2017).
[26] Galli-Cassese (1998).

are illegal dealings, especially when organised crime manages to be part of the equation. In most other cases, there are none, but this attitude impinges on the goal of increasing efficiency and competitiveness. Such connections, sometimes necessary for the company's survival, provide insiders with a competitive edge relative to new entrants who may be more dynamic but do not have the connections. Thus, the intricacies of law and bureaucracy act as a formidable obstacle to competition and are much more critical, in our view, than cartels or any other anti-competitive behaviour that are scrutinised by antitrust authorities.

In an article with the very indicative title *Merit in a Knowledge Society*, Cipollone-Visco (2007) showed that in Italy the wage earned by a university graduate was higher than that of a high school graduate by 53 per cent. This compared to 63 per cent in France and Germany, 74 per cent in the UK, and 81 per cent in the US. Together with the costs sustained for studying, this gives a rate of return to higher education estimated at 7.5 per cent in Italy. Such a return was about twice as much in the US and France and 18 per cent in the UK. As these authors say, 'merit must not only be adequately compensated in the labour market; it must be sustained, appreciated and appropriately evaluated primarily in education'. Many factors explain a relatively low graduate premium. As we will argue in Chapter 9, the structure of production, dominated by small family-owned companies, is an important factor.

1.7 Historical legacies and social capital

Lack of reward for merit is certainly not the only cause of Italy's problems. Other factors are very relevant, but they all interplay with the issue of merit. For instance, to understand why Italy has intricate laws and heavy bureaucracy, it is difficult to avoid looking at the low degree of trust between people and institutions, as we do in Chapter 3. The presumption of those who write the laws, who are civil servants in the various ministries acting under political mandate, is that Italians are *furbi*. It means cunning or smart, i.e. clever at finding ways around the law, which in many cases is true. For instance, tax authorities construct very complex legal systems to protect themselves from the possible accusations of making it easy for someone to evade taxes. Nevertheless, introducing more complex legislation does not reduce tax evasion. Indeed, it may even increase it, but it helps protect authorities and civil servants from blowback in possible scandals.

There is a sort of double presumption. Authorities do not trust people, and people do not trust authorities.[27] The more the government makes

---

[27] See Chapter 3.

complicated laws, the more people find it legitimate to evade taxes and bypass rules. The social stigma associated with tax evasion does not appear to be as significant in Italy as in other countries. In 2013, the former prime minister and then senator Silvio Berlusconi was convicted of tax evasion after three judgements. It was not the end of his political career. In 2019, he was elected into the European Parliament, with more than 560,000 personal preferences. Voters' behaviour also has to do with the low credibility of some institutions, including the judiciary.

Most politicians do not condemn those who evade taxes. On the contrary, even on the Left, which has traditionally taken the issue more seriously than the Right, many politicians think and sometimes state in public that, after all, small companies must evade taxes to survive. It is no accident that almost every year, with governments of all colours, there are small or big tax amnesties. The lobby of tax evaders, typically the self-employed, is one of the most powerful and is always well represented in the national parliament.

As for taxes, there is a high degree of tolerance for many other forms of illegality, such as flouting construction laws. Sometimes, it takes ages to get a building permit, even to make minor changes in one's home. Such slow proceedings are taken as a justification for building abuses. And when abuses become massive and involve millions of people, amnesties are almost inevitable, and indeed they are rather frequent. In turn, amnesties are a further incentive to disrespect rules and regulations.

The sociological literature describes the lack of trust between authorities and the population as a lack of social capital. Social capital is defined as the network of relationships among people who live and work in a particular society, enabling society to function effectively. Robert Putnam, a political scientist at Harvard, is the scholar who also made this concept popular among economists.[28] In the 1990s, the concept gained popularity, especially following extensive research on this topic by the World Bank.[29] A new field of study was opened, and it gave great insight into the role of institutions and social norms in shaping economic development. Robert Putnam himself applied his theory to Italy, claiming that central and Northern Italy developed faster than Southern Italy because the former is better endowed with social capital.[30] The lack of endowment of social capital across Italy has been highly persistent over centuries. Research carried out at the Bank of Italy tends to confirm Putnam's hypothesis.[31]

[28] Putnam-Helliwell (1995).
[29] See in particular Woolcock-Narayan (2000).
[30] Putnam (1993).
[31] De Blasio-Nuzzo (2006). Macchiati (2016) has a recent and very insightful application of the institutional approach to the case of Italy's decline, but he does not seem to consider meritocracy as a key factor shaping growth.

Nowadays, there are many standard indicators of social capital, mainly developed by Gallup for the United Nations and satellite organisations, which can be used to compare countries. By looking at these indicators, it is clear that Italy ranks very low under most potential dimensions of social capital (see Chapter 3). For example, trust in institutions is very low: government, politicians, and the judicial system. There also seems to be rather little interpersonal trust according, for instance, to the Prosperity Index, which is used extensively in the remaining part of this book.[32]

Given this evidence, it is hard to deny Putnam's hypothesis that history matters. Here, the mind goes to the fact that Italy has not been a nation for most of its history since the fall of the Roman Empire and was very often under foreign domination.

Various authors have cited the description given by Alessandro Manzoni, a nineteenth-century Italian novelist and poet, of the conditions of (Spanish line) Habsburg domination in the seventeenth century in his most famous novel *The Betrothed*.[33] Violence, injustice, and the arrogance of the powerful few against the peasants and their women were the norm, as were corruption, the ineffectiveness of laws in curbing abuses, prevarication and misbehaviour of the powerful, and complicity of institutions with the transgressors of the laws that these same institutions had promulgated. The rule of law was obviously an empty concept. The only way to be safe was to be under the protection of some powerful men.

Anyone who has read that novel understands why a person living under such domination would be uneasy in peacefully paying the taxes required by the authorities. When Alessandro Manzoni wrote that novel, first published in 1825, Milan and much of Northern Italy were again under (Austrian line) Habsburg—rulers of the Austrian Empire—domination. And he was probably writing about the seventeenth century to send a message about his own times.

Things got worse after Italy's unification in 1861 because many Southerners perceived unification as a conquest by the Savoy royal family, ruler of the northern region of Piedmont. For several years, the new Kingdom of Italy had to fight a movement called 'brigantaggio' (brigandage). It was de facto a phenomenon produced by criminals, but it was helped by some of the former rulers of Southern Italy, the royal house of Bourbon (again of foreign origin). For several decades after unification, and perhaps even today, many people in the South tend to recognise the various mafias as more legitimate, or at least more powerful, than the Italian state.

---

[32] See Chapter 2.
[33] Manzoni (1984). See also Capussela (2018).

1.8   The interplay of social capital and meritocracy

In any case, there is little question that Italy has a rather heavy historical legacy. But, of course, legacies are not forever; a country, like a person, can change its destiny.

In our interpretation, this has proven very difficult, essentially because the new ruling classes, especially after WWII, did not have the foresight to put competition and merit rather than connections, lobbies, and vested interests at centre stage in many fields of social life.

To be fair, in the Constitution that was drafted in 1948, 'merit' and 'concorso' appear several times: in particular, the document establishes that 'those who are capable and deserving, but without means, have the right to access the highest degrees of the education system' and that this right must be made effective through scholarships and other means. The Constitution also mandates that access to public office, including those of the judiciary, require a *concorso*, which implies that only the best candidates can get the job.

However, in practice, connections, patronage, and lobbies have been dominant. Hence, new leaderships lacked an essential element to be recognised as legitimate by the people.

This is also valid for elected politicians, especially since the populist revolt against the so-called technocratic elite has influenced Italian political development. The very sense of the protest was to bring ordinary people to the top because—so went the story—the competent ones had failed. One of the key slogans of the Five Star Movement, created by comedian Beppe Grillo, was 'one is worth one', which means that anyone can do the job of running the country, and no one should be more important than others. Indeed, that movement managed to bring to parliament very young people who had no previous experience in politics or, often, of anything else. Of course, as in any field of human activity, when the criterion of merit is abandoned, connections with the movement leader or other sorts of non-meritocratic selection processes become more relevant.

1.9   Egalitarianism and the 'long '68'

The question that one may ask at this point is why there has been such disregard for merit in Italian society and why such disregard has become more critical than in many other similar countries. This is a legitimate question. We, as economists, do not have much to add to what historians, sociologists, and political scientists have written on the topic;[34] we can sum up what seems to us the most relevant points.

Part of the answer seems to be that Italy's 1922–43 fascist regime had created a system in which loyalty to the regime itself or some political bosses was key to obtaining certain positions. This is what one would expect from any dictatorships. The key point is that, contrary to what happened, for instance, in Germany, there was not much discontinuity in many aspects of society: universities, public administration, justice, and even the army after the war. In June 1946, there was a general amnesty for almost all crimes committed during the war by the fascists as well as the partisans.

Palmiro Togliatti, then Minister of Justice and leader of the Communist Party, signed the amnesty. This was perhaps an inevitable choice as WWII turned out to be an internal civil conflict that divided the country. Some further minor and less publicised pardons and releases on parole took place in the following years, to the point that some commentators argued that the amnesty was turned into 'amnesia'.[35] Such amnesties and pardons did not take place in Germany.

The other explanation is that the first political elections in the newly founded republic, in 1948, marked the virtual disappearance of the liberal, market-oriented political parties. The main such party was headed by Luigi Einaudi, a member of the Mont Pelerin Society, founded by Friedrich Hayek, Karl Popper, and Milton Friedman among others. However, this party gained only 3.8 per cent of the vote, while the Democratic Christian (DC) Party, at the time strictly connected with the Vatican, won the elections with 48.5 per cent; second was the Popular Front, led by the Communist Party, at the time linked with the USSR, which got 31 per cent.[36]

Thus, the prevailing parties were inspired by the catholic and communist ideologies; both had a strong egalitarian drive and found a *raison d'être* in the opposition to the liberal ideology that had played an important role in Italy from its unification in 1861 until the advent of fascism in 1922. These two parties dominated the political scene until the early 1990s. Of course, there were enormous differences between the two ideologies and the corresponding parties. The DC Party was on the American side of the iron curtain, while the Communist Party was on the other side at least until the mid-1970s.

Nonetheless, they shared many aspects of egalitarian culture. For the Catholics, a certain degree of egalitarianism was present in the teachings of

---

[34] See among others Pavone (1995).

[35] Pombeni (2015).

[36] For an account of how pro-market ideas lost support in post-war Italy in favour of a mixed economy–corporativist model, see Micossi-Parascandolo (2010).

fathers of the church. Still, it became explicit with the publication, in 1891, of the Encyclical Letter 'Rerum Novarum' by Pope Leo XIII, which advocated economic distributism. The third paragraph of the letter is clear: '[W]orking men have been surrendered, isolated and helpless, to the hardheartedness of employers and the greed of unchecked competition.' The concept is further strengthened when the letter addresses 'the mischief [that] has been increased by rapacious usury, which ... is still practised by covetous and grasping men'. The notion that wealth must be redistributed is embedded in sentences like the following: '[T]he hiring of labour and the conduct of trade are concentrated in the hands of comparatively few; so that a small number of very rich men have been able to lay upon the teeming masses of the labouring poor a yoke little better than that of slavery itself.'

To be fair, the DC Party favoured regulated private property and was the key political party that prevented the advent of communism in Italy. In addition, the party was not monolithic, and its leaders had many different views on social issues. Nonetheless, the egalitarian teaching of Leo XIII, which was repeated and strengthened by his successors, was always rather strong.[37]

In the Communist Party also there were very different positions regarding social issues. Still, everybody agreed, at least in principle, that the party's ultimate goal was to eliminate exploitation embedded in the capitalistic system and establish a socialist regime of equal men.

The egalitarian culture, in its catholic and communist versions, penetrated deeply into society. It was one of the key factors behind the student movements that started in the late 1960s. Many of the leaders and militants of the student movements came from catholic organisations or the Communist Party, although they then took their own course and often turned harshly critical of traditional parties.

To give an idea of the egalitarian, anti-meritocratic culture of the 'Italian '68', one of the requests of some student movements was then called '18 political', which meant pass grades for all, independently of actual performance in an exam. This bizarre claim—obviously not shared by the DC Party or the Communist Party—was justified by the egalitarian idea that everybody has the right to a university degree.

As noted by Santambrogio (2021), anti-meritocratic criticism is not at all new in Italy. The rejection of meritocratic selection was rooted in the '68 movement. Santambrogio adds that 'there was no awareness that the impossibility of recognising skills leads necessarily to the inapplicability of the

---

[37] As noted in Amato (1992), the Democratic Christians defended private property mainly as a means to defend political liberty, rather than to promote efficiency and free markets.

principle of open careers to talents', a basic tenet of equal opportunities. 'Perhaps this is also why the typical practices of the *ancien régime* in the allocation of social positions have lasted much longer than elsewhere'.[38] We agree; the *ancien régime* found an utterly unexpected ally in the '68 movement because of the latter's prejudicial rejection of merit. It was probably an unintentional ally, but not without major responsibility. It should be obvious that the rejection of meritocracy goes hand in hand with—and is almost the same thing as—the acceptance of connections and nepotism.

In France, the student revolts that erupted in 1968 was challenged vigorously by President Charles de Gaulle and the entire French leadership, so it did not last long. In Italy, although it never managed to become an important political party in national elections, the student movements profoundly influenced many policies in the 1970s and later: this is the story of the 'long' Italian '68, that to some extent, is still with us. The Italian elites did not understand that certain ideas are incompatible with the proper functioning of modern liberal democracy and a market economy or, in any case, did not have the political will to contest them.

The success of the Italian '68 movement was also due to changes in other parts of society, especially among blue-collar workers. Trades unions became much more assertive, and the workers' movement started to be a key player on the Italian scene. Interestingly, the two major unions were the Confederazione Generale Italiana del Lavoro (CGIL), which was dominated by the communists and closely linked with the party, and Confederazione Italiana Sindacati Lavoratori (CISL), the house of catholic workers, with some links with the left wing of the centrist Democratic Christian Party.

An Italian economist, Paolo Sylos Labini, explained the strength of the worker movements in the late 1960s as a reaction to the condition of subalternity and poverty of the blue collars.[39] These conditions favoured reconstruction after the war and the so-called 'Italian economic miracle' of the 1950s and 1960s. But, over time, they had become unsustainable. They were not compatible with a decent standard of living and the values of equality and solidarity stated in the republican constitution of 1948.

These developments produced many changes in social conditions and reforms, some of which—it should be acknowledged—helped modernise Italy. In contrast, others had the effect of aggravating that lack of meritocracy that Italy had inherited from a troubled history. Positive changes included increases in wages, introduction of the right of workers to organise unions in

---

[38] Santambrogio (2021, 41); authors' translation.
[39] Sylos Labini (2015 [1974]).

factories, abolition of rigid contractual differences in wages between regions of the country, reform of the pension system to provide a decent pension for everyone, creation of a national public health system, and liberalisation of access to universities from all types of high school, including technical schools.

1.10 The 1975 wage indexation accord, inflation, and debt

The main mistakes or excesses of the 1970s were: elimination of factory level contracts and individual rewards to productivity that should have substituted the previous rigid regional differentiation; lack of a mechanism to calibrate pension benefits in relation to what could be afforded by the state of the economy (so-called baby pensions for public employees with seniority of only 18 years or even fewer!); generalised lack of cooperation between employees and employers, as the latter were often viewed as the enemy rather than a contractual counterpart; nationalisation or public support of many zombie firms; cancellation of debts of local authorities (municipalities, regions, health authorities); the enormous increase in public sector deficit.[40]

Perhaps the worst mistake of those years—and the most indicative of the prevalent culture—was the 1975 agreement on wage indexation. The agreement provided an equal wage increase in absolute terms in response to a given percentage increase in prices. The egalitarian idea underlying the deal was that a given increase in prices—say 10 per cent—did the same damage to a salary of 400,000 lire or 200,000 lire. Hence both should be compensated by the same amount, say 40,000 lire. The wages of one of the highest categories (400,000 lire in the above example; the contractual wage of a first category white-collar worker) was taken as the point of reference.

This (almost incredible) mechanism resulted in widespread reduction and eventually elimination of all differences among wages! According to Filosa-Visco (1977), this was an intentional goal of the agreement. Another consequence was that the indexation was more than 100 per cent for all lower categories and on average for the entire system.[41]

The leader of the Confederation of Italian Industry (Confindustria) who signed that agreement was Gianni Agnelli, the president and key shareholder

---

[40] Vivid descriptions of the damage done in these years can be found in Cipolletta (2012) and Rossi (2020).
[41] See Franco Modigliani and Padoa-Schioppa (1978), who harshly criticised the agreement.

of Fiat. He thought he could buy some social peace amid significant unrest in the factories, the Red Brigades, and far-right terrorism.

For a reader to grasp how serious the situation was, it is helpful to recall that in the 1970s, Italy was the advanced country with the highest rate of inflation and continuing devaluation of its currency's external value. Of course, all oil-importing countries were badly hit by the quadrupling of the oil price in 1973–74, but Italy was the only one with a rate of inflation that for several years remained close to 20 per cent. After the second oil shock of 1979, Italy reacted a little better on the inflation front because monetary policy was allowed to turn restrictive following the anti-inflationary move by Paul Volcker, Chairman of the Federal Reserve. But the 1980s became the worst period for the accumulation of public debt. In the 1970s debt had already risen from 35 per cent of GDP to 56 per cent. By the early 1990s it had grown to over 100 per cent. By and large, the distributive conflict that gave rise to inflation in the 1970s was the origin of the public debt increases of the 1980s, the largest among major advanced countries.

Many of the policy mistakes of the 1970s were corrected in subsequent years, with great pain and use of political capital, but these steps will not be illustrated here. This chapter does not intend to write an economic history of Italy but to provide some background as to why merit is so much disregarded in Italy and why the misguided incentive structure is at the root of Italy's poor economic performance. There may be other historical explanations than those given in this chapter, but there is little question that this is the big issue facing Italy today.

A significant part of the problem, as will be documented, is the blunder of the gender gap: Italy is one of the countries in the world with the highest gender gap in the employment rate. Of course, merit is not the only factor at play. Still, if merit were a careful consideration in hiring decisions, the gender gap would be closer to that of most advanced countries.

Another aspect of the Italian problem, as documented in Chapter 6, is the lack of social mobility. The most telling indicator is related to the offspring of parents who did not attain upper secondary education and have only a 6 per cent probability of achieving a university degree (one of the lowest in the OECD). They have a 64 per cent probability of attaining only a secondary education or lower (the highest in the OECD except for Turkey). In the much-criticised US system, these numbers are 13 per cent (more than twice Italy's figure) and 21 per cent (less than one-third), respectively. This is a rather strong indication that Ivy-League-plus universities are not the killers of equal opportunity.

Of course, in the prevailing egalitarian culture, men and women should be treated equally, and rich and poor children should have the same opportunities in life. Likewise, there should be no substantial difference in rights between an employee and a self-employed person who is asked to perform the same tasks as an employee. And more importantly, that culture should have been able to go a long way in reducing the gaps between the North and South of the country.

But the facts tell otherwise. In many cases, the egalitarian culture has produced the opposite of what it intended to do. In this book, we document the facts and give our explanation of why they occurred.

2

Italy's decline: stylised facts

Half a century of crises—The 1970s: inflation—The 1980s: public debt—The 1990s: crisis and hopes—The new millennium: the two original sins—From the GFC and the sovereign debt crisis to NGEU—Italy, the sick nation of the advanced world—The facts about growth and productivity—Why low productivity?—Facts about the debt and the budget—Methodology—The Prosperity Index—Appropriate use of international rankings—Italy's ranking

2.1 Half a century of crises

What follows is not an economic history of Italy. It is just a quick review of some key facts with the sole purpose of showing that Italy has been in a state of crisis almost without interruption since the end of the 1960s.[1]

It may seem an exaggeration. After all, Italy was recording periods of high growth in the 1970s and 1980s. However, many period documents clearly show a widespread perception, both in the country and abroad, that Italy has been an anomaly among advanced nations since the early 1970s.[2] And sometimes, specific situations were perceived as windows of opportunity for change.

Figure 2.1 displays total factor productivity (TFP) since 1954 in Italy and other major advanced countries.[3] TFP expresses the portion of growth in output that is not explained by conventionally measured inputs of labour and capital used in production. It hence reflects technological progress and innovation, as well as the allocative efficiency and organisation of the factors of production. It is also related to the organisational efficiency of public institutions. Together with labour productivity and capital deepening, it is directly associated with an extensive set of indicators that depict the prosperity of a country. In the three decades since the war, TFP has increased substantially

---

[1] For an economic history of Italy, see the Introduction in Toniolo (2013b) to the *Oxford Handbook of the Italian Economy since Unification*; also Castronovo et al. (1999), Bianchi (2013), Rossi (2020).

[2] The idea that Italy has been an anomaly for many years in the European context is central in Merler (2021).

[3] The data in the figure are based on the methodology of Feenstra et al. (2015).

Meritocracy, Growth, and Lessons from Italy's Economic Decline. Lorenzo Codogno and Giampaolo Galli, Oxford University Press. © Lorenzo Codogno and Giampaolo Galli (2022). DOI: 10.1093/oso/9780192866806.003.0003

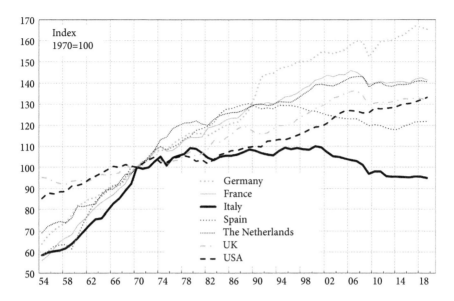

Fig. 2.1 Total factor productivity, selected countries
Source: University of Groningen, Penn World Table, authors' calculations, 1970=100.

but has stagnated and even declined somewhat since the 1970s. On the other hand, it continued to rise in other major countries, at least until the pandemic crisis.

In the 1970s and 1980s, Italy's GDP growth was in line with that of other countries, but it was not obtained through innovation. Figure 2.2 shows the striking divergence between real GDP and TFP. Essentially, TFP almost ceased to grow in the 1970s, around the time of the first oil shock, while GDP and GDP per person employed continued to increase.

Table 2.1 presents the full breakdown of the sources of growth for selected periods.[4] The sum of the last three columns in the table equals the first column containing real GDP growth. The period after WWII until around 1974 is sometimes called the 'golden age' of the Italian economy because GDP growth was very high (5.58 per cent per year, on average). In this period, the driving force of growth was (imported) innovation, as for other European countries: TFP grew at an average rate of almost 3 per cent.

Afterwards, and until the mid-1990s, GDP continued to grow, although at a much slower speed. However, the contribution of TFP was close to zero.

---

[4] TFP is measured as a residual from a Cobb–Douglas production function with constant returns to scale. As in Feenstra et al. (2015), the contribution of labour takes into consideration the number of persons employed, average hours worked, and an index of human capital that depends on years of schooling and returns to education. The contribution of capital is computed using the perpetual inventory method and asset-specific geometric depreciation; the relative price of the capital stock is computed by aggregating asset-specific investment prices using shares of each asset in the total capital stock.

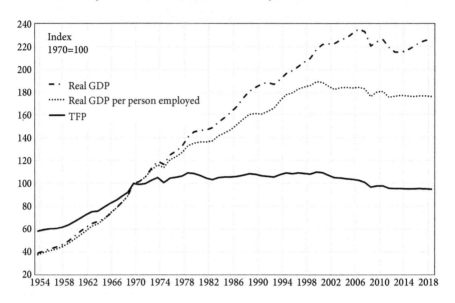

Fig. 2.2 TFP, real GDP, and GDP per person employed
Source: University of Groningen, Penn World Table, authors' calculations, 1970=100.

Table 2.1 Sources of growth of the Italian economy 1955–2019*

Selected periods	GDP	Contribution of labour	Contribution of capital	Total factor productivity
1955–1974	5.58	0.14	2.51	2.93
1975–1995	2.37	0.71	1.48	0.18
1995–2019	0.68	0.51	0.67	−0.51
1955–2019	2.70	0.46	1.49	0.75

* Percentage changes; yearly average in periods.
Source: University of Groningen, Penn World Table, authors' calculations.

Since 1995, GDP growth has been meagre, and the contribution of TFP negative. From the supply side of the economy, between 1975 and 1995, growth was driven mainly by the contribution from capital.

Large flows of investment and a major build-up of capital stock were in part due to substitution of labour, which had become too rigid, with machines (i.e. capital). It shows up in the productivity of labour as measured, for instance, by the variable 'GDP per person employed' in Figure 2.2.

On the demand side of the economy, in the absence of innovation, growth was obtained somewhat artificially through policy measures that pushed investment and both public and private consumption above the economy's growth potential. This meant essentially high inflation and continuous devaluations of the currency in the 1970s and high public deficit and burgeoning public debt in the 1980s.

In conclusion, the Italian anomaly did not start in the 1990s, as is often believed.[5] Instead, it began in the 1970s, when TFP, measuring innovation, ceased to grow. By then, it had no longer become possible to grow through low wages and by importing innovation from abroad, mainly from the USA.

2.2 The 1970s: inflation

High inflation, continuous depreciation of currency, price-wage spiral, high deficits of both the public sector and the current account of the balance of payments, public subsidies, and creeping nationalisation of zombie firms were all features that made Italy rather resemble an unstable Latin American country than an advanced western democracy.

In April 1974, Italy had to ask for a stand-by arrangement with the IMF and was forced to pursue a restrictive monetary policy. It then had to rush begging for lines of credit from foreign entities: the UK, the EC, the Federal Reserve, and the Bundesbank. The loan with the Bundesbank was backed by the Bank of Italy's gold, which made a great impression at the time. Despite these foreign aids, capital flight was massive. In January 1976, official reserves declined to just a few weeks' worth of imports; the Bank of Italy had to withdraw from the official foreign exchange market and let the lira depreciate freely.

Overall, in the 1970s, cumulated inflation was 230 per cent; the Deutsche Mark appreciated against the lira by 174 per cent. The 1975 agreement on wage indexation between the social partners (see Chapter 1) was one of the key factors behind these developments.[6]

The perception of crisis was so strong that in July 1976, a 'national solidarity government' was formed, with Giulio Andreotti as prime minister and the parliamentary abstention of the Communist Party. According to many commentators, it was the first window of opportunity for Italy's parties to leave aside political bickering and work together for the benefit of the country. It probably did bring some positive results but did not solve the deep structural problems of the country. In March 1978, Andreotti resigned to make room for a government with the Communist Party explicitly as part of the majority coalition, which materialised with a confidence vote on 16 March 1978.[7] The kidnapping on the same day and subsequent assassination of Aldo Moro, the then leader of the Democratic

[5] Toniolo (2013c) makes essentially the same argument.
[6] Among many others, see Codogno (2021).
[7] The Communist Party supported the government with a confidence vote, although it did not have any ministerial position in government.

Christian Party, by the terrorist group Red Brigades, eliminated the key moderate politician who was in favour of a government with the Communist Party.[8]

2.3 The 1980s: public debt

In 1979, with the second oil shock and the indexation of wages still in place, inflation started to rise again and in 1980 reached 20 per cent. In the 1980s, significant efforts were made to reduce inflation by participating in the newly defined European Monetary System, through the so-called 'divorce' between the Treasury and the Bank of Italy, and various attempts to reduce the stringency of the wage indexation mechanism. Inflation did abate but remained higher than in the rest of Europe, so that Italy was repeatedly forced to devalue its currency.[9] Reduction in the inflation tax was accompanied by a substantial increase in public debt-to-GDP ratio. Italy was the European country with simultaneous highest inflation and highest debt. Overall, the debt-to-GDP ratio rose from 55.9 per cent in 1980 to 94.3 per cent in 1990. Inflation was still at 6.6 per cent at the end of 1990.

In 1989, the Bank of Italy organised a major meeting of economists with the title 'Beyond the Crisis'.[10] There was some hope of seeing a new beginning. That hope translated into Italy's dismantling of capital controls and entering the narrow band of the European Monetary System (plus or minus 2.25 per cent instead of the plus or minus 6 per cent negotiated in 1979).

2.4 The 1990s: crisis and hope

That hope was again short-lived. In September 1992, the combination of considerable loss in competitiveness and high debt caused large capital flights and made it impossible to maintain the lira inside the European system. The period immediately following the September devaluation was another window of opportunity because all political parties agreed to rein in the deficit and lift the wage indexation mechanism. The government in charge at the time of devaluation (a centre-left government led by a socialist, Giuliano

---

[8] The then US ambassador in Rome wrote a vivid insider's account of that period, see Gardner (2005).
[9] For a lively account of the economy until the 1980s see Cingolani (1990).
[10] Ente Einaudi (1989).

Amato) did much to address Italy's long-standing issues, as well as the one that followed. In April 1993, in the midst of a major political crisis due to scandals linked to illegal financing of political parties, the president of the republic asked the then governor of the Bank of Italy, Carlo Azeglio Ciampi, to form a national emergency government. Initially, some ministers chosen by the former Communist Party, which had changed the name and political orientation in the meantime, were in government.

It was another window of opportunity, which raised great hopes and gave some results in tapering the conflict among social partners and substituting the old backward-looking wage indexation mechanism with a forward-looking system based on targeted inflation. It was indeed an important step, but not sufficient to create the climate of cooperation between workers and companies that prevailed in most other countries in Europe.

In 1995, another former central banker, Lamberto Dini, was called on to become prime minister after the brief parenthesis of the Berlusconi government, which had won the political elections held in 1994. The Dini government was another window of opportunity. It did achieve important results in finally stabilising the lira's external value and starting to reform an unsustainable pension system.

In the political elections held in 1996, the centre-left coalition, led by Romano Prodi, won and started a reform process that looked promising. Under the direction of Prodi and Ciampi, who became Treasury minister, the government managed to reduce the deficit below the 3 per cent threshold, which was an essential condition for Italy to participate in the single currency. In addition, the government started an important, but incomplete, programme of privatisation and liberalisation and introduced some timid reforms in the labour market.[11] For several of those that we consider the best policymakers of Italy at the time, 'European integration was a way to counterbalance centrifugal tendencies and to "anchor" national macroeconomic policies in a European framework'.[12]

In 2001, Paolo Onofri, an economist and consultant to Romano Prodi, wrote a book titled *An Unlocked Economy*.[13] Indeed, there was a perception that, with entry into monetary union, Italy had managed to make the necessary reforms to improve macroeconomic stability and economic growth.[14]

---

[11] On the merits and limit of such programme see Barucci-Pierobon (2010).
[12] See Maes-Quaglia (2003).
[13] Onofri (2001).
[14] For a very vivid description of the reforms implemented in the second half of the 1990s see Bassanini (2003).

2.5   The new millennium: the two original sins

This perception was soon to be proved wrong. Growth has been stalling since the mid-1990s due to the many reasons presented in this book: essentially, rents have dominated the economy, and there has been little reward for merit. Liberalisation has been only partial, and the labour market has remained rigid. Also, with entry into monetary union, interest rates converged towards German levels; this caused a relaxation of the so-called *vincolo esterno* (external constraint) that had been an essential factor in inducing governments to implement growth-enhancing reforms.[15]

In the UK, some economic literature and narrative argue that liberalisation went too far and workers' rights were too much restricted. Perhaps this is what happened in that country, but for sure, not in Italy.[16] To have a Tony Blair requires to have had a Margaret Thatcher. Italy had neither a Thatcher nor a Blair, although several centre-left leaders sympathised with him.

Macroeconomic stability was soon lost because of two major connected 'sins' or mistakes.

The first was an increase in wages not compatible with the new monetary regime, in which the European Central Bank (ECB) had the mandate to keep price stability, initially interpreted as a rate of inflation below 2 per cent, and then below but close to 2 per cent. Neither the government nor trades unions—or companies—including their representative organisations, fully understood that a new regime was in place. As is shown in Chapter 7, together with stalled productivity this fact caused a dramatic loss in competitiveness relative to Germany and most other European countries.

The second mistake was equally important. The governments that came after Prodi's squandered the inheritance of a large primary surplus accumulated by Prodi and Ciampi in the run-up to the single currency. The primary surplus was at 4.6 per cent in 1999 and had fallen almost to zero by 2005. In Brussels, this is still called 'the original sin of Italy' in the monetary union.

Some may reckon the second (2001–06) Berlusconi government (the first one, in 1994, lasted only eight months) as another missed opportunity for the country. Indeed, it was the first government with a clear pro-market stance and a pro-growth agenda, but it did not deliver for various reasons. Berlusconi and his Finance Minister, Giulio Tremonti, thought that by pushing on big infrastructure investments (*le grandi opere*) and unleashing the animal spirit of Italian entrepreneurs, they could generate the growth needed

---

[15] On *vincolo esterno*, see Chapter 3.
[16] This point is very convincingly made in Mingardi (2019).

to pay for higher public investment and current spending. However, without major structural reforms, this turned out to be a dramatic mistake and another missed opportunity for Italy, as became apparent with the Global Financial Crisis (GFC) in 2008.

2.6 From the GFC and the sovereign debt crisis to NGEU

The GFC of 2008–09 was particularly damaging for Italy because of its high exposure to the international trade of goods, which registered an unprecedented collapse. In the crisis, budgetary policy turned expansionary to support economic activity, more or less in line with most other countries. However, Italy's financial conditions were very fragile, and in 2011 Italy found itself fully immersed in the European sovereign debt crisis.

A comparison with Belgium, a country that in the 1990s started with public debt higher than in Italy, helps highlight why Italy was fragile. Sapir (2018) documented that when the euro was launched in 1999, public debt had been brought down considerably in the two countries to roughly 110 per cent of GDP. At that time, Belgium and Italy were also identical in terms of GDP per capita. However, afterwards, the situation changed radically. By 2018, the public debt ratio had reached 130 per cent of GDP in Italy against only 100 per cent in Belgium. Worse, in GDP per capita terms, Italy was 20 per cent poorer than Belgium at that point.

The key difference was that, after substantial fiscal efforts during a relatively brief period before the launch of the euro, Italy's commitment tailed off, while Belgium continued to consolidate its debt at an impressive pace. Italy also did too little to improve its growth performance, which lagged significantly behind Belgium's and that of all other Eurozone countries.

When the crisis hit the two countries, Italy was much more vulnerable to market forces than Belgium, especially when the sovereign debt crisis spread from Greece to other countries.

> Politics has been central to the contrasting debt dynamics in the two countries . . . Maastricht brought fiscal discipline to both countries, but the constraint proved more binding on Belgium than on Italy once the two countries joined the euro. During the crisis, Belgium fared better than Italy because its political class displayed an absolute commitment to debt sustainability and to euro membership that was at times lacking in Italy.[17]

---

[17] Sapir (2018).

The austerity measures undertaken in Italy in 2011–12 in response to the sovereign debt crisis are still a topic of heated controversy. According to many observers, those measures aggravated the situation. They caused a deep recession in 2012, with GDP falling by 2.4 per cent (3 per cent in the most recently revised data) and, consequently, a sharp increase in the debt ratio (from 120 to 129 per cent). We have a different view for two reasons.

First, we agree with the Bank of Italy, which in its annual report in 2012 stated that the sovereign debt crisis caused the recession.[18] The recession started in the summer of 2011 as a consequence of the sharp increase in yield spreads between Italian and German government bonds, which forced banks to drastically reduce lending to the economy. This was later called the 'doom loop', meaning the interaction of public debt and banks when they are major holders of government debt. The spread between Italian and German 10-year government bonds shot up from about 150 basis points in May 2011 to 300 in the summer, and then slightly above 550 in November. As a result, the growth of bank loans fell rapidly and turned negative in the last two months of the year. Effects on the real economy were immediate. By the year end, the carryover to 2012 was already at 1.0 percentage points, which means that almost half of the 2012 recession was the legacy of the previous year, before austerity measures were implemented. During 2012, the stock of bank loans continued to fall.

The second reason is that there were no alternatives at that time. Absent austerity measures, Italy could have ended up like Greece, losing access to financial markets. Nor could much support be expected from the rest of the Eurozone or the ECB. This was due to weakness in the Eurozone financial architecture and the general opinion that Italy's problems, like those of Greece, were essentially home made.[19] Indeed, only after Italy had acted on austerity measures was the ECB in a position to announce (on 26 July 2012) that it would have done 'whatever it takes' to save the euro.

In the absence of austerity measures, the debt-to-GDP ratio would probably have been higher than otherwise over the medium term.[20]

In any case, this chain of events caused considerable suffering for the economy. By 2013, GDP was 8.5 percentage points lower than in 2007. This

---

[18] Bank of Italy (2013).

[19] On the weakness of the financial architecture of the Eurozone see Baldwin-Giavazzi (2015), The Five Presidents' Report in European Commission (2015), Begg et al. (2015), Corsetti et al. (2015), and Codogno (2019b).

[20] The simulations performed by Gatteschi (2018) show that without the austerity measures enacted in 2012 (estimated by the IMF at 2.4 percentage points of GDP), the debt ratio would have been considerably higher in the following years. By 2018, the debt ratio would have been 142 per cent, instead of the actual value of 131 per cent. According to Alesina et al. (2019), the recession was due to the fact that the measures were mainly increases in taxes rather than reductions in spending.

is one of the reasons for the Five Star Movement's success in the political elections held in February 2013. And this is one of the reasons why the following governments in the 2013–18 legislature (led by Enrico Letta in 2013, Matteo Renzi until 2016, and Paolo Gentiloni until 2018) were all very cautious about public finance consolidation. They all followed what Pier Carlo Padoan labelled 'the narrow path', meaning that consolidation had to be done gradually to avoid damaging the economy.[21] From 2012 to 2018, the deficit was slightly reduced (from around 2.9 per cent of GDP to 2.2 per cent). However, it was done by less than was made possible by the reduction in interest payments, largely courtesy of ECB's monetary easing. The primary surplus was hence gradually eroded (from 2.2 per cent in 2012 to 1.5 per cent in 2018), and the debt ratio only stabilised at around 135 per cent. The growth rate improved somewhat but remained below 1.0 per cent on average. The rise in public, and to a lesser extent private debt, and the squeezing in banks' capital produced a prolonged 'balance sheet recession'. In turn, this made the adjustment in public finances much more difficult. The quasi-credit crunch further complicated the situation. Several local banks were in a state of crisis. That had to be resolved, according to the new European procedures calling for a partial bail-in of several categories of creditors of the banks.[22]

An account of this period would be incomplete if we did not mention that the government led by Matteo Renzi tried to implement important reforms in many different fields (education, cooperative banks, labour market). Nevertheless, he had mixed success, also because his term in office ended prematurely. In 2015, he tried to solve Italy's never fully addressed structural problems by changing the Constitution. The goal was to make decision-making and implementation of policies more effective. However, the attempt was defeated in a referendum held in 2016, after which Renzi had to resign. It was another missed opportunity.[23] A constitutional reform, with the same aim of reducing political instability, had also been attempted by the Berlusconi government and was defeated in a popular referendum in 2006.

In March 2018, two leading populist parties, the Five Star Movement and the League, won the general elections. They formed the so-called 'yellow–green' government, which did much of the opposite of what the country needed: decreasing the retirement age and worsening the budget with an

---

[21] Padoan (2019).

[22] These banks' crises made it clear the euro crisis was far from over; see Micossi (2016).

[23] For an account of economic reforms during the 2013–18 legislature, see Codogno (2018) and Leonardi (2018).

important new subsidy.[24] In August 2019, that government came to an end because Matteo Salvini, the League's leader, withdrew his support. The Five Star Movement decided to form a new government with the Democratic Party that, until the day before, was described as an enemy, responsible for all evils and corruption of Italy. The new 'yellow–red' government' marked a turning point in populism in Italy, at least in parliament, if not among voters.

The pure populist yellow–green government had been the only one in Europe that Donald Trump and even Steve Bannon blessed. But it had not managed to change Europe, break the euro, stop migrants from crossing the Mediterranean, or introduce any of the radical proposals of their electoral platforms. With Italy's high debt, the new rulers came quickly to terms with the need to cautiously deal with financial markets and European partners.[25]

At any rate, the new yellow–red government that took office in September 2019, although still supported by the Five Star Movement, proved to be moderate and completely redefined both in its domestic and international agendas.[26] The country became a reliable member of the European Union again, and tried to have a more reasonable approach to migrants. It also pledged to gradually reduce its public debt from its peak of almost 135 per cent of GDP. Even the League became less blatantly populist, perhaps because it too had learnt something from the experience of governing the country.

The real challenges for the new government started in February 2020 with the pandemic outbreak. From that moment onwards, it essentially had to face double sanitary and economic emergencies.

In 2020 the pandemic killed 74,159 Italians, according to official statistics. It caused an unprecedented fall in GDP (−9.0 per cent), forcing the government to approve support measures for as much as 108 billion euros (6.5 per cent of GDP). The public debt rose from 134.3 per cent of GDP in 2019 to 155.6 per cent at the end of 2020. According to a report by Helliwell et al. (2021), Italy was one of the countries that responded more promptly to the pandemic, together with Taiwan and Hong Kong.

On 13 January 2021, the government lost its majority in Parliament. The President of the Republic asked Mario Draghi, the former head of the European Central Bank, to form a 'high-profile government' to tackle the health, economic, and social crises related to the Covid-19 pandemic. He was also tasked to present a credible multi-year programme for using the funds agreed by European heads of government in the European Council of July 2020 and made available to Italy through the Next Generation EU plan.

---

[24] See Reichlin (2018).
[25] See Codogno-Merler (2019).
[26] See Codogno (2019a).

The Draghi government was formed in mid-February 2021 with both politicians and independent technocrats and was supported by a large majority in parliament, including the Five Star Movement, the League, Forza Italia (Berlusconi's party), the Democratic Party, the centrist Italia Viva (Matteo Renzi's start-up), and a far-left party called Article One.

Only Brothers of Italy, a far-right party, chose to stay in opposition, which helped it gain popularity. It had little more than 4 per cent of the votes in the 2018 political elections, while, according to opinion polls, it rose to around 20 per cent in 2021.

In any case, parties which until very recently considered themselves as enemies, or so it appeared, all stayed together in the same government. The Draghi government thus marked, at least for the time being, a further decline of populism and of the mutual demonisation that has been a constant of Italian politics over the past three decades.

A vital contribution to this political process came from the decision of the European Union to adopt the Next Generation EU (NGEU) plan. For Italy, this plan is essential for various reasons. The first is that it implies a common debt by the Union for unprecedented amounts (up to 750 billion euros), which relieves some of the pressure on national budgets, especially in high debt countries. Moreover, the grant component of the Recovery and Resilience Plan (which is the main item of the NGEU) is rather favourable to Italy (it amounts to 20 per cent of total funds, much higher than the 13 per cent share of Italy's GDP in the EU). Finally, Italy is the country of the Eurozone with the highest interest rates on government debt (except Greece), which allows it to take advantage of cheap borrowing via the EU instead of the market.

The attitude of the ECB and the EU towards Italy was different from the one that prevailed in 2012. They recognised that all countries were hit by a common shock, which called for common action. And it was generally acknowledged that fiscal and monetary stimulus measures should not be withdrawn too soon to let the economy recover fully from the pandemic-induced recession.[27]

These considerations explain why, after very troubled vicissitudes, the country seems to have a period of relative calm both politically and vis-à-vis Europe and financial markets.

However, it should not be forgotten that, according to the polls, populism is still high among voters. Italy remains with a public debt of about 150 per cent of GDP, long-dated growth problems yet to be solved, and 10-year yield

---

[27] See, among others, Buti and Messori (2021).

spreads vis-à-vis German bonds exceed 150 basis points, considerably higher than those of Portugal and Spain.

2.7 Italy, the sick nation of the advanced world

Summing up, a turbulent post-WWII history initially produced robust GDP growth for a couple of decades, the so-called 'Italian miracle', when Italy was still catching up with more advanced countries. Then followed two and a half decades characterised by social unrest, devaluation, high inflation, and rising deficits and debt, which temporarily maintained decent GDP growth. Since the currency crisis of the mid-1990s, the 'Italian disease' became increasingly evident. It became even more apparent in the new century, with China entering WTO, globalisation, and significant technological transformation that left Italy's economy on the sideline. Of course, development has not been linear. We will deal with that in detail in the remaining parts of this book. But before jumping into Italy's structural issues, it is important to set the stage of our discussion by describing in a stylised fashion the extent of the problem that has emerged since the mid-1990s.

Italy ended up in the 1980s with economic growth artificially supported by excessive public spending and a rapid increase in public debt. The preparation for monetary union required an adjustment of the economy to avoid continuing devaluation, bring inflation in line with other European partners, and rein back excessive deficits, which ended up slowing GDP growth. The successful entry into monetary union with the first group of countries marked some relaxation in economic policy. However, few fully understood what it would have taken for the Italian economy to survive and strive in a monetary union, giving up the degrees of freedom allowed by a national currency and national monetary authorities. In a nutshell, the country was not prepared to face all the consequences of joining the Economic and Monetary Union (EMU).

With dismal growth and very high debt, today's Italy remains the sick nation of the advanced world and one of the key risk factors for financial stability in the world economy.

2.8 The facts about growth and productivity

In the past quarter of a century, Italy has almost stopped growing. No other advanced country has fared worse than Italy; even countries such as Greece, with its tremendous debt crisis, and Japan, which used to be considered the sick nation of the world, have fared considerably better. The nations that have fared worse than Italy are those that have been devastated by wars or civil wars—like Yemen, the Republic of Congo, Venezuela, Zimbabwe—or natural catastrophes—like Haiti.

Within the EU, Italy used to be in the group of the richest countries and a net contributor to the EU budget. However, over the past 25 years, it has almost reached the group of poorer EU countries, which benefit from cohesion and convergence funds.

From 1995 to 2019, the cumulative gap in GDP's growth was 32.1 percentage points vis-à-vis France, 23.7 vs Germany, 29.5 vs the average of the Eurozone, and 64.5 vs the United States (Figure 2.3).[28]

Italy is also experiencing a demographic crisis, with the population having been shrinking since 2016. This has significant consequences in terms of debt sustainability in the long run. However, in terms of the effects of economic

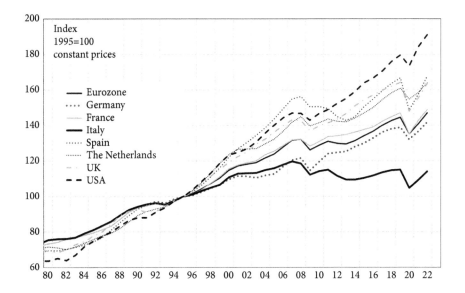

Fig. 2.3 GDP growth, selected countries

Source: Refinitiv (Datastream), European Commission AMECO database (forecasts for 2021–23), authors' calculations.

---

[28] Italy's stalled growth has been the topic of a vast literature. To the works already cited in specific chapters of the book, we should add the following references. In English: Codogno-Felici (2008), Mody-Riley (2014), Bank of Italy (2017), Zamagni (2018). In Italian: Kostoris (1993), Messori et al. (1998), Toniolo-Visco (2004), Saltari-Travaglini (2006), Padoa-Schioppa (2007), Tabellini (2008), Rossi (2009), Galli (2010), Schivardi-Torrini (2011), Nannicini (2011), Paganetto (2011), Simoni (2012), Spaventa (2014), Fubini (2014), Visco (2015), Felice (2015), Perotti (2016), Goldstein (2018), Leonardi (2018), Dell'Aringa-Guerrieri (2019).

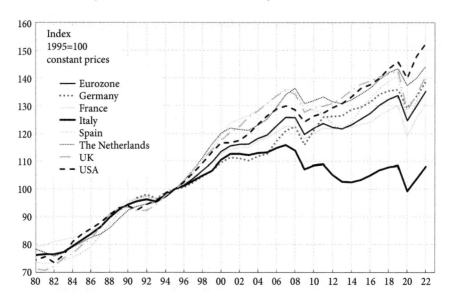

Fig. 2.4 Real GDP per capita, selected countries

Source: Refinitiv (Datastream), European Commission AMECO database (forecasts for 2021–22), authors' calculations.

growth, so far it has not played an important role due to increased female labour market participation, as explained below.

Indeed, even taking GDP per capita as a benchmark, i.e. partly stripping away the demographic trends, Italy has lost ground relative to the other major economies (Figure 2.4).[29] The loss has been even more staggering in recent years. In 2019, i.e. before the pandemic crisis, Italy's real GDP per capita was just marginally above its 1999 level, when monetary union started.

Table 2.2 completes the comparative picture of GDP components. Also Japan, a country that is more rapidly ageing than Italy, is included in the comparison.[30] All variables are indices with 1995=100. Since 1995, Italy's GDP (column 7) and GDP per capita (column 1) have grown by 15 per cent and 9 per cent respectively, the lowest values among the seven selected countries.

The problem clearly lies with GDP divided by total hours worked in the economy (GDP/TH). It has grown by only 7 per cent, against, for instance, 34 per cent for Japan and 29 per cent for Germany. Total hours worked as a share of the population (displayed in column 3) is not the problem since it has increased more or less in line with Germany or France. In Japan, it has decreased by 9 per cent because of an even larger fall in average hours per

---

[29] For a different view on the role of demography see Cottarelli (2019).
[30] On a comparison between the performance of Italy and Japan, see Fatas (2018) who reaches the same conclusion as we do.

Table 2.2 GDP per capita and its components in selected countries

	GDP/ POP	GDP/ TH	TH/ POP	TH/ EMP	EMP/ POP	POP	GDP	EMP	TH	MEG
	(1)	(2)	(3)	(4)	(5)	(6)	(7)	(8)	(9)	(10)
France	130	130	100	94	107	113	147	121	113	42
Germany	135	129	104	91	115	103	139	118	107	44
Italy	109	107	102	93	110	106	115	116	108	44
Japan	122	134	91	88	103	100	123	103	91	45
Spain	142	119	120	97	123	117	167	145	141	41
UK	141	132	107	97	110	117	164	128	124	41
USA	145	149	97	97	100	124	180	124	121	42

Note: GDP= real GDP national accounts; POP=population; TH= total hours worked; EMP= employment; MEG= Median age of workforce (average 2010–19).
Source: Authors' calculations on Penn World Table; ILO; index: 1995=100.

person employed (TH/EMP in column 4). This indicates that the low GDP per capita growth does not depend on more old persons being counted as 'capita' in GDP per capita but no longer contributing to the productive effort of the nation.

Neither does it depend on the fact that fewer working-age people actually work. The level of employment rate in Italy is very low (see Chapter 8), but its percentage change since 1995 (EMP/POP in column 5) has been positive (+10 per cent), more or less in line with France, Germany, and the UK and more than in Japan, where it has remained unchanged.

Contrary to what is often stated, in this period total employment increased in Italy, by 16 per cent, essentially because of steadily rising female participation in the labour market, from abysmally low levels.[31]

Finally, the median age (MEG in column 10) of the labour force (employed plus unemployed) is relatively high but no higher than in Germany and slightly lower than in Japan. In light of this fact and the prevailing literature, we feel reasonably confident that the culprit is not the population's age structure, although there might be some (negative or positive) effects of an ageing workforce in particular sectors and companies.[32]

These considerations should convince the reader that the productivity figures are not hiding other ongoing phenomena in the economy. Lack of productivity growth is the main factor that has held back economic performance. Figure 2.1, at the beginning of this chapter, showed that TFP has

[31] The source is the Penn World Tables. Total hours worked have increased much more in the Netherlands (+26 per cent), in the UK (+24 per cent), and in the USA (+21 per cent).
[32] See a Report of the US National Research Council (2012); according to this report, the aggregate effect of ageing is negligible and may even be a small positive number.

ceased to grow since the 1970s. However, only since the mid-1990s has the gap between Italy and the rest of the advanced countries also shown up in terms of GDP and GDP per capita. The reason, as we explained above, is that Italy's growth was obtained somewhat artificially through devaluation of the lira and accumulation of public debt.

So far, we have looked at the entire 1995–2019 period. Looking at sub-periods, we find deterioration in productivity almost everywhere in 2014–19 (Figure 2.5),[33] but the deterioration was more significant in Italy. The downtrend in labour productivity since the 1990s is evident. It is about a quarter of a century of stagnation for Italy, with further weakness in recent years. The so-called secular stagnation has produced low productivity and GDP growth worldwide, and Europe has been no exception. Still, this phenomenon has been far more pronounced in Italy than elsewhere, with country-specific causes.

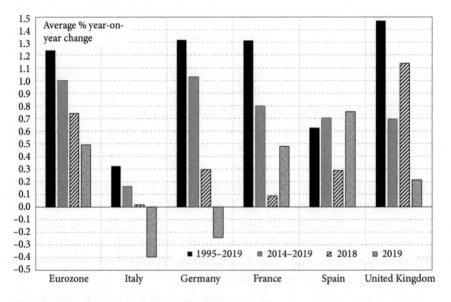

Fig. 2.5 Labour productivity in major European countries
Source: ISTAT (2020b), authors' calculations.

---

[33] In 2019, Italy's labour productivity even dropped below the zero line, which is hard to interpret as it is like regressing in the use of factors of production. Part of it has undoubtedly to do with the cyclical behaviour of productivity. It tends to weaken in cyclical downturns, as was the case for the weakening growth of 2019. However, productivity is hard to measure year by year, and what matters is the trend.

2.9 Why low productivity?

This question is the topic of the entire book. However, some considerations should be brought forward. First, the picture is segmented, and productivity dynamics differ substantially across macro-sectors.[34] In particular, especially since 2010, there has been structural adjustment and improvement in allocative efficiency within the manufacturing sector, but not in the non-financial services sector. The heterogeneity within each sector is even more important than among sectors. In terms of GDP and employment, the backbone of Italy's economy is a large number of small and micro-enterprises. These small enterprises have shown all their weaknesses over the past quarter of a century.

In Chapter 9, 'Why are companies so small?', we will delve into the chronic issues of Italy's corporate sector. The productive system is polarised,[35] with micro- and small enterprises generally old, with little appetite for innovation, less inclined to favour technological advances, and usually not involved in international markets. More importantly, most of them show a lack of managerial capacity and skills and a weak financial structure. This is the reason why these companies suffered enormously from globalisation and the credit crunch that accompanied the sovereign debt crisis.

Empirically, there is a strong correlation between size and productivity,[36] not only because size matters but also because micro-companies are, on average, less productive and dynamic than similar-size Eurozone counterparts.

Medium and large enterprises are less affected by these problems. In particular, a smaller set of medium- and large-size manufacturing companies are comparable to, if not even better than, their most successful European competitors. They innovate, are technologically advanced, and show a strong appetite for exporting. They have also opened up their capital structure and are well managed, despite all the headwinds and difficulties of the Italian business environment. As a result, they are very productive and provide valuable support to Italy's growth. However, their average size and share in value added is comparatively smaller than in other countries, and they are unable to grow. Thus, an unfavourable composition effect explains a large part of Italy's productivity problems. The gap in both labour and TFP productivity of micro-firms relative to large firms has widened from 55 per cent to almost

---

[34] See Galli (2010).
[35] See Bugamelli-Lotti (2018) and Lotti-Sette (2019).
[36] See Bauer et al. (2020).

65 per cent over 2000–15. Especially in construction and professional services, the higher number of smaller firms explains the productivity gap with the EU.[37]

Italy's structural weaknesses and its rigid and inefficient business environment are well known. They should be addressed by supporting product, process, and organisational innovation, adopting new technologies, and enhancing skills in the workforce. The capacity of the economy to efficiently allocate capital and labour towards the most productive firms should be improved. There should be an increase of what Bugamelli-Lotti (2018) call the 'up-or-out dynamics', i.e. the process by which new-born firms either grow to a reasonable size or exit the market early, and inefficient firms exit the market to free up resources. Instead, business dynamics have been modest and worsening, with the enterprise churn rate steadily declining across manufacturing and services sectors. The rate of entry has shown a widespread decrease since 2008.[38] Moreover, Italy is affected by so-called 'zombie congestion'. In the EU sample of countries available, it is second only to Spain in terms of the share of zombie firms. Zombie firms may prevent resources from being funnelled to other more productive firms, especially new ones. Their presence is a hurdle for the allocative efficiency of the economy and the process of creative destruction. In Chapter 9, we argue that most of these issues are closely intertwined with lack of meritocracy, even in the private business sector, and the misguided incentive structure in the economy.

Italy's innovation and technology gap versus other countries and the frontier is a crucial determinant of poor performance. It is reflected in underinvestment over several years: there is little scope for capital spending with little innovation. Looking at the capital side of the economy, Italy's growth in net capital stock has been at the bottom of the advanced countries group in the past decade (Figure 2.6). Since the 2008–09 crisis, public and private investment have fallen noticeably, partly because of restraint in the public budget, and capital stock has become increasingly obsolete. In some years, growth in net capital stock has slipped into negative territory. Obviously, with little capital investment, which can be seen as a bet on future growth, GDP growth has been increasingly dismal.

Human capital, closely connected to innovation, is another crucial driver of growth that is comparatively weak in Italy. There is negative feedback between the demand and supply of skilled labour, exacerbated by matching problems

[37] Bauer et al. (2020) and European Commission (2020c).
[38] Bauer et al. (2020) and European Commission (2021a).

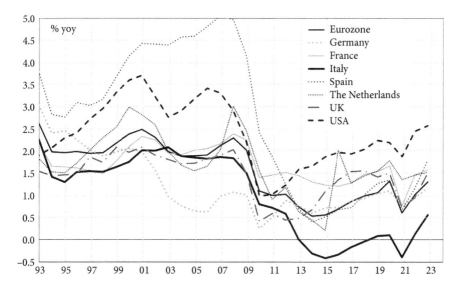

Fig. 2.6 Net capital stock growth

Source: Refinitiv (Datastream), European Commission AMECO database, forecasts for 2021–23, authors' calculations.

in the labour market. It is a catch-22 issue. Companies find it challenging to find qualified workers, but the return on education is low. Thus there is little incentive to invest in human capital by individuals and, more broadly, by society. We will go more deeply into this fundamental issue in the remaining part of the book.

We will also delve into ownership and management features that affect firms' performance. Let us just mention that there is much evidence to suggest that pervasive family management is detrimental to management practices, efficiency, and the propensity for internationalisation and innovation.

We will also show that underdeveloped capital markets and excessive reliance on banks to allocate resources within the economy are also very important for Italy's economic performance.

A lack of alternative forms of financial intermediation, such as venture capital and private equity, also impinge on the ability of the economy to nurture start-ups and innovative firms across sectors. Moreover, there is plenty of unrealised potential and plain evidence that companies are unable to grow due to rigid labour market legislation. It is, however, also a matter of incentives, as we explain in Chapter 9.

Insolvency procedures, the rule of law, and the inefficiency of civil justice are essential elements that influence productivity and innovation.

2.10 Facts about the debt and the budget

Along with dismal economic performance, or because of it, Italy's debt-to-GDP ratio has continued to increase (Figure 2.7). Before the 2008–09 crisis, the ratio was slowly decreasing and approached 100 per cent. It first worsened following that economic shock.

Then it rose even more following the sovereign debt crisis in 2011. Finally, it jumped due to the pandemic crisis in 2020, with the debt ratio exceeding 155 per cent of GDP.

In the 1970s and 1980s, debt increases were mainly due to high deficits. Since the 1990s, the crucial variable that prevented debt from falling was lack of growth, while the government has almost always run primary surpluses. A simple simulation may be helpful to illustrate this point. From 1995 to 2019, the growth gap with France was 32.1 percentage points in terms of real GDP. This implies that Italy's GDP would be higher by some 500 billion euros every year had the country grown like France. With the additional GDP, the debt problem would have disappeared long ago.[39]

To be precise, debt would have reached the 60 per cent Maastricht threshold by 2010 had the additional revenue stemming from higher growth

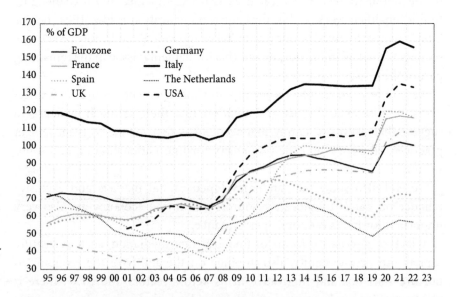

Fig. 2.7 Debt-to-GDP ratios, Eurozone and selected countries
Source: Refinitiv (Datastream), European Commission forecasts, authors' calculations.

[39] Pisani-Ferry (2018) made a symmetric exercise: 'Had France followed the same policy as its southern neighbour since the launch of the euro in 1999—that is, had it recorded, year after year, the same primary balances—its public debt today would be 45% of GDP, instead of 97%.'

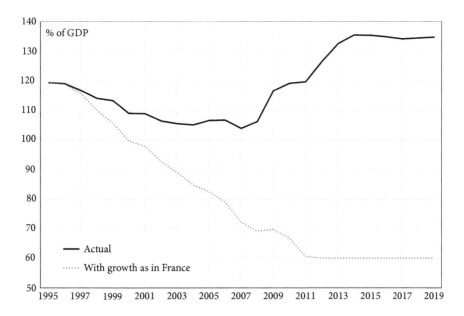

Fig. 2.8 Public debt-to-GDP ratio under alternative assumptions

Note: The assumption is that the extra revenue from higher growth is not used for more spending or lower taxes until the 60 per cent threshold is reached. The extra revenue can be used for such purposes from that point on.

Source: Eurostat, authors' calculations.

been used to reduce debt rather than increase spending (Figure 2.8). More-over, once the debt problem was solved, the 500 billion euros could have been used for private consumption and much needed public goods: allevi-ate poverty, finance the climate transition, modernise infrastructure, espe-cially in the South, improve education and research, accelerate the digital transition, etc.

Instead, the reality of the public budget is displayed in Table 2.3. Over the past ten years, total expenditure has been 49.7 per cent of GDP on average, higher than in Spain, Germany, and the whole Eurozone. In Sweden—usually classified as a high spender—the ratio is more or less the same as Italy's. Like-wise, revenues have been more or less in line with the Eurozone and less than in France and Sweden. However, tax evasion and the informal economy are substantial in Italy. Excluding from the denominator the official estimate of the informal economy (10.7 per cent of GDP[40]), the ratio of revenue to the regular part of GDP rises above 52 per cent.[41]

---

[40] The latest available estimate (on 2018) is contained in the Report of the Ministry of Economy and Finances on *Non-Observed Economy and Evasion of Taxes and Social Security Contributions*.

[41] This is an upper bound estimate of the ratio for honest citizens because it assumes the no taxes are paid in the non-observed economy.

Table 2.3 Expenditure by category, revenue, and deficit

General government, % of GDP, 2010–19 average	Italy	Euro-19	Germany	Spain	France	Sweden
General public services	8.7	6.7	6.2	6.2	6.4	7.3
Interest payment	4.4	2.6	1.7	2.9	2.3	0.8
Public order and safety	1.9	1.7	1.6	2.0	1.6	1.3
Justice (law courts)	0.3	0.3	0.4	0.4	0.2	0.3
Economic affairs	4.0	4.6	3.5	4.9	5.5	4.3
Environmental protection	0.9	0.9	0.6	0.9	1.0	0.5
Housing and community amenities	0.5	0.6	0.4	0.5	1.2	0.6
Health	7.0	7.2	7.1	6.2	8.1	6.9
Recreation, culture, and religion	0.7	1.1	1.0	1.2	1.5	1.3
Education	4.0	4.7	4.3	4.2	5.4	6.6
Social protection	20.6	20.0	19.3	17.3	24.1	20.1
Pensions	16.1	12.5	11.2	11.1	14.9	10.8
Unemployment	1.1	1.7	1.8	2.4	1.9	1.3
Total Expenditure	49.7	48.7	45.0	44.3	56.5	50.1
Total Revenue	46.9	46.1	45.2	38.2	52.5	50.0
Net borrowing requirement	2.8	2.5	−0.2	6.1	4.1	0.1

Source: Authors' calculations on Eurostat–COFOG classification.

However, two items are considerably higher than in the other countries: interest payments and pensions, respectively almost two and four percentage points higher than the average of the Eurozone. Higher interest payments result from higher public debt and higher borrowing costs, reflecting the perception of risk by investors. Pension spending reflects choices made by various governments under the pressure of trades unions and companies. The bulk of the union's rank and file were, and still are, retired baby boomers. For companies, facilitating early retirement has always been the easiest and sometimes the only way to reduce staff or downsize. As a result, spending on social protection outside pensions (unemployment benefits and income of last resort for the poor) and education is low. The latter is at 4 per cent of GDP versus 4.7 per cent in the Eurozone. Spending is also rather low in 'Recreation, culture, and religion', which includes all cultural activities, which in Italy are an essential asset for tourism and economic growth.

Other spending components are not very different from the Eurozone average as a percentage of GDP. In particular, health spending, which is usually considered badly underfunded, is more or less at the same level as in the Eurozone, Germany (where health insurance is more widespread), and Sweden. The same is true for Environmental protection, Defence and Public order and safety. The latter includes spending on the police, fire brigade, prisons, and law courts. Spending for Justice (law courts) is another item often considered underfunded, while it is in line with the other countries. It includes administrative, civil, and criminal law courts and the judicial system but excludes spending on prisons.

Another key feature of the Italian budget relative to other countries is its inflexibility.[42] As of 2019, 41 per cent of total spending was for welfare entitlements—mainly pensions—20 per cent for personnel—already much compressed and hard to further reduce. Only 7.1 per cent is for investment which declined by one-third in ten years, and 6.9 per cent is for interest payments. The remaining items include intermediate consumption (17 per cent), primarily related to necessary purchases by hospitals.

A serious spending review could still achieve meaningful results, but it would require much political support as the spending areas that could be streamlined without major reform are limited.

Finally, people do not usually consider spending as a share of GDP, as we have done here. Usually, the focus is on spending per citizen (or patient, student, etc.), which is far less favourable to Italy in respect of what this book is trying to explain: lack of growth. In all different areas (except pensions), people are right to complain that spending per capita has increased far less in Italy than in other European countries. If growth does not resume, complaints will inevitably mount and eventually become unmanageable.

2.11 Methodology

It would be nice if we were able to find a single variable (or a vector) measuring all the relevant dimensions of meritocracy and throw it into an econometric model to explain economic growth. Unfortunately, it does not appear possible. However, there is one study—the only one to our knowledge—that has tried to do precisely that. Pellegrino and Zingales (2019) is a rather formidable paper that has undergone many revisions since it first appeared in 2014.[43] The authors squeeze the whole world into a couple of variables that go into a single equation. Their methodology consists in regressing TFP[44] on the interaction between ICT capital contribution to TFP and meritocracy of managers across country and sectors.[45] The managers' meritocracy variable is constructed through country-level and firm-level surveys found in

---

[42] See Cottarelli (2015) and Perotti (2016).
[43] In what follows we comment on the last version we have seen, which is dated May 2019.
[44] In the Pellegrino-Zingales paper TFP is measured with EU-KLEMS data.
[45] Some technical aspects of the paper are not very convincing. For instance, it is not entirely clear why low management quality should not affect growth in the 1985–95 period or why it does not affect growth directly but only through its interaction with the ICT capital contribution to TFP.

the WEF and EFIGE datasets.[46] Respondents are asked if managers are chosen according to meritocratic or loyalty-based criteria. Interestingly, these data confirm our thesis (see Chapters 6 and 9) that in Italy, managers tend to be chosen according to loyalty rather than by merit.

The authors conclude that lack of meritocracy accounts for almost 80 per cent of the TFP gap that Italy had accumulated during the 1996–2006 period vis-à-vis the most meritocratic countries (which they identify as Germany and Japan). This is a startling conclusion, and it would be tempting to say that this is all there is to be told and stop here.

This paper is indeed heroic, and it reinforces our conclusions. However, one should be aware that it only measures the merit of corporate managers. In our view, merit, or lack of it, plays a key role in other sectors of the economy. Our book considers that merit is essential in many different aspects of society: education, judiciary, administration, etc. For example, if it takes ages to enforce a contract, this is a major impediment to doing business or starting new enterprises. Nor are we convinced that loyal, rather than capable, managers are able to overcome such impediments through their connections or illegal dealings. The same is true for the quality of education and of the public administration in general, which act as major external diseconomies. It is true that—as we will argue—loyal managers may be useful because, through a system of connections, they may be better equipped to deal with complicated bureaucracy. But we find it unlikely that they can completely overcome such formidable external diseconomies.

Indeed, even before the landmark book by Acemoglu and Robinson (2012), there were plenty of economic papers showing that many different institutions affect the incentive structure of an economy, hence potential growth.

The OECD developed a pioneering analytical approach to underpin its 'Going for Growth' project, grounded in findings from the economic literature on how policies influence GDP performance.

In February 2007, the Ecofin Council of the European Union underscored that 'monitoring and assessing reforms is an important factor for the success of the Lisbon Strategy. This calls for a clear and transparent approach based on suitable methods'. Then, with the support of the Economic Policy Committee, the European Commission launched a methodology to track,

---

[46] WEF stands for the World Economic Forum and EFIGE is a Bruegel/Unicredit database that combines measures of firms' international activities with quantitative and qualitative information on about 150 items, a representative sample (at the country level for the manufacturing industry) of almost 15,000 surveyed firms (above 10 employees) in seven European economies (Germany, France, Italy, Spain, United Kingdom, Austria, Hungary).

analyse, and model structural reforms carried out in the context of the Lisbon Strategy, and subsequently, the Europe 2020 Strategy. For a good summary of the literature and the methodology, see European Commission (2008). The methodology has broad coverage and captures the most critical drivers of growth, which in many cases can be linked to a more general concept of meritocracy. The metrics and the quantitative indicators form part of the analytical toolbox the EC uses on an ongoing basis to assess structural reforms.

In a nutshell, the starting point is an examination of the sources of GDP per capita differentials within the EU and the main drivers of growth. More specifically, twelve GDP components (three demographic, six labour utilisation, three labour productivity) are analysed in terms of levels and changes. Then an evidence-based analysis of performance is carried out in twenty policy areas which the economic literature has identified as relevant for GDP. They go from the labour market and demographic issues to pertinent policy areas for labour productivity as they deal with product and capital markets plus innovation and knowledge. Finally, a screening exercise examines whether there is a coincidence of underperformance in the relevant GDP components that have been identified in the literature survey. The outcome is a list of underperforming policy areas, quantified by appropriate links to GDP.

In the aforementioned document by the EC, the word 'meritocracy' does not show up. However, the concept is effectively all over the place. Many drivers of growth are linked one way or another to meritocracy.

In recent years, through their productivity or competitiveness councils mandated by the European Union, many countries started looking into ways to improve economic growth by intervening in its many drivers.

In light of these considerations, we proceed as follows. First of all, we provide plenty of evidence that (a) merit is disregarded in many fields of society, and (b) it is an essential ingredient for a knowledge-based economy to be competitive and produce prosperity. It was less critical when Italy, like several other European countries, could grow by imitation or through artificial demand stimuli such as public spending and currency devaluation.

In our view, cross-country comparisons are by far the best way to show the weakness of a country and how things can be done better. For instance, we want to show that the egalitarian anti-meritocratic ideology that has prevailed in Italy—especially since the 1970s—has produced the opposite of equal opportunities. We see no better way to do this than using top-level

OECD comparative data and research on social mobility and relating them to what we know about the educational system, the labour market, the characteristics of companies, etc. More generally, the method is summed up in three points.

First, we show that with the same amount of public money (or less), many countries do better than Italy in many fields (public administration, education, justice, corporate governance, equality of opportunities, etc.). In this regard, the data in paragraph 2.10 are quite useful.

Second, we show that merit is not adequately rewarded in these institutions for reasons we try to explain. For instance, because national labour contracts fix equal wages for everybody, or reforms to introduce evaluation and merit in schools have failed, or because families who own the companies prefer faithful to capable managers, etc.

Third, when the low quality of an entity concerns private companies, the effects on growth are self-evident (and, in any case, they are indicated in the listed literature). When it involves public institutions (such as education, justice, etc.), we rely on the large body of literature that shows how vital such institutions are for growth, which every person with common sense understands.

In the individual chapters, we bring to bear and quote top-level research. Although we do not offer a formal review of the literature because we think it would bore our kind readers, we use a vast body of research, most of it by the Bank of Italy or the OECD. For instance, we quote research that 'proves' or, to the very least, convincingly argues that connections produce inferior results in the corporate sector. There is evidence, besides Pellegrino-Zingales, that those firms entirely managed by the owner's family tend to have mediocre performances. They do less R&D, are less productive, and less likely to become internationalised. Politically connected firms tend to have better sales and profits but are less productive and innovative than their competitors, which is another rather convincing piece of evidence (see Chapter 9).

2.12 The Prosperity Index

To give some order to the discussion and base it on actual evidence, we consider an index that compares broad aspects of prosperity across a large number of nations. For this purpose, we have chosen the Prosperity Index produced by the Legatum Institute[47] since 2007.

Relative to more popular indices—such as the Competitiveness Report produced by the WEF or the World Development Indicators of the World Bank—the Prosperity Index has some relevant advantages for our purpose.

It aims to measure prosperity rather than just GDP. It thus has a broader perspective on many different aspects of society, such as Social capital, Governance, Education, etc. These are vital ingredients in our explanation of the Italian disease. It has a vast number of indicators (294 in the 2020 edition) taken from all the best available sources. It has about seventy different sources, although most of the indicators are taken from international organisations such as the United Nations and its satellite organisations, such as UNICEF, UNHCR, UNCTAD, and the World Bank, the IMF, and others. In addition, survey evidence, typically when hard data are not available, are taken from the international Gallup Polls, some of which are produced for various United Nations Reports and the WEF's Competitiveness Report.

While using a broad index of prosperity, we are primarily interested in a particular aspect: why Italy has almost stopped growing in the past quarter of a century. So, we use the rich set of indicators of the Prosperity Index to answer a well-defined and relatively narrow question. Our reading of the evidence is somewhat at variance with the index's aim of giving a broader view of the many different prosperity dimensions. The Legatum Institute aims to move the attention away from a narrow view of economic well-being, as measured typically by GDP per capita. Instead, we do the inverse, as we use a comprehensive set of indicators to answer a narrow question concerning a specific economic well-being aspect.

2.13 Appropriate use of international rankings

All international rankings suffer from various shortcomings. Several indicators are subjective and reflect the residents' perception of their country.[48]

---

[47] The Legatum Institute presents itself as 'a London-based think-tank with a bold vision to create a global movement of people committed to creating the pathways from poverty to prosperity and the transformation of society'. The Institute was founded in 2007 by the Legatum Foundation, the philanthropic arm of the Dubai-based investment firm the Legatum Group. It was given charitable status in 2015. The Legatum Institute is funded by over 40 donors including the Legatum Foundation. The institute is currently located in London. Philippa Stroud (formerly Executive Director of the Centre for Social Justice, and a Peer in the House of Lords) was appointed CEO of the Legatum Institute in 2016.

[48] D'Andrea-Ebano (2019).

The 'Doing Business' report of the World Bank was introduced to avoid this problem as it aims to be based exclusively on hard evidence.

However, on 16 September 2021, the World Bank announced that it had decided to discontinue the report because several data irregularities had been reported in internal audits and a report that the bank itself had commissioned to an independent legal office.[49] According to the audits, such irregularities were due to political pressure by some member countries (China in 2018, Saudi Arabia, Arab Emirates, and Tajikistan in 2020). In the case of the 2018 report, they involved the then Chief Executive of the World Bank, Kristalina Georgieva, who later became the Managing Director of the IMF. Georgieva criticised the report's findings as 'false and spurious'.

Whatever the truth, it is clear that these facts are grave and have undermined the trust in research carried out by the World Bank. Indeed, they have shaken the trust in research carried out by international organisations in general and perhaps also analysis performed by independent economists.

Together with our reading of a very authoritative independent economists' report[50] released by the bank in September 2021, before the scandal, and our own experience with the World Bank and the IMF, these facts indicate that international rankings are very useful. However, they must be taken with more than a grain of salt, which we do in this book.

In particular, the exact position of a country or the change from one year to the next is subject to an error term, which may depend on political pressure and the staff's mistaken understanding of certain features of a particular country. In the case of China, the alleged 'political error term' accounts for seven places as China managed to remain in the seventy-eighth position instead of being downgraded to the eighty-fifth.

Moreover, one should look inside the individual indicators to understand what is involved and must be able to tell a convincing story about them. For instance, it is helpful to know that Enforcing contracts takes 1.120 days in Italy and 216 days in New Zealand. At the same time, one looks at South Sudan and finds that it takes only 228 days, apparently as good as New Zealand. But, of course, this is not the whole story. By looking at the variable Quality of judicial process, South Sudan ranks very low, so that the overall rank in Enforcing contracts is only eighty-third.

Italy ranks fifty-eighth in the Doing Business ranking, which means it could well be fortieth or seventieth, taking into account the mentioned uncertainty. Italy should probably be in a better position than fifty-eighth because several low-income countries devastated by recent wars rank better than Italy, which

[49] WilmerHale Report (2021).
[50] Alfaro et al. (2021).

does not sound very plausible. However, it is equally implausible that Italy's rank suddenly becomes similar to New Zealand's or Denmark's. Most likely, Italy's ranking is below most major advanced countries and some emerging ones.

Throughout the entire book, we never give any relevance to minor differences across countries and time for any existing rankings, not just the World Bank's. Instead, we focus on very significant differences, especially across countries. Furthermore, we look inside these indexes and try to tell a story to explain why a given indicator may have a particular value for Italy. Indeed, this is why we wrote the book. Otherwise, we would only have published tables and graphs.

2.14 Italy's ranking

Table 2.4 shows the ranking of the thirty-one best countries according to the Prosperity Index.[51] The absolute winners are the European Nordic countries. Italy's overall rank is thirty-first out of 167 countries, with a score of 71.8 (normalised so that the best-performing country can reach 100 and the worst zero). This ranking is not very different from those of the World Bank, the UN Human Development Report, or the WEF. Interestingly, it is not very different even from that of the World Happiness Report based on a completely different methodology.[52]

Rarely is Italy above thirtieth position, which means that most advanced countries and sometimes some emerging ones rank better. And again, the best performing countries generally are the European Nordic countries. The only Western European country with a lower ranking than Italy is Greece (forty-first).

Table 2.5 summarises the main headings (called 'pillars') in which the Prosperity Index indicators are aggregated.

The second column shows the ranking of Italy relative to all 167 countries included in the index. The third column shows Italy's ranking versus the subset of thirty-four countries defined by the IMF as advanced (excluding very small ones).[53]

[51] The data were downloaded on the 22 March 2021 and correspond to those published in the Report: *Legatum Prosperity Index 2020.*
[52] See Helliwell et al. (2021) and Galli et al. (2021a). The Happiness Report is based on a Gallup survey in which people are simply asked how they rank their life on a scale between zero and 10. On average in the period 2017–19, Italy ranks thirtieth out of 153 countries.
[53] The thirty-four advanced countries are: Australia, Austria, Belgium, Canada, Cyprus, Czech Republic, Denmark, Estonia, Finland, France, Germany, Greece, Ireland, Israel, Italy, Japan, Latvia, Lithuania,

Table 2.4 Prosperity Index, top countries

	Rank	Score
Denmark	1	84.4
Norway	2	83.8
Switzerland	3	83.3
Sweden	4	83.1
Finland	5	83.1
Netherlands	6	82.0
New Zealand	7	81.1
Germany	8	81.1
Luxembourg	9	81.0
Austria	10	80.4
Iceland	11	80.2
Ireland	12	80.2
UK	13	80.1
Canada	14	79.8
Singapore	15	79.5
Australia	16	78.6
Hong Kong	17	78.4
USA	18	77.5
Japan	19	77.3
Taiwan	20	77.1
Estonia	21	76.9
France	22	76.5
Belgium	23	76.1
Spain	24	75.8
Malta	25	75.5
Slovenia	26	74.6
Portugal	27	74.1
South Korea	28	73.4
Czechia	29	73.1
Israel	30	72.0
Italy	**31**	**71.8**

Source: The Legatum Institute (2020), and authors'
calculations.

This latter ranking is perhaps more meaningful since it compares countries similar to Italy. Italy's ranking is relatively low among the entire set of 167 countries considered in the index and is close to the bottom of the thirty-four advanced nations. The same message emerges from Figure 2.9, in which

Luxembourg, Malta, Netherlands, New Zealand, Norway, Portugal, Singapore, Slovak Republic, Slovenia, South Korea, Spain, Sweden, Switzerland, Taiwan, United Kingdom, United States.

Table 2.5 Ranking of Italy relative to 167 countries and 34 advanced countries

Pillar	Italy/167	Italy/34	Top Country
Social Capital	64	25	Denmark
Economic Quality(*)	51	32	Switzerland
Natural Environment	46	27	Sweden
Investment Environment	40	32	Singapore
Governance	39	33	Finland
Education	35	30	Singapore
Enterprise Conditions	31	26	Singapore
Living Conditions	30	28	Denmark
Infrastructure	24	21	Singapore
Personal Freedom	24	21	Norway
Safety and Security	23	20	Switzerland
Health	10	9	Singapore

* A weighted average of the main economic indicators such as GDP growth, unemployment, inflation, public debt, productivity, female participation, various measures of innovation. *Source*: Legatum Institute (2020), and authors' calculations.

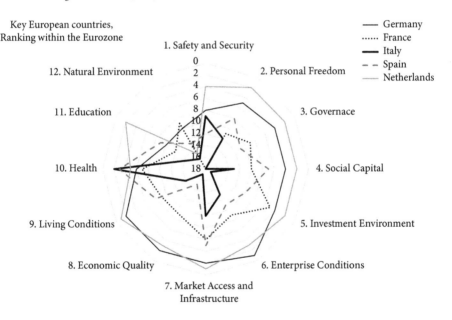

Fig. 2.9 Prosperity Index's pillars, Italy vs main Eurozone countries
Source: Authors' calculations on Legatum Institute (2020).

Italy is compared with the main Eurozone countries: except for health, Italy's spider's web is entirely inside those of other countries.

The relative ranking of Italy has not changed much in the past thirteen years since the index was created (Figure 2.10). Almost all countries have a better score in 2020 than in 2007. Italy was in a rather low position in 2007, and it

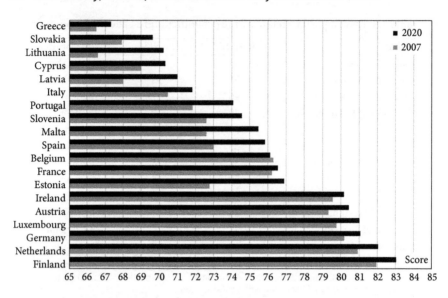

Fig. 2.10 Prosperity Index's overall score in 2007 and 2020
Source: Legatum Institute (2020), authors' calculations.

did not change much in 2020, suggesting that most problems are not new and still present.

At this level of aggregation, it is hard to pinpoint the critical problems of Italy. Still, they lie in Social capital, Economic quality (a variable which captures the key economic indicators such as GDP growth, unemployment, inflation, public debt, productivity, female participation in the labour market, measures of productive innovations), Natural environment, Investment environment and Governance.

Therefore, we need to dig deeper into each of these items. To do this, we first look at the fundamental long-run and primarily non-economic determinants of growth: Social capital, Governance, and Education. We then look at those economic variables that are more closely related to competitiveness and growth: Economic quality, Investment environment, and Enterprise conditions. Thus, our journey into the indicators is meant to move from the long-standing causes of low growth to their likely effects on the standard economic variables.

PART II
COMPARATIVE EVIDENCE: SOCIETY

3
Legacies of a troubled history

Low mutual trust—Historical legacy and trust—Democratic legitimacy and meritocracy—Some unpleasant truths about SMEs

3.1 Low mutual trust

We start our journey into the comparative numbers with Social capital. Among the twelve fundamental pillars into which the Prosperity Index is divided, Social capital is where Italy has the lowest rank. It is sixty-fourth over the entire set of one hundred and sixty-seven countries and twenty-fifth over the subset of the thirty-four advanced countries. According to the official definition, 'Social capital captures the personal and family relationships, social networks and the cohesion a society experiences when there is high institutional trust and people respect and engage with one another'. Thus, it is strictly related to the notions of civicness and civic and social participation.

Although the definition seems pretty straightforward, Social capital is a very complex concept. For instance, distinguishing between low trust in institutions and privileging personal ties of trust and loyalty is crucial. This distinction is (imperfectly) captured in Prosperity indicators of Institutional trust, Civic and social participation and the other sub-indices.

Moreover, there is a difference between what 'trust' means in different cultures and for different people. For instance, in the Anglo-Saxon world Institutional trust is closely interconnected with the role of the state, and freedom is seen as freedom 'from' the state. However, the opposite seems to be true for most Southern European political cultures, where the expectation is that the state drives economic development and the road to prosperity.

All these complications seem to wane when one looks at the case of Italy, as displayed in Table 3.1. Italians declare that they have very little confidence in virtually all sorts of institutions: banks, government, politicians, the judicial system. Nor is there much trust in the local police, strangers, and even other Italians. Even for Personal and family relationships, Italy does not rank very well, especially among advanced countries. All the items measuring trust

Meritocracy, Growth, and Lessons from Italy's Economic Decline. Lorenzo Codogno and Giampaolo Galli, Oxford University Press. © Lorenzo Codogno and Giampaolo Galli (2022). DOI: 10.1093/oso/9780192866806.003.0004

Table 3.1 Social capital

Element	Indicator	Italy /167	Italy /34	Top country /167
Institutional Trust	Confidence in financial institutions and banks	164	33	Singapore
Institutional Trust	Confidence in national government	160	34	Singapore
Institutional Trust	Public trust in politicians	149	34	Singapore
Interpersonal Trust	Helped a stranger	145	25	USA
Institutional Trust	Confidence in judicial system and courts	127	29	Multiple—3
Civic and Social Participation	Voiced opinion to a public official	123	23	Denmark
Civic and Social Participation	Volunteering	119	25	New Zealand
Personal and Family Relationships	Family gives positive energy	80	25	Greece
Personal and Family Relationships	Help from family and friends when in trouble	79	32	Multiple—2
Social Networks	Helped another household	74	17	Cyprus
Social Networks	Opportunity to make friends	60	23	Singapore
Institutional Trust	Confidence in military	51	13	Finland
Civic and Social Participation	Donated money to charity	51	22	UK
Institutional Trust	Confidence in local police	46	22	Singapore
Interpersonal Trust	Generalised interpersonal trust	46	23	Multiple—2
Civic and Social Participation	Voter turnout	40	9	Malta
Social Networks	Respect	39	11	Multiple—3

The notation 'Multiple—n' indicates that n countries are in the top position.
Source: Legatum Institute (2020), and authors' calculations.

are necessarily subjective; most of them come from Gallup's surveys. One of the sub-indices—trust in politicians—comes from the World Economic Forum Survey of chief executives. It is instructive to look at how the question is formulated: 'In your country, how would you rate the ethical standards of politicians?' This is a more helpful question than asking whether one trusts politicians.

A particularly important item is the first one in the table, which shows that Italians do not trust financial institutions and banks. This may be somewhat puzzling in light of the fact that Italy has not had financial scandals of the magnitude experienced in many other countries. In particular, Italian banks were not involved in the Global Financial Crisis (GFC) of 2008–09 because they had a small portfolio of derivatives and virtually no exposure to US sub-prime mortgages; also, Italian banks have not been involved in the major scandals of the international banking system such as the one linked to the manipulation of the Libor and Euribor interest rates that emerged in 2012. Nevertheless, admittedly, the case of Monte dei Paschi, the Venetian banks, and some other smaller banks somewhat dented confidence in the banking sector.

As extensive literature has suggested, low trust in financial institutions is an indicator of low social capital in general. Hence, to some extent, it is a consequence of low trust in the population. In turn, such low trust in financial institutions has important consequences because it hampers the development of a healthy market economy.[1] Objective indicators, such as the relevance of venture capital or the equity market size, tend to confirm that mutual confidence is not high.

The very fact that Italy has a bank-centric financial system, where other forms of financing play a minor role, might be due to a lack of trust. Banks are more equipped than common shareholders to monitor what the firm is doing and whether it will be able to provide an appropriate return to capital.

Other telling indicators are:

a. Volunteering, which measures the percentage of people who answered that they had 'volunteered time to an organisation in the past month'; Italy ranks 119th over 167 countries and 15th over 34 advanced nations. This fact may seem puzzling, but we see no particular reason for arguing that there might be negative bias in the answers of Italians.

b. Helped another household, in which people are asked to say whether their 'household sent financial help to another household in the last year'. Here again, there seems to be no reason for a particular type of bias.

c. Helped a stranger, where people are asked to answer the question: 'Have you helped a stranger or someone you didn't know who needed help in the past month?' Here Italy ranks 145th over the entire set of 167 countries and 25th over 34 advanced countries. It is probably better to compare Italy's rank to advanced countries than the overall sample, as people are more likely to answer this question positively if they do not live in an advanced country. This seems to confirm that there may be quite a difference between social capital relative to institutions and that relative to interpersonal relations for many countries.

3.2 Historical legacy and trust

The level of social capital of a country is usually attributed to historical vicissitudes. It is a legacy of many centuries of history. The low level that seems to be observed in Italy is hard to explain without appealing to a long history of foreign domination. It has made it challenging to create a strong feeling of national identity and has generated distance between the elite and the bulk of the population.

---

[1] Guiso et al. (2004b).

However, the question in this context is whether a country can get rid of such a negative historical legacy. Is such a legacy a condemnation forever? The answer is quite obviously no. History has forged a country in a particular way and has left a negative legacy. In the same way, a different path of history can change that legacy. Especially in the past few decades, a vast number of countries have radically changed their destiny. Italy itself made dramatic changes in the three decades after WWII. It became an advanced industrial economy, starting from a condition in which most of the working population was employed in agriculture. Apparently, the old negative legacies have reappeared in the last quarter of the century.

Meritocracy may play a role in changing the path for the better. Consider again the items that penalise Italy from the point of view of social capital. They all have to do with confidence in parts of the country's elite or leadership: banks, politicians, government, judges. Quite clearly, such a low degree of trust cannot only depend on ancient history. It must also be a function of how competent is the country's leadership and whether it is perceived to pursue general interest rather than its own.

Both these factors are connected with the perception of patronage and clientelism. In other words, if a person does not get a fair chance because 'they' look after their friends, she/he does not expect meritocracy and does not behave in expectation of meritocracy, which may well compound the problem.[2]

In any case, the various components of a country's leadership will be trusted only if selected according to meritocratic criteria. This is undisputable when applied to professions that require high skills, such as bankers, civil servants, doctors, pilots, engineers, teachers.

3.3 Democratic legitimacy and meritocracy

It is less obvious when it is applied to politics. After all, in a democracy, it is the people who elect politicians. It must be presumed that those who win the majority of the votes must be those the voters trust the most.[3] In the past thirty years, after 'mani pulite' (a major investigation, started in 1992 into illegal financing of political parties), Italians experimented with several new

---

[2] It is the argument of a 'social trap', inhibiting escape from a state–society relationship that creates reciprocal patterns of misguided behaviour; see Bo Rothstein (2011).
[3] Many of the arguments of this section are inspired by Keefer-Khemani (2005), Persson-Tabellini (2005), Giovanni Sartori (2015), and Dambisa Moyo (2018).

political parties and sent to power people with no previous experience in politics. This was the case with the League, which became part of a centre-right national government in 1994. It was the case with Berlusconi's party, which was created in a few months in 1994 and won that year's political elections. It was the case with the Five Star Movement created by Beppe Grillo, which got 26 per cent of the popular vote in the 2013 national elections and went to power forming a majority with the League after winning the election of 2018 with 33 per cent of the votes. Most political parties often changed their leaders and many of their representatives in Parliament because they had to appear new. Matteo Renzi, who has been the Prime Minister from 2014 to 2016, was very successful initially because he was perceived as an outsider, bringing new life to an existing political party, the Democratic Party. Despite all these changes, Italians still declare themselves to be highly dissatisfied with their politicians. When asked why they are dissatisfied, the typical answer is that politicians are incompetent and do not care for the people but only for their own interests.[4]

However, whenever there was a severe crisis, the presidents of the republic decided to appoint as prime ministers individuals who were generally recognised as being highly competent. These outsiders gained ample support in Parliament.

Mario Draghi, the former President of the European Central Bank, formed a government in 2021 during the deep economic crisis caused by the Covid-19 pandemic. It was also the case for Mario Monti, an economist and former EU commissioner for competition, who formed a government in November 2011 during the sovereign debt crisis when Italy was on the verge of losing access to financial markets. Both the Draghi and Monti governments started with a very large majority in parliament, including almost all political parties from Left to Right. A similar story had happened in 1993 with the government headed by Carlo Azeglio Ciampi, the then-governor of the Bank of Italy, who took office in the midst of one of Italy's worst financial and political crises. Again, a similar story happened in 1995 when Lamberto Dini, a former Director-General of the Bank of Italy, formed a government because the League's departure from the Berlusconi government triggered new political and financial turmoil.

To sum up, whenever there was a crisis, Italy resorted to leaders perceived as competent. Whenever the game became challenging, the tough men who

---

[4] This is a common feature in many advanced countries. See Ipsos Mori (2019) and PEW Research Centre (2021).

played the game were the ones who had acquired merit in the public perception because of their achievements in their previous activities. When a lot is at stake, meritocracy becomes king in terms of human lives and livelihood.[5] Consider again the government formed in February 2021 by Mario Draghi: it is almost unbelievable that it managed to get the support of all political parties, from far Left to Right (with few exceptions). How is it possible? Until the day before, the same parties had been not just opponents but true enemies, accusing each other of the worst misdeeds, if not crimes. In addition, how is it possible that Draghi is popular among voters who had given their preference to populist parties just three years before, in the elections of March 2018?

The only possible answer to these questions is that, in the end, both political leaders and the public recognise that competence and merit are essential for ruling a country. This was particularly true when the political elites perceived that Italy was facing the *vincolo esterno* (external constraint), a concept made popular by Guido Carli, Governor of the Bank of Italy between 1960 and 1975 and Treasury Minister between 1989 and 1992.[6] Financial markets often worked as a *vincolo esterno,* as did Europe in many circumstances. As a result, competent technocrats were seen as a must to avoid unmanageable troubles for the country. So yes, democratic legitimacy is given by voters, but such legitimacy is weak if it is not supported by merit.

Returning to where we started, Italy, like any other country, can change its destiny and improve its social capital. Meritocracy may not be the only answer, but it is undoubtedly an essential part.

Of course, this leaves us with some big open questions: why does Italy resort to its best leaders only in times of crisis? Why do voters not elect people who have merit in normal times? We leave these questions to political scientists who certainly can give better answers than we can. We can only suggest that in the case of Italy, there may be more than a grain of truth in a famous and highly controversial sentence by Jean-Claude Juncker, the former President of the European Commission, who once said: 'We know how to do the right things, but we do not know how to be re-elected afterwards'.[7] The point is that Italy needs reforms that are rather unpopular, both

---

[5] Indeed, all the above-mentioned prime ministers enjoyed a high level of trust in public opinion polls, especially at the beginning of their mandates.

[6] Guido Carli (1996). For a discussion of the external constraint in the context of European integration see Giavazzi-Pagano (1988), Dyson-Featherstone (1999), Featherstone (2001), and Maes-Quaglia (2003).

[7] While politicians may indeed share Juncker's belief, this belief may be wrong. Empirical research suggests that electorates under specific circumstances will reward reformist politicians. Those specific circumstances pertain to the functioning of the financial system. If it functions well, the future growth bonus generated by reform will be discounted in current asset prices. See Buti (2009) and Buti et al. (2010).

because of its high public debt and because it needs to fight acquired privileges in order to restore sustainable growth. Any competent person is aware of these facts and does not dare to deny them. 'Incompetent politicians' can instead promise the moon to the electorate. Voters may be mindful that they will not get the moon, but they may think it is better to kick the can down the road than face the problems straight on. A crucial part of the League's manifesto in the political election of 2018 was about lowering the retirement age. Of course, competent people know that this is nonsense given the ageing of the Italian population and the already very high expenditure on pensions. Voters probably knew it as well. However, the people who managed to retire at age 61, rather than waiting until 67, made a good deal and preferred short-term personal gains rather than worrying about Italy's long-term issues.[8]

As a note of caution, we should recall that Italy is a divided country. The level of social capital is likely to be different between North and South (see Chapter 6), which may also have implications for the feasibility of unpopular reforms.

3.4 Some unpleasant truths about SMEs

In the list of indicators displayed in Table 3.1, there are some surprises concerning interpersonal trust and the role of SMEs.[9]

Italians are usually considered cordial and hospitable people, while, according to these indicators, they tend to have relatively little interpersonal trust. Indeed, Italy does not have a high percentage (twenty-third among advanced countries) responding 'Most people can be trusted' to the question 'Generally speaking, would you say most people can be trusted, or you can't be too careful?' The percentage has remained fairly stable since 2007: about 29 per cent of respondents say that 'most people can be trusted', and twenty-two advanced countries have a higher score. Some scores are much higher: for instance, all European Nordic countries have percentages between 60 and 80 per cent. Denmark, Norway, Finland, and Sweden are at 77.4, 75.1, 72.2, and 67.4 per cent respectively. Switzerland is at 59.4, New Zealand at 56.8.

---

[8] This is one of the central arguments of Dambisa Moyo (2018): 'Voters generally favour policies that enhance their own well-being with little consideration for that of future generations or for long-term outcomes. Politicians are rewarded for pandering to voters' immediate demands and desires.'

[9] Apparently there is surprise also about the role of families (items 8 and 9); however, by looking at the time series from 2007 (the start date of the Prosperity Index), we found that both indicators about families have a high variability over time, possibly suggesting the Gallup sample was not large enough to give reliable answers.

Moreover, all these percentages are fairly stable over time. Italians may find some comfort in the fact that France is a little below Italy, with a percentage of 28.1.

Psychologists are better equipped than economists to reconcile these answers and the perceived situations or traditions. However, we can guess that there may be a simple story: there may be a difference between how people behave and how they feel. Thus, Italians may have the habit of exhibiting more friendliness than other nationalities towards strangers, but they trust strangers less than others. This is entirely possible and does not mean that Italians are not sincere. On the contrary, they have been educated to behave in a friendly way with strangers, which matters from the viewpoint of a foreign tourist who visits Italy.

The question is what matters for the smooth functioning of the economy. And here, the answer does not seem too difficult. What matters are actual sentiments, not behaviour or appearances. In the World Economic Forum (WEF) survey of executives' opinions, it is asked 'In your country, to what extent do companies collaborate in sharing ideas and innovating?' In this sub-index, Italy's ranking among advanced countries is also very low: the top countries here are the US, Israel, the Netherlands, Sweden, Finland, Canada, and Germany. A few years ago, a survey asked top executives to what extent they trusted executives of their own country, and here again, Italy's ranked very low. Italian executives do not seem to trust each other.

These answers induce us to reconsider a traditional view of Italian companies collaborating with each other in clusters ('distretti' or districts).[10] Plenty of false perceptions were formed in the 1970s and 1980s. The common perception was that many small companies that manufactured similar products gathered together in some geographical locations (e.g. Prato, a town near Florence, for shoes and textiles) to collaborate and operate almost as if they were a single larger company. In this sense, clusters were viewed as a way around the problem of the dwarfism of Italian companies. They were small, indeed too small to withstand international competition, but they collaborated and, in the end, managed to overcome their limits.

For anyone who knows the reality of the 'distretti', this is only half-true, and probably is more false than true. Typically, companies in the clusters that make the same products are fierce competitors and have no intention

---

[10] This reconsideration of the traditional view was already present in Quintieri (2006). For a broad discussion of the role of districts in industrial development see, in English, Pyke et al. (1990) and, in Italian, Brusco (1990), Beccattini (1998), Traù (2000), and Galli-Paganetto (2002).

whatsoever of collaborating. Rarely, they create common facilities for the execution of some industrial functions. For example, they do not perform R&D together, and very rarely do they conduct marketing together.

However, clusters are useful for different reasons. For example, companies in the same sector can find skilled workers in a particular industry and find many suppliers in that sector. They can also lobby for common goods supplied by public authorities, such as roads or railways, local banks or specialised professional schools.[11]

Today, many traditional manufacturing clusters are in deep crisis because they have not been able to withstand globalisation and competition from low-cost producers. Nonetheless, some of the companies born in a cluster have become global and are doing well; in these cases many other small companies in the same cluster can prosper as providers of intermediate goods or services for a larger, more successful company.

An example is Luxottica, an eyewear conglomerate that started in the early 1960s in the cluster of Belluno and is now a successful global company. Most of the other companies in the district have remained small, and many have now disappeared.

The policy attempt to overcome the dwarfism of Italian companies through monetary incentives to create 'networks of companies' had some success in the past. These companies could form a single legal entity and perform some functions, including financing themselves in the market, as a single entity.[12] There is some evidence that joining a network is sometimes a profitable opportunity.[13] However, these agreements never took off and rarely convinced companies to move to the next stage, i.e. a fully-fledged merger.

---

[11] See Galli-Paganetto (2002).
[12] Such networks of companies have been introduced by Law n. 33 of 9 April 2009.
[13] See Cabigiosu-Moretti (2020).

4

Lobbies in government

Trust and governance—Difficult transitions of power: Berlusconi and the 'red togas'—The rise and fall of populism—The government, ubiquitous and untraceable—Lobbying by rule-makers—Attempts at institutional reforms—Powerful lobbies: magistrates—Is Italy corrupt?

4.1 Trust and governance

The next pillar of the Prosperity Index is Governance[1] (Table 4.1). It did not appear at the top of our list of pillars because Italy, being a western democracy, ranks high on some essential items, in line with all other democracies: Military involvement in rule of law and politics, Democracy level, and Political participation and rights.

Of course, democracy cannot be taken for granted, and in Italy, there have been some attempts to challenge or even suppress it.[2] Probably the main risk for democracy comes from Italy's dismal economic performance. The sequence of crises since 2008 has had the effect of delegitimising a large portion of the country's leadership. The situation has, of course, been enormously aggravated by the pandemic in 2020–21. If Italy did not manage to solve its economic problems, it might have no choice but to levy a major wealth tax or restructure its debt with new austerity measures. In that case, the democratic fabric of the country might not resist. However, as of today, democracy is thriving.

The interesting and somewhat appalling aspect of Table 4.1 is that Italy ranks among the worst advanced countries in virtually all other items. It is hard to attribute this fact to anything different from the two forces described above. On the one hand, the historical legacy of lack of social capital explains why mutual trust between citizens and institutions is deficient. In turn, this explains why the opinions of people on government action are so negative.

---

[1] In Table 4.1, we include the item Natural environment because we consider it as part of a broader issue of poor governance. In the Legatum index, this item is instead treated as a separate pillar.
[2] Faini, M. (2021). On the risks to liberal democracies today, see Salvati-Dilmore (2021).

Meritocracy, Growth, and Lessons from Italy's Economic Decline. Lorenzo Codogno and Giampaolo Galli,
Oxford University Press. © Lorenzo Codogno and Giampaolo Galli (2022). DOI: 10.1093/oso/9780192866806.003.0005

Table 4.1 Governance

Element	Indicator	Italy /167	Italy /34	Top country /167
Executive Constraints	Transition of power is subject to the law	35	28	Denmark
Executive Constraints	Government officials are sanctioned for misconduct	32	27	Denmark
Executive Constraints	Executive powers are effectively limited by the judiciary and legislature	31	23	Norway
Executive Constraints	Government powers are subject to independent and non-governmental checks	29	25	Denmark
Executive Constraints	Military involvement in rule of law and politics	1	1	Multiple—19
Government Effectiveness	Efficiency of government spending	156	33	Singapore
Government Effectiveness	Policy coordination	67	33	Multiple—23
Government Effectiveness	Prioritisation	58	32	Multiple—23
Government Effectiveness	Implementation	54	32	Multiple—22
Government Effectiveness	Policy learning	51	32	Multiple—22
Government Effectiveness	Government quality and credibility	48	33	Singapore
Government Effectiveness	Natural Environment	46	27	Sweden
Government Effectiveness	Efficient use of assets	45	33	Multiple—22
Government Integrity	Transparency of government policy	148	34	New Zealand
Government Integrity	Diversion of public funds	79	29	New Zealand
Government Integrity	Publicised laws and government data	40	32	Australia
Government Integrity	Use of public office for private gain	40	32	Denmark
Government Integrity	Right to information	28	23	Sweden
Government Integrity	Budget transparency	22	13	New Zealand
Political Accountability	Complaint mechanisms	65	34	Netherlands
Political Accountability	Consensus on democracy and a market economy as a goal	36	30	Multiple—29
Political Accountability	Democracy level	1	1	Multiple—23

Continued

Element	Indicator	Italy /167	Italy /34	Top country /167
Political Accountability	Political participation and rights	1	1	Multiple—29
Regulatory Quality	Efficiency of legal framework in challenging regulations	155	33	Finland
Regulatory Quality	Delay in administrative proceedings	93	33	Singapore
Regulatory Quality	Enforcement of regulations	43	33	Austria
Regulatory Quality	Regulatory quality	41	33	Singapore
Rule of Law	Efficiency of dispute settlement	157	34	Singapore
Rule of Law	Judicial independence	63	29	Finland
Rule of Law	Civil justice	58	33	Germany
Rule of Law	Integrity of the legal system	46	31	Multiple—8

Note: The notation 'Multiple—n' indicates that n countries are in the top position.
Source: Prosperity Index, 2020, and authors' calculations.

On the other hand, the success of old elites and lobbies in rejecting merit makes it challenging to get rid of such a heavy historical legacy. The end result is that people are very unhappy with the bureaucracy, and public sector workers have become a powerful lobby and one of the most successful in impeding change.

When the level of trust is so low, it may well be that democracy is solid, but some critical junctures of a democratic system may not be functioning well. This problem is exemplified by the first four items in the table concerning Executive constraints: Transition of power is subject to the law, Government officials are sanctioned for misconduct, Executive powers are effectively limited by the judiciary and legislature, and Government powers are subject to independent and non-governmental checks. On all these items (taken from the Rule of Law Index of the World Justice Project[3]) Italy's score among advanced countries is relatively low. But probably the most worrying aspect is the first one, which is a composite measure of (a) whether government officials are elected or appointed in accordance with the rules and procedures set forth in the Constitution, and (b) the integrity of the electoral process, including access to the ballot, absence of intimidation, and public scrutiny of election results.

It is indeed true that political parties have resorted to reciprocal delegitimation and even demonisation. Journalists were sometimes removed from

[3] World Justice Project (2021).

their positions, typically in the state-owned main TV channels the government controls. It was also the case for the leading private TV (with three national channels) owned by the Berlusconi family, which played a role in Berlusconi's success. Various attempts were made to approve a law barring conflict of interest, but such attempts had no success.

Two key aspects of the recent political history of Italy help to better understand the issue of the transition of power. The conflict between the pro- and anti-Berlusconi camps lasted from 1994 until 2011, and that between the populist movements and the so-called establishment from 2012 to 2020. The quick review that follows does not pretend to be a political history of Italy, but only highlights those aspects of such history required to understand the crucial issue of the transition of power.

4.2 Difficult transitions of power: Berlusconi and the 'red togas'

To put the issue in context, Italy has never seen episodes such as the 2020 assault on Congress in the United States at the end of the Trump administration. The losers always accepted the results of elections, as proclaimed by the Minister of Interior. However, elections were almost always contested in the sense that the losers accused the winners of manipulating electors through their influence on the media or the judges. Most importantly, these features have lasted for an extended period, a quarter of a century. It is thus useful to dig deeper into this issue.

In 1996, the centre-left coalition, led by Romano Prodi, won the elections and formed the government. The opposition, led by Silvio Berlusconi, forcefully argued that the government was not legitimate because Berlusconi was the victim of persecution by the judges, which he called the 'red togas', thus implying that they were close to the 'reds', i.e. the (former) communists that were in government. The 'red togas' had sent him notice of an investigation at a very critical moment in November 1994. Prime Minister Berlusconi was presiding at a G7 meeting in Naples when the news hit the tape. Unknown sources sent copy of the notice to the leading Italian newspaper. In turn, when Berlusconi won the 2001 elections, several opposition politicians considered he was not a legitimate prime minister because he had been indicted for a large number of crimes. These alleged crimes included tax evasion, corruption of fiscal authorities, bribery of judges, complicity with the mafia, induction to prostitution, etc. The lawsuits were a considerable number (100), also counting all those against the companies Berlusconi controlled. For him, this disproportionate number was a confirmation that he was a victim of persecution.

According to his political opponents on the other hand, this was proof that he could not rule Italy. Also, many foreign observers thought that Berlusconi was unfit for office. In April 2001, a few days before the general elections, *The Economist* put Berlusconi on the cover with a big title 'Why Silvio Berlusconi is unfit to lead Italy'. Similar articles appeared in many other international media such as *El Pais* in Spain, *Die Welt* in Germany, and *ABC News* in the USA. The conflict between the two camps became heated as Berlusconi's government approved many laws widely deemed *ad personam*, i.e. made to help him escape from trial. In July 2003, *The Economist* sent an open letter to Berlusconi signed by the editor, Bill Emmott, asking him to respond to no less than fifty-one questions about his trials and the laws that his government was approving.

The opposition (mainly Left or Centre-Left) used these arguments to delegitimise Berlusconi. He did the opposite. He called it a plot against him organised by the Left together with the 'red togas'. In the political elections of 2008, the leader of the Centre-Left, Walter Veltroni, made an effort to avoid mutual demonisation, which was doing enormous damage to the integrity of the democratic institutions. However, the attempt did not succeed. Berlusconi won the elections and ruled Italy until the end of 2011, when the sovereign debt crisis induced him to resign in favour of a national emergency government headed by Mario Monti.

4.3 The rise and fall of populism

In more recent times, the transition of power, though always subject to the law, became difficult because of the rise of the populist parties that considered the so-called establishment essentially illegitimate.[4] In the political elections held in February 2013, the Five Star Movement became the second political party, almost with the same number of votes as the Democratic Party. The Five Star Movement, at the time, presented all the characteristics that would allow a careful political scientist to label it as 'populist'. It did not have what could be called a programme to run the country. Still, it had clear ideas as to how the establishment, particularly the political establishment, could be punished: cutting pension benefits of members of parliament, reducing their number and many of their presumed privileges. As background, recall that Italy was coming out of two major crises: the GFC of 2008–09 and the sovereign debt crisis of 2011–12. At the time of elections, available economic

---

[4] For an analysis of the deep origins of populism in Italy and Europe see Guiso et al. (2019) and Panebianco-Belardinelli (2019). For a review of literature on populism see Nouri-Gerard (2020).

data were indeed abysmal: GDP was 7 per cent lower than in 2007, and the poverty rate, as measured by the national statistical office, had risen from 4.1 per cent in 2007 to 5.9 per cent in 2012.[5] There was widespread resentment against the EU and the parties that had supported the Monti government in 2011–12. That government had to cut the deficit and enact essential labour market reforms to reduce some of the rigidities inherited from the 1970s. Even today, pension reform is still a matter of great resentment against Monti himself and even more against his courageous Minister of Labour, Elsa Fornero. The Five Star Movement capitalised on the nation's tense social situation and promised to punish those who were deemed responsible. One of the movement's slogans was: 'we will open parliament like a can of tuna'.

At the same time, the League, originally a regional party advocating autonomy for the more prosperous northern regions of the country, changed leadership. After a major scandal and health problems of its historical leader, Umberto Bossi, the League fell into the hands of Matteo Salvini and rapidly became a national and nationalistic party. Also the League exploited the discontent of many social groups and accused mainly the EU, the euro, the European Central Bank, and Germany. Other main enemies of the League were immigrants, particularly those that came illegally crossing the Mediterranean from the coasts of Libya and Tunisia.

In the end, these two parties, the Five Star Movement and the League, managed to create an anti-establishment climate, which deserves to be defined as a climate of true hate. Once again, the political landscape was characterised by mutual demonisation, and the transition of power became difficult.

After the general elections of February 2013, the leader of the Democratic Party, Pierluigi Bersani, tried to engage with the Five Star Movement but was rather brutally rejected. In the end, the only possible government turned out to be the one based on a coalition, led by Enrico Letta, between the two historical enemies: the Democratic Party and, despite all his indictments, Silvio Berlusconi. Obviously, in this situation, there was no way that 'a government official be sanctioned for their misconduct', an item in which Italy ranks twenty-seventh among advanced nations. Berlusconi was the leader of a centre-right coalition that had received almost 30 per cent of the popular vote, and his support in Parliament was essential to forming a government. On 1 August 2013, three months after the government gained a confidence vote in Parliament, Berlusconi was convicted for fiscal evasion in the third

---

[5] Percentage of individuals who live in families that cannot afford a minimum acceptable standard of living, as defined by the national statistical office.

and last degree of judgement. It also quickly became a fundamental problem for the stability of Letta's government. Berlusconi's conviction made it necessary for the Senate to declare his dismissal as a member of that house, which occurred in the following month of November after very tense political convulsions.

After 2013, the opposition was formed by the two populist parties, whose support in the country was bound to rise. To complete this quick overview, it was not clear at that time whether Italy had managed to overcome its financial problems. The spectre of the Greek drama was vivid in consideration of the traditional parties, and many of the country's economic elites feared the advent of populist parties.

In February 2014, in view of the European elections, the Democratic Party decided to change horses and tried the card of Matteo Renzi, a young, very determined and initially very popular leader who had previously been mayor of Florence.

The Renzi government was initially very successful in mixing two elements of his political strategy: a bit of populism, which he probably thought was a necessary ingredient at a time of rising populist feelings in the country, and the rather unpopular reforms that Italy needed—for instance, introducing evaluation and merit in the school system, eliminating residual rigidities in the labour market, enhancing efficiency in public administration, and transforming the large and inefficient mutual banks into joint-stock companies.

Renzi tried to solve the institutional problem through a combination of electoral and constitutional reforms (see below). The change of the Constitution required a referendum; that ended with resounding defeat in December 2016. Renzi resigned and was replaced by his foreign minister Paolo Gentiloni, also a member of the Democratic Party, who managed to bring the country to the crucial political elections of March 2018 in a relatively orderly way. In these elections, the Five Star Movement became the first party with 32.7 per cent of the popular vote; second was the Democratic Party with 18.7 per cent, just a little more than the League, which managed to get 17.4 per cent of the vote.

After three months of complex negotiations and amid fears of a repeat of the Greek drama, the Five Star Movement and the League finally formed a government on 1 June. The two parties' leaders became deputy prime ministers in a government led by Giuseppe Conte, a lawyer who had never been in politics until then and was unknown to Italy's public.

Italy finally had a government entirely formed by populist parties who proclaimed themselves, with more or less strength, as 'the people', not just representatives of a majority of the voters. They declared that they no longer cared about budget discipline, Europe, and the euro.

During their government, the spread between Italy's and Germany's ten-year government bond yields rose from about 120 basis points to values between 250 and 300 basis points. At one point, it looked as if the real intention was to exit the euro and change Italy's international alliances, shifting towards China or Russia.[6]

In any case, the experience and responsibility of governing were very instructive for the two populist parties because, in a short time, they became much more moderate. Anti-European and especially anti-euro positions rapidly became marginal. Many of the slogans and totems that had contributed to the success of populism fell into disgrace or were forgotten.

The coalition between the Five Star Movement and the League ended with Conte's resignation on 20 August 2019, following the withdrawal of the League's support from the government. A new coalition was formed with the Democratic Party and the Five Star Movement, and Conte was sworn in for a second mandate as Prime Minister on 5 September 2019.

This date was a turning point for politics in Italy. It became more evident during 2020 when the Covid-19 pandemic forced everybody to face the nation's real issues pragmatically. This was a tremendous maturity test for the Five Star Movement; it was as if an adolescent was suddenly given an enormous responsibility that obliged her/him to rapidly become an adult.

In February 2021, after a crisis of the Conte II government and in the midst of the tremendous sanitary and economic crisis caused by the pandemic, Mario Draghi, former president of the European Central Bank, was called on to form a national unity government. He had the support of almost all political parties, with the main exception of Brothers of Italy, a far-right nationalist party.

This marked a further step in the retreat of populism in Italy since both the Five Star Movement and the League became part of the Draghi government. The Five Star Movement lost its identity and much of its support in public opinion; the League still had a marked right-wing identity with its position against immigrants and for a quick reopening of the economy after the extended lockdowns caused by the pandemic. But the League also lost part of its popular support in favour of Brothers of Italy.

With the formation of the Draghi government, the risks for Italian democracy—in terms of the first item of Table 4.1, Transition of power is

---

[6] Exit from the euro, in our view, would be disastrous. See Codogno-Galli (2017) and Codogno-Merler (2019).

subject to the law—should have reduced sharply. The long journey since the war between Berlusconi and the 'red togas' and the rise and fall of populism appears to have ended, making democracy safer.

However, this does not mean that the problems were over. Populist parties were still strong in opinion polls, Italy was left with public debt at 150 per cent of GDP and long-standing structural issues; and a political situation still far from being settled.

4.4 The government, ubiquitous and untraceable

Another worrying indicator is the composite index Complaint mechanism, where Italy ranks last among all advanced countries. This variable measures whether individuals feel that they have effective mechanisms to complain about government's performance (again from the World Justice Project). People think that institutions are far from them and not prepared to listen to their complaints. There is hardly any question that this is a fair description of the situation. Administration is everywhere except where it is needed. As Sabino Cassese (1998), a former judge of the Supreme Court, wrote:

> the State is nowhere to be found[. . .], a state that remains ambivalent, half developed, half backward; it is still dualistic, authoritarian and liberal; and above all, it is ingested in everything, without then being able to assert the public interests that motivate such interference.

According to Barucci et al. (2010b), there is too little government where it is needed and too much where it is not. We agree; the government is absent and untraceable, or hard to trace, when citizens need it. It is everywhere in terms of regulating too many aspects of social and economic life as well as in terms of running businesses on which it has no expertise, especially at the regional and local levels.

Reducing the distance between institutions and citizens has always been one of the objectives of various public administration reforms tried in the past. For example, the 2009 reform had the intention of transforming public service users into 'clients', as in the private sector.[7] There were also some (failed) attempts to reward public employees according to some measure of 'client satisfaction'.

---

[7] So called Brunetta law (from the name of the minister who proposed it): legge delega 4 March 2009, n. 15.

Scrolling down the list in Table 4.1, one finds some of the key items that damage the competitiveness of Italian companies. All items under the heading Government effectiveness see a very low ranking for Italy. On Efficiency of public spending, Italy is ranked 156th out of 167 countries. But the score is low on all other items in this list: Policy coordination, Prioritisation, Implementation, etc. One of the critical reforms included in Italy's National Recovery and Resilience Plan, and correctly so, is public sector reform. According to the EC, the low efficiency of public administration and its perceived distance from individuals and companies is one of the key factors that hamper competitiveness and growth in Italy.

We agree with Di Mascio et al. (2021) that

> Whilst the institutions are inspired by the French model, Italian administration has also long displayed features typical of what has been labelled the Southern European bureaucratic model: clientelism in the recruitment of low ranking officials; an uneven distribution of resources, institutional fragmentation, and insufficient mechanisms for policy coordination; formalism and legalism complemented by informal shadow governance structures; and the absence of a typical European administrative elite.

In addition, as they say, a 'distinctive historical feature of the Italian bureaucracy is its "Southernisation", meaning that public administration was used as a social buffer to reward the loyalty of Southern clientele via the particularistic distribution of selective benefits, including jobs'. As Cassese (1998) put it, '[the administration] constituted an "ossified world", elderly and with a relatively low level of professionalism, in which promotions were rewards for age and length of service, with limited horizontal and vertical mobility'. It goes without saying that in this context, merit is virtually non-existent.[8]

A poor score on Regulatory quality is an obvious consequence of poor governance. The only indicator we find difficult to reconcile with reality concerns the Efficiency of legal framework in challenging regulations. Almost all investment projects are delayed by recourse to administrative justice, and typically, the immediate act of the judges that follows is the stopping of works. Perhaps this indicator, which comes from the WEF survey, captures chief executives' and entrepreneurs' complaints about national and local governments that tend to take decisions to achieve short-term electoral benefits rather than those that would help competitiveness and growth.

---

[8] A detailed analysis of how public sector employees are selected and promoted can be found in Giorgiantonio et al. (2016).

4.5 Lobbying by rule-makers

Items 14 through 19 are interesting. They all measure the perceived integrity of the government and public officials. Again, here we find the abysmal distance between people and institutions. In particular, Italy ranks last among advanced countries on the item Transparency of government policy, which is a WEF question formulated in the following terms: 'In your country, how easy is it for companies to obtain information about changes in government policies and regulations affecting their activities, from extremely difficult, to extremely easy?' Here the fact is that the laws are written in such a way that they cannot be easily understood except by super experts of each particular sector. Members of parliament, who have to approve or amend the laws, do not understand them until parliamentary offices produce a precious document that translates each article of law into a readable format and explains the status quo and what changes are introduced by the law.[9] Those who write the laws are not members of parliament, but a small number of 'mandarins', typically administrative magistrates, who work in the cabinet or legislative office of the ministries. They form the powerful lobby of rule-makers. By writing unreadable laws, they preserve their power; they are almost the only ones who understand the laws and see what they imply for firms and citizens. They are the ones whom interested companies or citizens must consult.

Why rule-maker mandarins have such great power is not an easy question to answer. Still, for the present purposes, it is sufficient to note that this is primarily a consequence of the distance between governments and citizens, which in turn has an important effect on the functioning of public administration and the judicial system.

A much more severe comment was that of Giovanni Giolitti, several times Prime Minister of the Kingdom of Italy from 1882 and 1922. He once said the laws are complex because they 'are to be applied to enemies and interpreted for friends'. It is the opposite of the Roman law principle, according to which *in claris non fit interpretatio*, i.e. there should be no room for interpretation in a well-designed law. Hence, it is the opposite of what in the Anglo-Saxon world is known as the rule of law.

In practice, companies are often unsure which law should apply to a particular case, which means they are in the hands of some public employees or politicians for the 'right' interpretation. If they manage to have good connections with those who make decisions or interpret the laws, they may have

---

[9] This is a well-known fact which is confirmed by personal experience as well as by a large body of literature. See for instance, Galli-Cassese (1998).

an easy life; otherwise, they are lost. 'Connections' is the keyword. As we will argue in Chapter 9, connections are often more important than good marketing, R&D, innovation, and competitiveness for a company's domestic success.[10] Companies with connections may not have high productivity, but they will have a number of more important advantages than productivity: having someone who gives them a favourable interpretation of the law. Connections may be helpful for many other reasons: speeding up processes requiring administrative approval, having a favourable law being approved, and selling products to public administration. Sometimes, a connection must go beyond public employees or politicians and reach the police, the Ministry of Interior, the judges.

4.6 Attempts at institutional reforms

For much of the last thirty-year period, there have been attempts to solve many of these problems through institutional reform, both electoral and constitutional.[11] The idea was that at the root of many Italian issues there was a lack of political stability and excessive dependence by the central government on other powers, particularly a very fragmented system of political parties and regional governments. Indeed, Italy has had sixty-seven governments since the start of the Republic in 1946, almost one government per year.[12] In the latest legislature, which started with the elections of 2018, there have been three governments: Conte I (with the Five Star and the League), Conte II (with the Five Star and the Democratic Party), and Draghi.

For the entire republican period until 1993, Italy had a purely proportional system, which was thought to be the reason for the extreme political fragmentation and the high number of parties. That system gave rise to what many have called 'partitocracy', i.e. a system dominated by short-term party dealings that resulted in corruption and pork-barrel politics.

Following the 1991 referendum that promoted the idea of a majoritarian system, a new system was approved in 1993 (called 'Mattarellum' from the

---

[10] See Akcigit et al. (2018a).

[11] Useful accounts of institutional reform in Italy can be found in Amato (2015), Cassese (2015), and Leone (2020). A updated list of reforms, both proposed or approved, can be found on the site of the Italian Parliament: Parlamento Italiano (2021). According to Mieli (2017) the problem of political instability has been plaguing Italy since unification in 1861.

[12] In Italy, as in several other countries, government reshuffles involving more than one minister are usually counted as changes in government due to the constitutional procedures involved, and thus the number of governments since WWII may be slightly overstated relative to countries in which the prime minister or the president have the power to change ministers. Even taking this into account, changes in government have been very frequent.

name of the proponent). It had a strong majoritarian twist: 75 per cent of the seats in both the Senate and the Chamber of Deputies were allocated according to the first-past-the-post system. The remaining 25 per cent were allocated by a proportional system. This reform changed the political scene in the sense that it helped substitute the old system in which one party (the Christian Democratic Party) was always in power, with a system in which two camps could alternate in power: the Centre-Left and the Centre-Right. Essentially, the reform was inspired by the English system in which two main parties followed one another in power. The goal of creating alternation in power was achieved, but the system did not become more stable. The average duration of governments after reform remained very short. Coalitions formed to win elections with the new majoritarian system were very heterogeneous and could not form cohesive governments. This was the main reason for the failure of the new system in its attempt to increase stability. Indeed, the first government that won the election after reform (the Berlusconi government of 1994) lasted less than one year because the League (at the time the Northern League) had a very different programme.

In 2005, Berlusconi, who was back in government, approved a law that was again proportional but with a substantial majority premium: the coalition that received the relative majority of the popular vote would win a premium so that it could reach an absolute majority both in the Senate and in the Lower House. This law was harshly criticised. It came to be remembered as the 'porcellum' because its main proponent defined it as porcata (rascality). Essentially this law introduced very large constituencies with long lists of candidates, and did not allow voters to express their preferences on candidates of a given coalition. In 2013, the Constitutional Court declared this law unconstitutional. In any case, even this law did not produce political stability. The first coalition that won the election after its approval (the Prodi-led coalition in 2006) lasted fewer than two years. Again, it was a heterogeneous coalition ranging from the radical Left to the former Christian Democrats and was not apt to support the government.

After very intricate vicissitudes, a new law (the third one since 1993) was approved in 2017, called 'Rosatellum', from the name of its proponent. This law, which is still in force, is again a hybrid system between proportional and first-past-the-post. Almost everybody considers it an imperfect solution, including their original proponents. It was applied for the first time in the elections of 2018, and since then it has not increased stability. The result was widespread expectation that parliament would approve a new law sooner or later.[13]

Overall, the story of electoral reform is the story of the illusion of the reformist movement that a law leaning towards an English-style majoritarian rule would produce more stability. We are among those who had many hopes that this would be possible, but it has not happened.

Another route to solving problems of government instability has been the reform of the Constitution. After discussions that lasted several decades, two attempts were made, one by Berlusconi and one by Renzi; both were rejected by voters in two referenda, in 2006 and 2016. The two proposed reforms were very different, although both aimed at reducing political instability: making the legislative process more efficient by eliminating the pure bicameral system according to which the two chambers have exactly the same tasks and both must approve all laws; clarifying the powers of central government and those of the regions. Both reforms had positive aspects. We voted in favour of them in the referenda.[14]

It is worth highlighting that both reforms were rejected for reasons that had nothing to do with their content. In both cases, the dominating force with the electorate was partisan politics. In 2006, Silvio Berlusconi and his ideas were the evil to be defeated. In 2016, it was the desire to kick Matteo Renzi out of the political scene, which is what de facto happened for some time.

Too bad; today's Italy would be a somewhat better country had one of the two reforms been approved.

Nonetheless, we would not want to give too bleak a picture of the Italian political system. Here, we should reflect what we wrote in Chapter 3, that whenever there was a crisis Italy resorted to leaders perceived as competent. And we made examples of the governments led by Ciampi in 1993, Dini in 1995, Monti in 2011, and Draghi in 2021. This means that the political system is still capable of seeing when it is time to go beyond its limits and recognise merit.

4.7 Powerful lobbies: magistrates

Last but not least in this inglorious list are items under the heading Rule of law. Italy ranks among the worst countries globally, and the last among advanced countries, concerning Efficiency of dispute settlement. This is a well-known fact documented by data collected by the World Bank and

---

[13] See D'Alimonte (2021).
[14] For an excellent account of why change was needed see Cassese (2016).

Table 4.2 Enterprise conditions, civil justice

Element	Indicator	Italy/ 167	Italy/ 34	Top Country
Contract Enforcement	Time to resolve commercial cases	151	32	Singapore
Contract Enforcement	Legal costs	89	31	Luxembourg
Contract Enforcement	Alternative dispute resolution mechanisms	60	34	Norway
Contract Enforcement	Quality of judicial administration	23	15	Multiple—2
Property Rights	Protection of property rights	67	33	Finland
Property Rights	Intellectual property protection	48	30	Finland
Property Rights	Lawful process for expropriation	43	30	Germany
Property Rights	Procedures to register property	26	12	New Zealand
Property Rights	Quality of land administration	11	8	Multiple—4
Property Rights	Regulation of property possession and exchange	1	1	Multiple—32

Source: Prosperity Index, (2020), and authors' calculations.

other organisations. It is why companies, like politicians, often find it useful, though it is obviously illegal, to have close connections with members of the judiciary. Magistrates are organised in powerful lobbies. So far, they have managed to resist attempts to introduce evaluation and merit into promotions and careers.

To get a more precise picture, we look at two other indicators in the Prosperity Index classified in the pillar Enterprise conditions (see Table 2.5 for an overall view): contract enforcement and property rights (Table 4.2).

Items under the heading Contract enforcement come from measures performed by the World Bank, except for the third one (on alternative dispute resolution) that results from the Rule of Law Index of World Justice.

The worst item for Italy is the first one, Time to resolve commercial cases. The score is relatively low or very low on all other items, therefore it is not surprising to find a low score on the item Protection of property rights (from the WEF survey): executives of Italian companies or Italian branches of foreign companies consider that property rights are not sufficiently protected.

Returning to Contract enforcement, the World Bank provides the following definition: 'The average time it takes to make a commercial case through the courts, including the time for filing and service, trial and judgement'. In Italy, it takes twice the time it takes in France and about three times that in the USA.

Similar results hold for penal proceedings, which may well take ten or more years. This is why the EC, and many others, consider reform of the justice system one of the key reforms to be implemented within the Next Generation EU framework. Slow justice, together with inefficient administration, is considered a key obstacle to investment and growth.

Italian magistrates seem not to be aware of this problem as they do not seem to realise that slow justice is one of the key reasons why Italy does not grow. When asked to explain the inefficiency of the justice system, they typically say that it is underfinanced and that Italians are very litigious and resort to tribunals too often.

The first claim is de facto not true. Eurostat data show that Italy's spending on tribunals is more or less in line with the European average (0.33 per cent of GDP), which is more than France (0.24 per cent) and a little less than Germany (0.39 per cent).[15] What instead seems to be true is that there are fewer magistrates than in most other countries and that these fewer magistrates have higher salaries.[16]

As for litigiousness, attempts to reduce recourse to tribunals (introducing an access fee or a penalty for petty or frivolous cases) are typically rejected on the grounds that the Constitution guarantees access to justice for all: the two lobbies of lawyers and magistrates are pretty powerful. As it goes, only in the city of Rome are there more lawyers than in the whole of France.

The real problem is that there is no reward for merit. A judge who works hard and is highly productive cannot expect to be treated differently from his peers. The careers and salaries of judges depend almost exclusively on seniority. In theory, the CSM *(Consiglio Superiore della Magistratura* [High Council of the Judiciary], the body of self-government of the judiciary) provides assessment, but practically all magistrates receive a positive evaluation.[17] In the period 2017–21, 7,394 magistrates (99.2 per cent of the total) received a 'positive evaluation', 24 (0.3 per cent) a 'non-positive evaluation', and 35 (0.5 per cent) a 'negative evaluation'.[18]

---

[15] Frattola (2020).

[16] Council of Europe (2020).

[17] 'Positive' means pass (and gives the right to a promotion), 'non positive' means that the evaluation is repeated the following year, 'negative' means that the evaluation is repeated after two years. In case of a repeated 'negative' evaluation the magistrate is removed from office. The evaluation is performed every four years. Only the 1st, 3rd, 5th, and 7th evaluations give the right to a salary increase.

[18] From testimony by the Minister of Justice, Marta Cartabia, at the Chamber of Deputies' question time of 20 October 2021.

Some tribunals are relatively efficient, and this depends on the attitude of the tribunal president, who in principle has some tools at her/his disposal to give judges the appropriate incentives. It so happens that tribunals are considerably more efficient in the North. The average duration of a first-degree civil proceeding is 1,142 days in the South and 671 days in the North.[19] Some tribunals (Trento, Turin, Milan) are much more efficient than others. Statistical analysis performed by researchers at the Bank of Italy shows that such differences are not due to differing availability of resources.[20]

The point is that the tribunal's president can act as a passive bureaucrat who does not evaluate and reward merit (including time employed for the proceedings) or be more similar to a manager. Most magistrates do not accept the idea that a tribunal is a complex organisation that needs a managerial style of direction. But the reform must facilitate that. And it must introduce incentives for more productive tribunals, where productivity also includes how much time is employed for an average proceeding.[21]

To these problems, it must be added that, in recent times, several scandals have emerged that have badly shaken the prestige of the judicial system and have made it clear that radical reform is needed. Such scandals mainly concern connections between magistrates and politicians, and highlighted that connections and patronage are essential to a successful career.

The incredibly slow machine of Italian justice and its system of connections are some of the most devastating consequences of the general rejection of the principles of evaluation and meritocracy. This situation has wide-reaching implications for the competitiveness of Italian companies, beyond what could be grasped by simply looking at the evidence we have presented. It is usually mentioned among the top problems facing multinational companies willing to invest in Italy, de facto increasing entry barriers and reducing competition.

Finally, for a fair evaluation of the system, one cannot forget that many magistrates, perhaps the majority, do their work with 'diligence and honour' as required by the Constitution of all civil servants. Several of them risk their lives fighting against organised crime; many have died while in office.

4.8 Is Italy corrupt?

An essential aspect of the Italian scene is the perception that corruption is widespread. Indeed, going back to Table 4.1, Italy has a low ranking in most

---

[19] Cascavilla (2020).
[20] Giacomelli et al. (2017).
[21] See De Nicola-Cottarelli (2019).

items under the heading Government integrity; particularly in the critical Diversion of public funds, Italy ranks seventy-ninth among all countries and twenty-ninth among advanced nations. The source is a WEF survey in which executives are asked the following question: 'In your country, how common is illegal diversion of public funds to companies, individuals, or groups?' The interesting aspect is that answers reflect the opinion of companies' executives, who should know more about the issue than most of the population.

The most cited index of corruption is the Corruption Perception Index, compiled by Transparency International. This index tries to reflect the views of the entire population. It gives Italy an even worse ranking: fifty-third, after all advanced and most East European countries, former USSR, and many less developed countries. At the top of the least corrupt countries, one finds Denmark, New Zealand, Finland, Singapore, Sweden, Switzerland, Norway, the Netherlands, and Germany. The UK is in eleventh position, France in twenty-third, the USA in twenty-fifth, Spain in thirty-second.

Hence, there is little question that Italians perceive Italy as a rather corrupt country, which is an essential piece of information because perception matters, especially for such a critical issue as the legitimacy of a country's leadership. Much of Italian political history of the past thirty years is intertwined with the perception of corrupt leadership. Operation *mani pulite* (clean hands) brought by the Milan magistrates in 1992 against a number of top politicians had an enormous rate of approval from the population and was the critical determinant of the end of the political parties that had ruled Italy for decades. Many changes in the political scene have emerged since then, in the form of new parties appearing or old parties changing identity and leaders. The success of populist movements, notably the Five Star Movement, in the political elections of 2013 and 2018 was very much due to the perception that the establishment was corrupt. Most magistrates would say that corruption and organised crime are pervasive in all aspects of Italian society.[22]

The very explanation developed in this book about lack of merit, connections, and lobbies may induce the reader to believe that Italy is indeed a very corrupt country. We do not entirely share this view, and we think the perception is somewhat exaggerated relative to reality. In the following paragraph, we bring some evidence in this respect.

In addition to the indices of perception, there are those of experience of corruption. Transparency International itself provides one in a publication

---

[22] Barbieri-Giavazzi (2014) document the corruption that exists in public procurement, with particular reference to the construction of 'Mose', a system of retractable mobile floodgates at the lagoon port inlets to protect the city of Venice and the entire lagoon ecosystem from high waters.

called the Global Corruption Barometer.[23] Contrary to the indices of perception, it is not updated every year and does not receive as much publicity. However, it is very carefully estimated, and it is unclear why it is known only to scholars and not to the general public.

The Global Corruption Barometer asks respondents in a selected number of countries about their experiences of bribery or those of other household members over the past twelve months. It refers to contacts with the following eight typologies of public service: the road police, public agencies issuing official documents, the civil courts, public education (primary or secondary), public education (vocational), public health care, public agencies in charge of unemployment benefits, and public agencies in charge of other social security benefits. The result is a variable called Bribery rate, based on those who have had contact with at least one case in dealing with these public services.

Table 4.3 shows data from the Global Corruption Barometer. Italy ranks twentieth in terms of the experience of corruption and seventy-fifth in terms of perception.[24] Note that several western countries (those marked ** in the table) are not listed in the dataset on experience. We have conventionally set them at the same value as Germany: they all rank in fourth position, with a score of 2 per cent. In this ranking, Italy is below most western democracies but is above most Eastern European countries, those of the former USSR, and those of Africa, Asia, and South America.

A similar conclusion can be drawn from the results of the Eurobarometer 2020 Report from the European Commission (Table 4.4); Italy is again below almost all Western European countries (except Greece and Austria), at the same level as Belgium and above most Eastern European countries. With 7 per cent of people who respond that they have experienced or witnessed corruption cases in the past twelve months, it is slightly above the EU average of 6 per cent.

In Italy, corruption is above that in the best Western European countries but is not as bad as most emerging and low-income countries. This conclusion seems sensible to us, in light of our personal experience as persons in reasonably high positions in public administration or lobbying organisations in Italy and with some knowledge of what happens in other countries.

An obvious question is why Italians perceive their country is more corrupt than it actually is. There may be many answers to this question.

---

[23] Transparency International (2021).
[24] This number (75) differs from that of the Corruption Perception Index (53) because the Global Corruption Barometer does not report a summary measure of corruption perception; as a proxy for that summary measure we have used the perception of corruption of Government Officials.

Table 4.3 Corruption: experience vs perception

Countries	Experience of corruption	Perception of corruption (*)
Japan	1	32
Hong Kong	2	7
Mauritius	2	12
Belgium(**)	4	20
Cyprus	4	44
France	4	46
Germany	4	1
Korea	4	109
Netherlands(**)	4	9
Portugal	4	29
Slovenia	4	24
Spain	4	12
Sweden(**)	4	4
Switzerland	4	7
UK(**)	4	29
USA(**)	4	50
Australia	17	9
Jordan	17	59
Georgia	19	2
Estonia	20	2
Italy	**20**	75
South Africa	20	93
Taiwan	20	12

(*) Corruption of government officials. (**) Countries for which there are no data on experience; they are all conventionally set equal to Germany.
Source: Authors' calculations on Transparency International, Global Corruption Barometer 2021.

Figure 4.1 shows the scores of the entire set of 113 countries of the Global Corruption Barometer. In the graph, the triangular symbol represents Italy with 5 on the x-axis (experience of corruption) and 40 on the y-axis (perception); the squares are advanced countries, and the circles are developing countries.

There are sharp differences between perception and experience of corruption in many other countries, in one sense or another (dots above or below the 45-degree line). They may be related to the different metrics used in the two surveys or measurement issues, and thus we should not rely too much upon these differences. At low levels of experience of corruption, the perception is almost always higher (above the 45-degree line); this is the case for nearly all advanced countries. As experience increases, perception also increases, but less than proportionally.

Table 4.4 Corruption in the EU

Country	%	Country	%
Germany	2	Belgium	7
Finland	2	Czechia	7
Portugal	3	Italy	7
Sweden	3	Malta	7
UK	3	Lithuania	8
Denmark	4	Greece	9
Estonia	5	Cyprus	9
Spain	5	Romania	9
France	5	Slovenia	10
Latvia	5	Slovakia	10
Netherlands	5	Bulgaria	11
Poland	5	Hungary	12
UE	6	Austria	14
Ireland	6	Croatia	15
Luxemburg	6		

Source: Authors' calculations on Eurobarometer 2020, % of people who experienced or witnessed corruption.

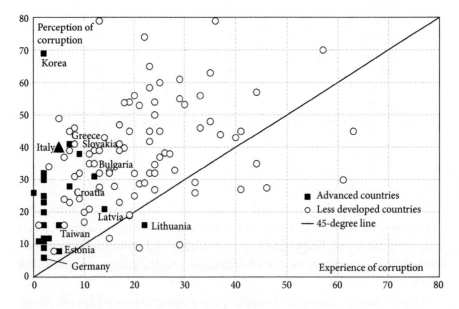

Fig. 4.1 Experience and perception of corruption
Source: Authors' calculations on Transparency International; Global Corruption Barometer, 2021.

At any rate, at the top of the corruption scores we find Lebanon and Yemen, followed by Moldova. Apart from South Korea, Greece, and Slovakia, Italy stands out as no other developed country for its higher (positive) difference between perception and experience among developed nations.

South Korea is the most striking example since it is set conventionally 4th in terms of experience (2 in the score), in line with Germany, but it is 101st in terms of perception. Experience of corruption may indeed be much higher than our assigned score, but the gap between experience and perception would still be massive. Greece and Slovakia have scores similar to Italy for perception, although those for experience are somewhat higher.

A possible reason for such differences is the varying degree of tolerance towards corruption: it may be that Italians and Koreans have low tolerance to corruption, but it does not appear convincing.

Another reason we find rather compelling is provided by a Bank of Italy study, which shows that day after day, in each province of Italy, the perception of corruption changes when some scandal hits the front pages of local newspapers and TV news—so when magistrates are very active, people perceive that there is much corruption, and vice versa.[25] And there seems to be little question that magistrates have been quite active in past decades. Even more importantly, magistrates' actions have been exploited by all political parties, one against the other, and this is the real reason why their actions made headline news. Even minor episodes appeared, at least at first, as major scandals. Hence, the phenomenon cannot easily be dismissed as a distortion due to the media.

All in all, Italy definitely has problems of corruption, and more severe than most other developed countries, although probably less than generally perceived by its overly pessimistic citizens.

In light of these considerations, we find that the interpretation of Italian problems by Capussela (2018), though well presented, is somewhat of an exaggeration. He sees Italy as a country plagued with corruption and ruled by criminals. We agree with his crucial claim that 'Italy has not yet completed its transition from an illiberal, hierarchical society, as it still was in 1945, to an open, liberal democracy governed by the rule of law and served by an economy driven by competition and innovation'. However, we disagree with the argument that politics and the economy are bound together, and illegality is not an exception but an instrumental component of a 'harmonious' whole.

For example, let us take universities. Can we say that university professors are criminals or that they are corrupt? Honestly, we do not think so. They are all part of a semi-feudal system in which merit is often less important than personal loyalty. We explained that university professors are often labelled as *baroni*. We should add that younger researchers usually perceive them as *maestri* (masters or teachers) because they feel that they owe to them their

---

[25] Rizzica-Tonello (2015).

knowledge as well as their careers. We can undoubtedly say that the system is inefficient, but not that professors are generally corrupt or criminals.

Similar reasoning applies—we believe—to most other aspects of society: public administration, the judiciary, schools, politics, etc.

Likewise, we disagree with Zingales (2012), who sees the corporate world as inefficient and highly corrupt. To be sure, Zingales also labels American companies as corrupt. Still, in the Italian version of his book, he immediately clarifies that he sees a fundamental difference between American and Italian companies. In the USA—he says—companies pay lobbyists to receive favourable regulation. In Italy, 'they directly pay public officers to avoid complying with the rules and evade taxes'. Thus, in his view, corruption, illegality, lack of moral standards, and meritocracy are the real reasons for the decline. Of course, we agree with him that lack of meritocracy is the key problem, but we do not think that Italy's entrepreneurs are generally corrupt or criminals.

Overall, we like the metaphor that Bill Emmott (2013) has used in his wonderful book on Italy. Corruption is for Italy like cancer is for a person. It can be perilous. However, cancer is an enemy of the person, but it cannot be identified with the person. So likewise, corruption is not the nation of Italy; it is its enemy, meaning that the bulk of its population and its institutions are not corrupt.

5
Lobbies in education

Low level of education—Egalitarianism for whom?—Funding of universities—Ranking of universities—Attempts at reform—Lobbies against merit—The North–South divide in education—Low return to education

5.1 Low level of education

Many Italians misleadingly believe that Italy has one of the best educational systems in the world. After all, Italian schools inherit a great tradition that goes back to the ancient glories of the Roman Empire. Classical high schools (*licei classici*), where much time is spent on Latin and Greek, were considered superior to scientific and technical high schools, where more time is devoted to mathematics and science. The essential imprint of the Italian schools system goes back to the reform of 1923 that Giovanni Gentile conceived.[1] He was then minister of the Mussolini government. Together with Benedetto Croce, he was a key proponent of the philosophical school of idealism—with Hegel as the reference philosopher—and considered scientific subjects as ancillary to the more profound knowledge represented by philosophy itself. Hence, the future ruling class had to be educated according to humanistic and classical criteria. Mussolini stated that this was 'the most fascists' of all reforms.

Some significant changes were introduced in the post-war period. In 1962,[2] middle high schools (from 6th to 8th grade) were unified with the abolition of professional schools. More recently, education was made compulsory up to the age of 16. Nonetheless, the essential imprint of the 1923 reform was not abandoned.

OECD's PISA (Programme for International Student Assessment) tests show relatively poor results for Italy, especially in the South. Table 5.1 shows

---

[1] For a history of the Italian schools system see De Giorgi et al. (2019). For an overview of recent problems, see Sestito (2014), Gavosto (2019). The Agnelli Foundations and the TREELLLE Foundation have websites in English with useful information on the Italian schools system.

[2] Law 1859, 31 December 1962.

Meritocracy, Growth, and Lessons from Italy's Economic Decline. Lorenzo Codogno and Giampaolo Galli, Oxford University Press. © Lorenzo Codogno and Giampaolo Galli (2022). DOI: 10.1093/oso/9780192866806.003.0006

Table 5.1 Education

Element	Indicator	Italy /167	Italy /34	Top Country /167
Adult Skills	Digital skills among population	73	33	Finland
Adult Skills	Education inequality	55	24	Norway
Adult Skills	Education level of adult population	53	33	South Korea
Adult Skills	Adult literacy	41	26	Multiple—21
Adult Skills	Women's average years in school	28	21	Israel
Pre-Primary Education	Pre-primary enrolment (net)	27	20	France
Primary Education	Primary completion	72	21	Multiple—8
Primary Education	Primary enrolment	54	26	Norway
Primary Education	Primary education quality	24	16	South Korea
Secondary Education	Lower-secondary completion	46	27	Multiple—21
Secondary Education	Secondary education quality	39	29	Singapore
Secondary Education	Secondary school enrolment	25	19	Canada
Secondary Education	Access to quality education	24	18	Japan
Tertiary Education	Skillset of university graduates	51	29	Switzerland
Tertiary Education	Tertiary enrolment	47	29	Multiple—2
Tertiary Education	Tertiary completion	45	31	Multiple—5
Tertiary Education	Quality of vocational training	44	25	Switzerland
Tertiary Education	Average quality of higher education institutions	11	10	Multiple—2

Note: The notation 'Multiple—n' indicates that n countries are in the top position.
Source: Legatum Institute (2020), authors' calculations.

indicators beyond the OECD's and are taken from various sources, including the Unesco Statistical Institute and the Barro-Lee dataset.[3] The worst score concerns Digital skills among the population, where Italy ranks thirty-third out of thirty-four advanced countries. This result is confirmed by the impressive set of data collected by the EC (DESI index).[4] To make sense of this result and the low level of Adult literacy, one should probably look at the third indicator: Education level among the adult population. This is a composite measure based on (a) percentage of the population without any education, (b) proportion of workers with secondary education, and (c) proportion of workers with tertiary education.

Few Italians reach university-level education, and even fewer manage to complete their studies.[5]

There is clear discrimination against children with low-income backgrounds. This is still in place today, as is apparent by looking at the flow of new students who complete all school levels. In particular, the ranking of Italy

---

[3] Barro-Lee (2020).

[4] European Commission (2020a).

[5] According to Mandler (2020), mass education is antithetic to meritocracy. As is clear from what we have written, we think that mass education is the best way to promote equal opportunities, hence true meritocracy.

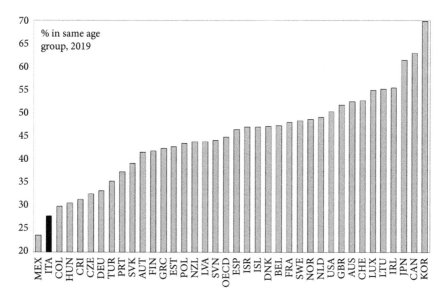

Fig. 5.1 Population with tertiary education 25–34 year-olds
Source: OECD, authors' calculations.

is relatively low when looking at Primary completions, meaning that many children do not finish primary school; Lower secondary completion; and especially Tertiary enrolment and Tertiary completion (Unesco Statistics).

The most telling indicator is the one produced by the OECD, which measures the population between 25 years and 34 years who have a tertiary diploma (see Figure 5.1). In Italy, the number is 27.7 per cent. Only one OECD country (Mexico) fares a little worse than Italy. In many countries, the share is around or above 50 per cent. In South Korea, it is at 70 per cent. This means that the situation will not change in the near future, at least relative to most other advanced countries.

5.2 Egalitarianism for whom?

The low level of adult education is somewhat difficult to reconcile with the egalitarian principles that, as we argued in Chapter 1, inform much of Italian laws and institutions. In the USA, which is usually considered a highly meritocratic society, high schools are not differentiated up to the age of 17.

Instead, there are still several types of high school in Italy, which to some extent are attended by students who have different family backgrounds: classical schools, scientific schools, technical schools.[6] Students from low-income families are likely to attend technical schools, which are supposed to prepare students for lower-income technical jobs.

Why is this the case? Why is an egalitarian society so far away from equal opportunities for all, regardless of family background?

To answer this question, we must acknowledge the simple truth that egalitarianism, as practised in Italy, is the opposite of the concept of equal opportunities. The pursuit of equal opportunities in a modern society requires that virtually the entire population has the opportunity to enrol in tertiary education. The education system is instead the result of the other major force that shaped Italian institutions: the lack of meritocracy as a means of self-preservation for a conservative elite.[7]

To be sure, there have been some efforts to move in the right direction. For example, in 1969, reform allowed students to access universities from all high schools, whether from 'noble' classical high schools or technical schools.

The remaining distance relative to most other countries indicates that the egalitarianism shaping much of Italian culture is for the happy few who can afford to study until 25 years of age or more. In 1968, these same happy few, supposedly left-leaning students asked for the so-called '18 politico', meaning a passing grade (18/30) for not well-specified political reasons. It is for these same happy few that university fees are extremely low.

For this same false egalitarian culture, no one has ever succeeded in creating top-level universities where only the best students and best scholars can have access. If there are top-level universities, there must also be universities that are not top. However, in the current prevailing culture, not just among many students and professors but also in the political establishment, all universities should be equal. If in a parliamentary committee or the national government someone proposes to reward the best universities, for instance, with more research funds, the objection would be that whatever funds are available must be given to the worst universities to allow them to improve.

---

[6] This distinction also exists in other countries (France, Germany, and Spain); in Italy, choice of the type of high school depends very much on family background.

[7] It is sometimes argued that this is the result of low demand for higher education by households. This may be true, but such demand is to be considered largely endogenous relative to the driving forces that are identified in this paragraph.

5.3 Funding of universities

Table 5.2 summarises the sources of public sector financing of universities in the group of countries that contributed to the latest available Report on Performance-Based Funding of University Research.[8] Again, Italy stands out for the low number at the bottom of the table (19 per cent). In the words of the report, 'the bottom line of [the] table indicates the degree to which university research funding is "contested": either through external competition or via a Performance-Based Research Funding System (PRFS)'.

This number is the sum of two items. The first is State external research funding. According to the report definition, it 'typically comes from research councils, innovation agencies and other government agencies and ministries. We include EU structural funds where they support the budgets of these organisations (or similar arrangements) because they are under the control of the national government as well as containing a small element of national funding'. All the funds in this item are considered to be acquired

Table 5.2 Distribution of universities' total income from the national state

	Austria	Czechia	Estonia	Italy	UK	Finland	Norway	Sweden
State external research funding	9	11	40	1	37	26	13	20
Undifferentiated block funding	85	0	0	78	0	0	60	0
Teaching, block funding	0	47	44	0	36	0	0	49
Teaching, performance-based	5	12	10	3	0	51	20	0
Research, block funding	0	18	0	0	0	0	0	28
Research, performance-based	1	12	6	17	27	23	7	3
Total funding	100	100	100	100	100	100	100	100
Of which, total institutional funding	91	89	60	99	63	74	87	80
Sum of state external research funding plus PRFS as a % of total funding	10	22	46	19	64	49	20	23

Source: Authors' calculations on European Commission (2018). Per cent 2015–16.

[8] European Commission (2018). The table does not consider financing from private sources.

through open competition. Institutional financing is instead the funding coming directly from central government. In Italy, External state funding is 1 per cent of total financing, which means that Institutional financing, the part that comes directly from the government, is at 99 per cent.

The second item is the share of funding classified as a PRFS. This is not low in Italy (17 per cent), but the sum of the two items (19 per cent, due to rounding) places Italy as one of the two countries (with Austria) with the lowest share of competitive funding. The bulk of funding for Italy's universities (78 per cent) is Undifferentiated block funding, which is 'essentially without conditions' and may be 'influenced by history, the size of the institution, its particular costs and so on but is not driven by its previous performance and tends to be rather stable or to grow in line with the university cost base'.[9] It is 'undifferentiated' because it makes no distinction between funding for research or teaching.

Some government experts and many professors do not agree with the picture that emerges from the data mentioned above. The claim is that data refer to 2016 and that things have changed since then. Performance-based funding has increased from 19 to 30 per cent—so goes the story—because of the lagged implementation of the 2008 reform, and because of a law of 2016 that gives extra resources to so-called 'excellent departments'.[10] In addition, it is claimed that it is difficult to reward the best departments in a situation in which total government funding is below that of most other European countries.

The latter claim is correct. According to the latest OECD data (relative to 2018), total public spending for tertiary education is only 0.9 per cent of GDP, against a European average of 1.2 per cent.[11] However, this number is the same as in Portugal and greater than in Greece. More to the point, there are countries where government funding is much lower than in Italy and universities have excellent performances (for instance, in Israel and Korea). Those who use this argument implicitly admit that merit is not rewarded.

As to the first part of the claim, the question is straightforward. How is the performance-based funding actually distributed across universities? According to the law, allocation is supposed to be based on performance. Unfortunately, detailed data are not yet available, nor are international comparisons performed by such *super partes* organisations like OECD or the European Commission. The latest available analysis was performed in April 2021 by two Italian economists, Tito Boeri and Roberto Perotti.[12] These authors gathered detailed budgetary data of fifty-seven universities in 2019.

---

[9] European Commission (2018), p. 28.
[10] Law 232 of 2016, which devolves extra resources to 180 departments deemed to be excellent.
[11] Eurostat data.
[12] See Boeri-Perotti (2021) and their article in *La Repubblica*, 12 April 2021.

They distinguished between items that could, in principle, be linked to quality and the rest. In their dataset, items related to quality amounted to 23 per cent of total government funding and included the funds distributed according to the law of 2016. The remaining part depends primarily on students' fees and the size of the university, i.e. block funding in the language of the European Commission. According to their estimates,[13] the funds that should be distributed according to performance, in line with what the law prescribes, are de facto almost evenly distributed across all universities.

As a check, the authors did the same exercise for the top fifty-seven universities in the UK (chosen according to the Times Higher Education rankings). They first showed that the UK's share of performance-based funding[14] is about the same as in Italy. They then found that the concentration of *performance based* funding is high.[15] They conclude that the introduction of performance-based funding in Italy had no practical effect in terms of rewarding the best departments.

This was also the conclusion of the European Commission Report mentioned above. On page 38, the report stated: 'Italy, Austria, Sweden and Norway have strong block funding traditions. Italy uses almost no state external research funding but quite a strong PRFS, which may have compensated to some degree for the lack of external competition but which would appear more likely to preserve the status quo within the universities.'

So the picture is one in which governments are trying to introduce performance-based evaluations, but in practice, they are just a way 'to preserve the status quo'. This is reminiscent of a famous dictum in the novel *The Leopard* by Tomasi di Lampedusa: 'If we want everything to stay as it is, everything has to change'.

5.4 Ranking of universities

Since there is little reward for merit, it does not come as a big surprise that Italian universities do not appear in any of the many available rankings of the best world universities.[16] Table 5.3 displays the number and position of Italian universities in the four most widely used international

---

[13] They computed the Gini concentration index of the two items. The result is that the Gini index is only 0.10 for the funding which is supposed to be based on performance. This is lower than the concentration index for the items not linked to performance: 0.16 for student fees and 0.11 for block funding.

[14] Computed as the sum of funding from research councils and research grants provided by the government through 'Research England'.

[15] The Gini index is 0.45, while it is 0.13 for tuition fees and 0.29 for other sources of income.

[16] This paragraph is based on Galli-Ricciardi (2021). For a comparison of the different rankings see Fauzi et al. (2020).

Table 5.3 Ranking of Italian universities

	THE	QS	ARWU[*]	Leiden[**]
Total number of rated universities	1,662	1,300	1,000	1,225
Position of the best Italian University	172°	142°	151°–200°	83°
Number of Italian universities				
1°–150°	0	1	0	4
151°–200°	3	2	4	1
201°–250°	3	1	2	2
251°–300°	0	0	2	1
301°–350°	3	2	1	1
351°–400°	4	2	1	0
401°–500°	11	6	9	6
Total(<500°) (A)	24	14	19	15
>500° (B)	27	27	26	27
Total (C)= (A) + (B)	51	41	45	42

* In this ranking, the ranges are (a) 201–300 (4 Italian universities) and (b) 301–400 (2 Italian universities) with no indication of the exact position of each institution. They have been equally split into two semi-intervals.
** Ranking based on research impact; publications attributed pro-quota in cases of collaboration.
Source: Authors' calculations on THE (2022), QS (2022), ARWU (2021), and Leiden data (2021); latest available version of each ranking.

rankings: Times Higher Education (THE) World Universities Ranking, produced by a specialised independent magazine in collaboration with Elsevier; Quacquarelli Symonds (QS) Ranking, produced by a British company specialised in education; Academic Ranking of World Universities (ARWU), produced by Shanghai Ranking Consultancy; and Leiden Ranking produced by the University of Leiden in the Netherlands.

These four rankings differ very much by coverage, nationality, weights given to different factors (reputation, teaching, research, internationalisation of teachers, internationalisation of students, citations, number of teachers per student, external financing, etc.) and methodology to aggregate individual indicators. In particular, the Leiden ranking is based only on impact factors of research and does not consider the quality of teaching. Despite such significant differences, all rankings are uniformly negative for Italian universities. In the THE ranking, there are 51 Italian universities out of a total of 1,662; only 24 are among the first 500. The first is number 172. In the QS Ranking, there are 41 Italian universities out of a total of 1,300; the first is number 142. In the ARWU Ranking, there are 45 Italian universities out of a total of 1,000, and the first is in the range 151–200. Finally, in the Leiden Ranking, there are 42 Italian universities (chosen because they are considered the best from the point of view of 'intensity of research') out of a total of 1,225, and the first is number 83. In all rankings, most Italian universities are ranked below position 500.

Table 5.4 lists the countries which have universities ranked among the first 100. US universities dominate all rankings (with an average of 35), followed by those in the UK (10 on average), and then Germany, Holland, Australia, and China. Italy appears at the bottom of this list, together with Brazil and Mexico. In Europe, Italy is below the UK, Germany, Holland, France, Switzerland, Belgium, Denmark, and Sweden.

Table 5.4 Number of universities in the top 100 positions by country

Country	THE	QS	ARWU	Leiden
USA	38	27	40	34
UK	11	17	8	6
Germany	7	3	4	1
Netherlands	7	2	3	2
Australia	6	7	7	5
China	6	6	7	26
Canada	5	3	4	4
Hong Kong	4	5	0	0
France	3	4	4	2
Switzerland	3	3	5	2
Belgium	2	1	2	1
Japan	2	5	3	4
Singapore	2	2	2	2
Korea	2	6	0	4
Denmark	1	2	2	1
Sweden	1	2	3	1
Argentina	0	1	0	0
Malaysia	0	1	0	0
New Zealand	0	1	0	0
Russia	0	1	1	0
Taiwan	0	1	0	1
Israel	0	0	3	1
Finland	0	0	1	0
Norway	0	0	1	0
Italy	**0**	**0**	**0**	1
Brazil	0	0	0	1
Mexico	0	0	0	1
Total	**100**	**100**	**100**	**100**

Source: Authors' calculations based on THE (2022), QS (2022), ARWU (2021), Leiden (2021). Ordering based on THE, and then QS, ARWU, and Leiden.

The picture would be incomplete if we did not mention that individual departments are in a good position in some international rankings for particular subjects. This is apparent in the QS ranking, which is the most disaggregated and considers fifty-one individual disciplines grouped into five broad areas (see Table 5.5). Departments of Italian universities can be found: in the top position worldwide for Classics and Ancient History, in fifth position for Art and Design, seventh for Business and Management, tenth for Archaeology and for Architecture & the Built Environment, thirteenth for Civil and Structural Engineering, fourteenth for Finance, and eighteenth for Economics and Econometrics.

Overall, there are few top universities; still, some departments may be excellent in particular fields. With his unmatched ability to sum up, Bill Emmott (2013) put it this way: 'Universities are one of Italy's greater tragedies: a proud history, many fine individuals, but a mediocre collective outcome.'

To be fair, there is anecdotal evidence that Italian students who go to the best world universities tend to perform comparatively well, whether out of

Table 5.5 The best Italian departments

Discipline	Position of the top Italian department	Number of Italian departments in the top 100 positions
(A) Arts and Humanities		
Archaeology	10°	2
Architecture & Built Environment	10°	4
Art & Design	5°	3
Classics & Ancient History	1°	9
(B) Engineering and Technology		
Engineering—Civil and Structural	13°	4
Engineering—Electrical, Electronic	22°	3
Engineering—Mechanical	15°	3
Engineering—Petroleum	15°	1
(C) Life Sciences & Medicine		
Dentistry	39°	2
Veterinary Science	39°	1
(D) Natural Sciences		
Mathematics	54°	2
Physics & Astronomy	41°	2
(E) Social Sciences & Management		
Accounting & Finance	14°	2
Business & Management Studies	7°	2
Economics & Econometrics	18°	2

Source: Authors' calculations on QS data (2021 rankings).

good preparation or 'desperation' and strong motivation as they want to stay in non-Italian university systems.[17]

5.5 Attempts at reform

The Italian education system has been the target of many reforms over the past three decades. This fact suggests that various governments were aware of the severeness of the problem. However, virtually all reform attempts were vehemently opposed by crowds of teachers and students protesting in the streets of Italian cities, and achieved very partial results.

The two (most recent) reforms that tried to introduce merit into education are the 2008 reform,[18] proposed by the then-minister of education Maria Stella Gelmini, and the 2015 reform, presented by the Renzi government, and labelled *'La buona scuola'* (The good school).[19]

The 2008 reform was very complex and dealt essentially with universities. An important aspect of it was the attempt to introduce mechanisms to reward merit for universities and individual professors. It also allowed for some disincentives, in the form of exclusion from seniority wage increases for unproductive professors. Ideas were good, but the reform was de facto not implemented, and thus merit remained unrewarded. The attempt to introduce merit in hiring new researchers and professors failed. Stringent rules were introduced to give an advantage to those candidates with the best publications in internationally recognised journals. However, the law could not prevent a slight margin of discretion from being given to the national committees in charge of deciding whether a candidate deserved hiring or advancement. The committees exploited that tiny margin to an extreme, bypassing the spirit of the law in a truly outrageous way. The *ancien régime* continued to rule, as is certified by several inquiries into what is commonly labelled *concorsopoli*, meaning alleged illegal manipulation in the selection process.

The European University Institute, an international organisation founded in 1972 by the six original members of the European Union, provides information on academic careers in a large number of countries. On Italy, it says that 'access to an academic career and progression up the career ladder

---

[17] Capano et al. (2017) argue that part of the problem is the great dispersion of productive researchers across universities, so that there are few attractive research centres.

[18] Law 240 of 2010.

[19] Law 207 of 2015.

is strongly conditioned by the fact that the Italian academic system is not very open'. In particular, 'there are incentives for universities to hire internal candidates, since hiring an external candidate means higher costs to the university. Because of this, mobility across universities in Italian academia is very low'. On evaluation and merit, it states that 'recently Italy has seen the introduction of an evaluation system for Universities, with the aim of improving the existing University system [. . .] The problem is that the evaluation process is still at a very experimental stage and the financial resources attached to it have not materialised'.[20]

Finally, in most departments the system remains the old one: hiring and promotions depend largely on connections.[21] A young scholar must be faithful to a powerful professor. In the common language of Italians, professors, especially the powerful ones, are called *baroni*, barons. Indeed, this is a word that captures the essence of a system that, with some exceptions, is essentially feudal. Sometimes, instead of the word *barone*, people in universities use the word *maestro* which is a nicely ambiguous term that can be translated as 'teacher', but also as 'master'. If one wants to be optimistic, this term is used by the student in recognition of the teachings he has received from the *maestro*. But it is somewhat strange to hear professors aged 50 or more, often not yet full professors, who continue to refer to a particular person as a master, which often suggests that they feel dependent on her/his benevolence for their careers.

The reform of 2015 tried to introduce merit for schoolteachers. The starting point was that salary progressed only with seniority, as had always been requested by teachers' unions.[22] The pay is more or less in line with OECD levels. The initial salary (average of different school levels) is about 70 per cent of GDP per capita, in line with the average of the OECD countries, and the final one is 110 per cent of GDP per capita. This is less than the OECD average (124 per cent), but very close to the US and France (113 and 114 per cent, respectively), and somewhat higher than in the UK and most Nordic countries. However, progression remains very slow, as it takes 35 years to reach the maximum level, and merit does not play any role.

The 2015 law tried to find a remedy, by allocating 200 million euros for bonuses based on merit.[23] The system had only partial success for various

---

[20] Although, as we have seen, the share of funding which is theoretically based on performance has been considerably increased in the last few years.

[21] Part of the anti-meritocratic distortion derives from promoting internal candidates, who are less costly for the university than appointing external candidates. Official selections (*concorsi*) are launched only when universities are rather confident that the internal candidate will win.

[22] The information that follows is based on Favero-Stella (2021) and Liaci (2021).

[23] Art. 1 c. 126 of law 107of 2015.

reasons. First, the allotted amount was less than 1 per cent of total funds for schoolteachers' salaries. Second, a large part of this sum was used to finance contractual wage increases for all teachers, so that in the end, the merit bonus could count only on 111 million euros in 2018 and 131 million euros in 2019. The allocated amount for 2020 (143 million euros) was again hijacked to finance contractual wage increases. Third, the remaining funds were used to give one-time bonuses for one year. No decision was taken regarding a structural progression of salary based on merit. According to a survey by the Ministry of Education, in the first year of application of the new law, 40 per cent of teachers received the bonus. This corresponds to about 300 euros per teacher/year, which is not much.[24] Moreover, the funds were distributed more or less equally among all schools, in proportion to the number of teachers.[25] There was no alternative to such allocation as no information about the quality of the different schools was publicly available.

The flip side of the coin is that several governments have recognised the need to reward merit. Also, an articulated system was set up to do the evaluation. At first glance, this system is an impossible comitology (three representatives of teachers, two of parents, one of students, and an external member). Still, finally the decision had to be taken by schoolmasters. This is one of the tiny bits of power that remained in the hands of schoolmasters after crowds of teachers (and their students) demonstrated in the streets against the reform, shouting that schools are not companies and do not need managers to run them.

To complete the picture, teachers have succeeded in avoiding evaluation of schools (which in principle are measured through INVALSI tests) being made public. This means that students and their parents have essentially no way of knowing which are the good schools.[26] There is no evaluation of individual teachers so that school heads are not only powerless but also cannot try to attract good teachers because they do not know who they are.

In conclusion, the quality of teaching is almost exclusively left to the goodwill of individual teachers; sometimes, this is enough to provide a good and even excellent service to the community. But it cannot be the basis for the sound functioning of such critical institutions as schools in a modern democracy.

---

[24] The data from the ministry are available at the following link: https://snv.pubblica.istruzione.it/snv-portale-web/public/docenti.

[25] Larger shares of the fund are allocated to schools in disadvantaged areas.

[26] In fact, people tend to use Eudoscopio, a system provided by a private foundation (Fondazione Agnelli).

5.6 Lobbies against merit

The analysis of Boeri and Perotti discussed above concluded with the need to give greater consideration to merit as measured by peer review and international standards. As a reaction to this proposal, several professors wrote a manifesto in the form of an open letter to the Prime Minister.[27] They said that the proposal would increase existing inequalities, especially between North and South, and would be plainly illegitimate in light of the general principles of equality stated in the Constitution. In addition, they noted that the best international standards for the ranking of universities are not trustworthy, and in any case cannot be the basis for financing universities because 'they do not reflect the relationship between universities and their local communities'. They also claimed that international rankings are distorted because they are based on peer reviews and, for this reason, are 'self-referential'.

What is most revealing in this manifesto is the rejection of the very concept of peer review and international standards and the reference made to universities' connections with local communities. Peer review is, of course, an imperfect method, and sometimes it is 'self-referential'. Nonetheless, who else can judge scientific research but other researchers? Of course, these professors do not want to be assessed according to international standards. They prefer to be judged based on their connections with local communities, where they are often important and well-respected members. The rejection of international standards is entirely a priori. It does not distinguish among the many different standards that are adopted abroad.

> It is by now plainly acknowledged that such standards have a very low reliability [...], and there is no merit in the argument that this is 'what is done abroad' in Europe and the world. In fact, the specific Italian context must be taken into consideration [...] The last thing we want to do is adding to our own vices those of others.

In other words, it is a university system folded in on itself.

We have offered this rather long quote, not so much because we see this as a scandal, but because hundreds of professors have signed this manifesto, and some of them are well known. It shows how deep is the damage of the anti-meritocratic culture and how immensely difficult it is to introduce change.

---

[27] *La Repubblica*, April 12 2021.

The critical point is that connections, rather than merit, are once again at centre stage. Fortunately, these powerful professors' lobbies are indeed quite powerful, but they do not represent the universe of professors.

A similar rejection of merit is carried out by an association called 'Roars', with internet site address www.roars.it. It has the mission to reject any attempt to objectively evaluate merit in schools. Its main enemies are the INVALSI tests run by the Ministry of Education,[28] the Agnelli Foundation (which produces the only existing evaluation of Italian high schools[29]), the TREELLLE Foundation, which promotes evaluation and merit in schools,[30] and the PISA tests of OECD (routinely performed in almost eighty countries). The purpose of the PISA tests is to measure a 15-year-old's ability to use their reading, mathematics, and science knowledge and skills to meet real-life challenges.

A discussion about the value of these tests, their limitations, and how they can be improved is entirely legitimate and useful. Indeed, there are ongoing discussions inside OECD and among participating countries, often leading to improvements in the tests. However, the Roars association rejects the legitimacy of the tests at their source because they deny the possibility of comparing an Italian student with an American or Chinese one. Its members seem to reason as if we were living in a closed world where international competition—in science, technology, organisation, culture, etc.—did not exist.

They deny that a student can be evaluated based on standardised tests, no matter how sophisticated. Of course, it may indeed be true that a student who scores poorly in a standardised test can be an excellent citizen and may turn out to be successful in life. Or that a student can even turn out to be a genius, as did Albert Einstein. Nonetheless, standardised tests are the only way to compare students from different schools or even classes within the same schools, and compare various regions and countries. On the Roars site, one can find sentences like the following: 'reducing the complexity of education to standardised tests is unacceptable [. . .] An effective system of evaluation must fully appreciate the human and cultural aspects [of teaching].' This may well be correct, of course, but nobody has found a way to do this in an objective and comparable way. Again, this shows that evalua-

---

[28] These tests are rather similar to the PISA tests. In light of widespread hostility against them, the results for individual schools have never been published. In 2020, their score was made irrelevant for the final overall student scores. In 2021, with the excuse of the pandemic, they were suspended. For sharply opposing views on such decisions, see Puleo (2020) and Gavosto (2021a).

[29] Eudoscopio (2021).

[30] http://www.treelle.org/english-site.

tion and merit do not have a good reputation even at the highest levels of society. The rejection of merit is the self-preservation of the elite, but—we must acknowledge—it is also a sincere conviction of some honest and intelligent persons. The egalitarian ideologies of the 'long' Italian '68 appropriately adapted to the new circumstances, are still alive.

These matters are indeed very complex, and we do not pretend to be experts in evaluation. Yet, it is clear that critiques on methodologies are often more or less hidden ways to undermine the very concept of evaluation and meritocracy.

5.7 The North–South divide in education

One of the results of the domestic system of evaluation is that grading systems are different across regions of Italy. Secondary and tertiary education students often receive the top grades in most southern areas. In 2019, grades at graduation (13th grade) were 0.7 per cent higher than Italy's average in the South and 1.3 per cent lower in the North-West (Table 5.6). The PISA tests or their Italian equivalent, the INVALSI tests, are much more telling. Table 5.6 presents scores of the latest round of PISA tests (2018) in the various regions of Italy and the mean for Italy and the OECD. Italy is below OECD in all three subjects: reading (−2.3 per cent), mathematics (−0.4), and science (−4.3). Its rank ranges from 23rd to 29th. However, this result hides significant differences across regions. In the North-West and North-East, scores are above the OECD average and close to the top ten countries. In the South and the Islands (Sicily and Sardinia, considered part of Mezzogiorno), scores are between 6 and 12 per cent lower than the OECD average. This implies that these regions are at the bottom of the OECD ranking.

Table 5.6 Scores in PISA tests and at graduation

PISA: % distance from OECD average.
Graduation: % distance from Italy's average

Region	PISA tests			Graduation
	Reading	Math	Science	Grades
North-West	2.3	5.1	0.4	−1.3
North-East	2.9	5.3	1.6	−0.3
South	−7.0	−6.3	−9.4	0.7
Islands	−9.9	−9.0	−12.1	0.0
Average Italy	−2.3	−0.4	−4.3	-

Source: Authors' calculations on INVALSI (2019) and Ministero dell'Istruzione (2020).

The critical point is that local systems of evaluating students (based on the subjective judgements of their teachers) cannot be compared across regions, schools, and teachers.

Of course, without a common measurement standard, it is impossible to reward merit. This implies that human resources departments cannot and do not rely on school grades in their hiring practices. In any case, they have to make a rough adjustment for regional differentials.

The other consequence of such a system is that families and students have almost no way of finding out which are the good schools. There is hence no incentive to improve. If one asks a teacher about a good school in town, the answer would likely be the same school with a good reputation 50 years ago or maybe 100 years ago. That school has a good reputation typically because it is located in the city's centre and was attended by persons who later become famous or well off. The likelihood that a new school or a school on the periphery acquires a good reputation is virtually zero. The system is de facto frozen. It is also highly unjust because it rewards wealth rather than merit (typically, the more affluent people live downtown).

Another channel that depresses quality is that schoolmasters have no way of attracting the best teachers; indeed, in the absence of an evaluation system, they do not know who are the best teachers.

5.8 Low return to education

There is another critical piece of evidence for the lack of reward for merit. For individuals, the return on higher education is lower in Italy than in most other countries. Cipollone-Visco (2007) showed that in Italy the wage earned by a university graduate was higher than that of a high school graduate by 53 per cent. This compared to 63 per cent in France and Germany, 74 per cent in the UK and 81 per cent in the USA. As these authors say, 'merit must not only be adequately compensated in the labour market; it must be sustained, appreciated and appropriately evaluated primarily in education'. As we argue in Chapter 9, one of the reasons is that merit is not in high demand in the corporate sector for a number of structural reasons.

Recent data from the OECD's report 'Education at a Glance' provide a message similar to Visco-Cipollone's, although with a different and updated database. Higher levels of education usually translate into better employment opportunities and other social benefits that are sometimes intangible.

As for earnings, the OECD states that 'in Italy, 25–64 year-olds with a tertiary degree with income from full-time, full-year employment earned 37 per

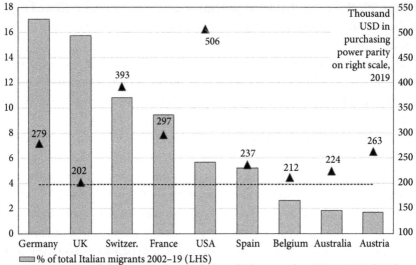

Fig. 5.2 Net gains from a tertiary degree in countries of destination
Source: Galli et al. (2021b), and authors' calculations on OECD and AIRE data.

cent more than full-time, full-year workers with upper secondary education compared to 54 per cent on average across OECD countries'.

Figure 5.2 displays OECD estimates of the gains from tertiary education (black triangles, right scale) in the countries which host the largest numbers of recent Italian migrants.[31] The triangles measure the benefits (net of all costs, including foregone income while studying) from attaining a tertiary degree relative to only a higher secondary degree. The net benefits are measured in $US in PPP, i.e. correcting for differences in purchasing power parity across countries. The net return in Italy is US$198,000, while in Germany and France it is US$279,000 and US$297,000 respectively. Looking at the entire set of OECD countries, in only five (Latvia, Sweden, Estonia, Turkey, and Slovakia), the return to tertiary is lower than in Italy.[32]

---

[31] Brazil and the Netherlands, which are important destinations of Italian emigrants, are excluded because the return on higher education is not available for these countries. Data are from the registry of Italians who reside abroad (AIRE) which probably underestimate the phenomenon because often Italians abroad do not change residence for many years after they have effectively left the country. This lag is significant when the numbers are increasing. The shares of each country of destination are based on data available for the period 2002–19.
See: Istat (2021a) https://www.istat.it/it/archivio/252732
[32] The low return in Sweden and other Nordic countries is considered rather puzzling by the OECD. Possible explanations are a very high number of graduates, a high number of students with masters or higher degrees (who might displace those with a simple bachelor's degree), a higher probability of being

The grey rectangles (left scale) in the figure represent the share of Italians who have migrated to each of the countries displayed in the last twenty years. Today, 5.5 million Italian citizens reside abroad, a significant jump from 2.5 million in 2000. The main countries of destination over the past twenty years have been Germany (17 per cent), the UK (16 per cent), Switzerland (11 per cent), USA (6 per cent). Overall the countries displayed in the figure account for 70 per cent of total emigration from Italy. About one-third of the migrants have a tertiary degree.

According to OECD, the potential to earn more and increase earnings over time is a powerful societal incentive for individuals to pursue education and training, and adults with tertiary education have a higher probability of being employed. By contrast, smaller economic gains from higher education could potentially reduce students' incentives to pursue and complete higher education.

Despite Italy suffering today from one of the least educated populations in the OECD, low returns may be one of the reasons for the still low tertiary enrolment, which implies that the situation could further worsen. It may also be related to the migration of young talents, although it is not a mechanical factor and several other variables, such as the prestige of individual universities, must be considered.

One of the apparent reasons for the relatively low returns is that Italian companies are typically very small and have rather rudimentary organisational structures centred on the controlling family.[33] However, it is difficult to say if the problem starts with the low supply of skilled labour or low demand. There seems to be a vicious circle in which low demand and low supply reinforce each other, as contended in Sestito (2014).

To sum up, there is plenty of evidence that Italy's education system does not provide the right incentives to teachers and professors and does not recognise or reward the most talented students. Most importantly a school system that abhors evaluation prepares new generations for a society in which protection and equality of outcomes are definitely more important than merit and competition.

---

employed, higher non-monetary benefits. Also, in many of these countries, but not in Italy, lifelong learning is a reality: people with only a higher secondary degree may have a chance to further improve their skills and education at professional schools after a period of work.

[33] This fact is so well established that it is stated in official documents. See for instance Italy's Recovery and Resilience Plan in European Commission (2021b) at page 172.

PART III
COMPARATIVE EVIDENCE: ECONOMY

6
Key problems and inequities of Italy's economy

Confirmation and some surprises—The blunder of the gender gap—Schumpeter forgotten—Professional managers?—Antitrust versus many large and small lobbies—Exports: good, not excellent—The drama of the North–South divide—Quality of government in the regions of Italy—Inequality and social mobility—Gerontocracy

6.1 Confirmation and some surprises

Continuing our journey through the comparative indicators of Italy, we now enter the specific field of economics. The Prosperity Index has a pillar called Economic quality, which summarises the key indicators of an economy. For Italy, it is the second-worst pillar: its ranking is 51st out of 167 countries and 32nd out of the 34 advanced countries.

Using the official definition, Economic quality captures how well a nation's economy is equipped to generate wealth sustainably and fully engage its workforce. A strong economy is dependent on the production of a diverse range of valuable goods and services and high labour force participation. Its components are Fiscal sustainability, Macroeconomic stability, Productivity and competitiveness, Dynamism, and Labour force engagement.

Table 6.1 contains some apparent confirmation but also some food for thought. Confirmation concerns the low rankings in GDP growth per capita (average over the last five years), government debt (as a percentage of GDP), unemployment, youth unemployment, labour force participation, and productivity. It is also no surprise to see a low ranking in the country risk premium and credit rating (both towards the bottom among advanced countries). These are indeed the very facts that this book is trying to explain: why Italy does not grow and has accumulated an enormous debt relative to GDP. We view high unemployment as being essentially a consequence of low growth, although there are some specific aspects of the labour market that

Meritocracy, Growth, and Lessons from Italy's Economic Decline. Lorenzo Codogno and Giampaolo Galli, Oxford University Press. © Lorenzo Codogno and Giampaolo Galli (2022). DOI: 10.1093/oso/9780192866806.003.0007

Table 6.1 Economic quality

Element	Indicator	Italy /167	Italy /34	Top Country /167
Dynamism	Capacity to attract talented people	130	29	Switzerland
Dynamism	New business density	54	28	Estonia
Dynamism	Patent applications	27	23	Multiple—3
Fiscal Sustainability	Government debt	160	31	Estonia
Fiscal Sustainability	Gross savings	93	25	Singapore
Fiscal Sustainability	Government budget balance	72	26	Norway
Fiscal Sustainability	Country risk premium	53	31	Multiple—12
Fiscal Sustainability	Country credit rating	47	32	Multiple—7
Labour Force Engagement	Youth unemployment	145	32	Japan
Labour Force Engagement	Unemployment	129	32	Czechia
Labour Force Engagement	Labour force participation	113	34	Switzerland
Labour Force Engagement	Female labour force participation	105	34	Sweden
Labour Force Engagement	Waged and salaried workers	56	32	USA
Macroeconomic Stability	GDP per capita growth	108	28	Ireland
Macroeconomic Stability	Inflation volatility	15	10	Malta
Productivity and Competitiveness	High-tech manufactured exports	32	21	Singapore
Productivity and Competitiveness	Labour productivity	19	14	Luxembourg
Productivity and Competitiveness	Export quality	16	15	Luxembourg
Productivity and Competitiveness	Economic complexity	15	14	Multiple—5

The notation 'Multiple—n' indicates that n countries are in the top position.
Source: Legatum Institute (2020), authors' calculations.

can help explain both low growth and high unemployment, especially for the young. Another important fact about the malfunctioning of the labour market is revealed by the item Waged and salaried workers, which measures the percentage of the workforce in waged and salaried roles. Italy ranks almost last among advanced economies because the labour market does not function as it should, and employers try to avoid hiring people.

Essentially this variable is a stark example of what is sometimes called the law of unintended consequences.[1] Labour laws are meant to protect workers and treat them equally. The result is that companies find ways around such strict rules by using self-employed workers rather than salaried workers. In this way, they can reward merit as they should and punish unproductive workers. We will come back to this in Chapter 8 of the book.

The real surprises in this list are Female labour force participation and Dynamism.

6.2 The blunder of the gender gap

Female labour force participation measures the percentage of the female working-age population (aged 15–64) who are economically active, either by working or looking for work. Italy's rank is 34th out of 34 advanced countries and is only in 105th position when considering the entire set of 167 countries. The surprise is not that female participation is low, which is well known, but that it is one of the lowest in the world. This is a telling indicator that merit is the missing factor in Italian society. Although merit is not the only factor at play,[2] if employers looked exclusively for the best workers, they would hire roughly the same number of men and women or, at least, the gap would be closer to that of similar countries in the OECD. In addition, if politicians, employers, and trades union wanted to provide equal opportunities for all, males and females, they would have come up with some solutions to make it possible to better reconcile family and working life for males and females. Employment gives women emancipation and social integration, independence, and decision-making capacity. Low female labour market participation undermines future growth prospects, also considering low fertility rates and greater longevity.[3] Women account for only 27.3 per cent in top managerial positions, almost seven percentage points below the EU average. The gender pay gap is about 10 per cent, net of individual and employer's characteristics.[4]

The gender gap should be classified under the pillar of Social capital. There is little social capital in a country that discriminates against women in such an extreme way. Figure 6.1 gives the exact picture of Italy's distance from the rest of the advanced world. In Italy, women who are active in the labour market

---

[1] See Hayek (1978).
[2] As argued in Foschi (1996).
[3] 'Gender quality to support growth', speech by Alessandra Perrazzelli, Deputy Governor of the Bank of Italy, at the 14th National Conference of Statistics, 1 December 2021.
[4] Leythienne and Pérez-Julian (2021).

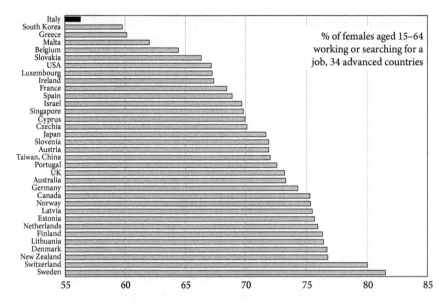

Fig. 6.1 Female participation in the labour market
Source: ILO, authors' calculations, 2019 data.

(either working or searching for a job) were 56.5 per cent of total women aged 15–64 in 2019. In the Nordic countries, they are at 79–80 per cent. In two catholic countries such as Spain and Portugal, they are around 70 per cent. The average of all EU countries is 68.1 per cent.

Of course, this is but one dimension of the gender gap. Others are the wage gap between male and female and the number of females in top positions, who are very few, although they have a higher level of education on average. The gender gap is a double blunder; because women are discriminated against, and because their contribution to the productive effort of the country is limited.

6.3 Schumpeter forgotten

The other rather surprising fact concerns Dynamism. As can be seen, in the three variables measuring Dynamism, Italy's rank is rather low.[5] This means that the dynamics of Schumpeterian creative destruction are essentially impeded and confirm our findings in Chapter 2 about stalling TFP.

---

[5] On the lack of innovation in Italy, a key reference is Daveri (2006).

As documented by Aghion et al. (2021), creative destruction is the key to economic growth.

In particular, Italy ranks 130th over the entire sample and 29th among the 34 advanced countries in terms of Capacity to attract talented people.

The other two items measuring Dynamism are New business density and Patent applications. Here again, some myths need to be dispelled. Italy is no longer the country where small new companies are created, and entrepreneurs pop up everywhere with new brilliant ideas. New business density is a World Bank measure of the number of newly registered limited liability corporations in a calendar year (as a ratio of working population). Italy ranks twenty-eighth among advanced countries, which means that many more new companies are founded every year in countries such as the UK (which ranks sixth), Australia (seventh), Denmark (ninth), Norway (tenth), United States (eleventh), and many others. In the UK, twice as many companies as in Italy are founded every year.

Patent applications is 'the rate of applications for the exclusive rights to an invention, covering both products and processes per 1,000,000 population' as measured by the World Intellectual Property Organisation (WIPO). It captures applications submitted by residents in the home country office as well as abroad. Here Italy scores a little better; yet it is twenty-third among advanced countries. There are 535 new patent applications per million people in Italy, while Switzerland has more than ten times this number. In many advanced countries, there are about 2,000 (Taiwan, Sweden, Denmark, Germany, the Netherlands, Finland, and Israel).

Again, the point here is that entrepreneurship requires talent and the rewarding of merit to create innovation. This was not a major constraint when Italy was growing mainly by imitation. But today it is. Without adequate reward for talent, it is challenging to create new patents and innovate.

A set of data that confirms that Italy is not among the top countries in terms of innovation is the Global Innovation Index produced by WIPO, in collaboration with Cornell University and the European Institute of Business Administration (INSEAD). In the latest index (2020), Italy ranks twenty-seventh among high-income countries and twenty-eighth globally. It is useful to list the countries in the first ten positions: Switzerland, Sweden, USA, UK, the Netherlands, Denmark, Finland, Singapore, Germany, and Korea. Before Italy, one also finds, among others, France, Israel, China, Ireland, Japan, Canada, Luxemburg, Austria, and Norway.

Italians proudly think they are creative people. This may be accurate, but it does not translate automatically into better performance in terms of innovation. It may be painful for Italians' pride to discover that Switzerland, Sweden, and most Northern European countries are considered more innovative than Italy.

This is one of the main reasons for Italy's lack of prosperity, because Schumpeterian creative destruction is impeded. In Italy, there are few new firms and less innovation. Few companies fall out of the market because governments almost always find ways to bypass European rules on state aid to subsidise ailing companies.

6.4 Professional managers?

According to the WEF survey, managers would not seem very different from professors. This results from the following item: Reliance on professional management. In such an essential aspect, Italy ranks 107th over 144 countries. The score is based on answers given by top executives to the survey question: 'In your country, who holds senior management positions in companies?' The answers can range from 1 (usually relatives or friends without regard to merit) to 7 (primarily professional managers chosen for merit and qualifications). As we argue extensively in this book, this is one of the critical areas where lack of merit is apparent, and the damage is greater.[6]

Lack of merit criteria at the top gives a bad example to the entire company and conveys the message that loyalty is more important than merit. As we will show later in the book (see Chapter 9), extensive research work has demonstrated that this answer does reflect hard facts: Italian companies are unique in that a larger share of managers compared to other countries is typically chosen inside the owner's family. This fact magnifies the Italian problem enormously because loyal managers are unlikely to innovate and grow in international markets. However, this choice of company owners is partly endogenous, in the sense that it is a reaction to a hostile environment. Since connections are key to success (in domestic markets), owners choose managers with whom they can confidentially share such connections.

These statistics mainly reflect the situation of companies in the service sector. As is well known and we will argue in Chapter 9, in the manufacturing sector, Italy has several hundred companies that export and withstand the competitive challenges of international markets.

---

[6] This is one of the measures of meritocracy used in Pellegrino-Zingales (2019).

6.5 Antitrust versus many large and small lobbies

Lack of competition in many domestic markets is a large part of the prob-lem and is not a new one.[7] In March 2021, the Italian Antitrust Authority sent to the government and Parliament a document of more than 100 pages filled with proposals to enhance competition.[8] According to this document, pro-competition reform in the service sector can increase productivity in manufacturing by more than 25 per cent. The key sectors that need reforms are: public procurement,[9] the more than 8,000 companies held by local authorities, public transport, the exit of protected zombie firms, liberalisation of retail commerce, elimination of entry barriers for large retailers, auctions for the distribution of natural gas and for hydroelectric power, and private pension funds.

According to the OECD and the EC, the problems are essentially in the service sector. Figure 6.2 shows that Italy and Belgium have the highest bar-riers to entry in the service sector. This is an interesting metric because it is constructed very carefully based on a questionnaire to the national authori-ties comprising some 200 questions. Looking at the individual questions, the issues which are most penalising for Italy are retail trade, sale of pharmaceu-tical products, distribution of gas, local transport, taxis, regulated professions (in particular, notaries), business services, energy, and limited authorisations ('concessions') for the use of public goods.

What a president of Italy's antitrust authority said many years ago is probably still true:

> [As an antitrust authority] we are weak, and we have to tackle waves of old legis-lation that reflect on everything except the principles of competitive markets, with corporations which are protected through laws which apparently deal with other matters; with laws which provide for authorisation and closed numbers of possi-

---

[7] See, in English, Padoa Schioppa (1993), Galli-Pelkmans (2000); and in Italian, Grillo (1996), Baldas-sarri et al. (2002), Pammolli et al. (2007), and Ravazzoni (2010).

[8] AGCM (2021).

[9] 'The incomplete implementation, uncertainty and complexity of the public procurement and con-cessions framework undermine the ability of administrations to use tenders efficiently, especially at local level, and weigh on planning decisions of private firms, especially SMEs. Late payments by public admin-istrations, including at local level, and long tendering procedures (public tendering procedures last 200 days in Italy compared to some 120 days on average in the rest of the EU) also discourage businesses from participating in public tenders (some 30% of tenders only receive one bid). The framework for local public services (e.g. transport, utilities) does not always guarantee that competitive tenders are prioritised over direct awarding or in-house solutions, resulting in inefficiencies of service management'. Commission Staff Working Document, Analysis of the Recovery and Resilience plan of Italy, SWD (2021) (European Commission 2021a) 165 final.

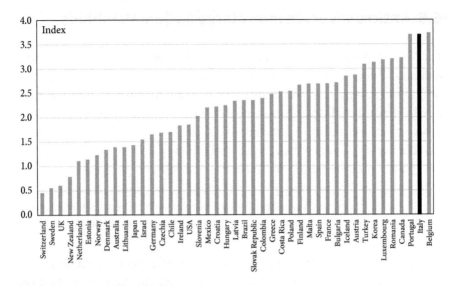

Fig. 6.2 Barriers to entry in the service sector

Note: The index varies between zero (no barriers to entry) and four (maximum barriers).
Source: Authors' calculations on OECD (2018).

ble entrants and give protection to categories which already have that number of members, thus not allowing entry of others nor changes in the configuration of the market.[10]

As in the OECD data, the reference here is to the many small but powerful lobbies that populate Italy.

But probably the big lobbies are elsewhere. Quite appropriately, the March 2021 document of the Authority proposes to 'reduce bureaucratic burdens which represent a relevant obstacle to doing business and create barriers to entry in the market'. As we will argue later in the book (see Chapter 9), the combination of obscure bureaucracy and a complex legal system is indeed the key obstacle to competition in domestic markets. It is why, even in the corporate sector, connections are more important than merit, which is itself a major obstacle to economic growth. According to the European Commission (2021a), 'the length, complexity and unpredictability of administrative procedures, remaining restrictions to competition, and some sectoral over-regulation weigh on firms' productivity and competitiveness, discouraging investment'.

[10] Amato (1995).

6.6 Exports: good, not excellent

It is often argued that Italy is a successful exporter despite its weaknesses. Indeed, its export share is not performing poorly; in the past ten years, the share of Italian export in world trade has remained constant (at 2.8 per cent), despite the rise of China and many other emerging markets.

However, as shown in Table 6.2, in the entire period 1995–2019, the volume of Italian exports of goods grew at an average annualised rate of 3.3 per cent, less than those of Germany (9.6 per cent), Spain (8.5 per cent), and France (5.5 per cent). The relatively low performance of Italian exports also remains if one looks at the period after the GFC, i.e. between 2010 and 2019; in this period, the distance between Italy and other countries is less marked, but it remains true that Italian exports display the lowest growth. The picture improves somewhat if one looks at values in current prices (euro) rather than in real terms. This suggests that Italian companies likely have enhanced quality,[11] which may not be fully captured in the statistics or may have increased prices in markets with low price elasticity.[12] They have also moved up the quality ladder in traditional 'Made-in-Italy' products, such as food, fashion, and furniture.

Italy hosts among the most innovative and competitive firms in the global market for niche products. In the Italian context, exporting companies are the

Table 6.2 Goods exports[1]

	Italy	France	Germany	Spain
Volumes[2]				
1995–2020	3.3%	5.5%	9.6%	8.5%
2010–2019	3.1%	3.4%	3.8%	4.7%
2019–2020	−9.8%	−14.9%	−8.3%	−8.9%
Values at current prices				
1995–2020	6.7%	6.3%	10.2%	12.9%
2010–2019	4.4%	4.2%	4.7%	5.9%
2019–2020	−10.3%	−16.3%	−8.9%	−9.9%

Notes: (1) Annualised average growth rate: cumulative growth rate, divided by the number of years; (2) Chain-linked with 2015 as the reference period.
Source: Authors' calculations on Eurostat databank, percentage annualised average growth rates

[11] See Codogno-Paganetto (2011) *Measuring Italy's External Competitiveness*.
[12] Bugamelli et al. (2018) and Bank of Italy Annual Report (various years).

most productive, better organised, and efficient; in these companies, merit and human capital are considered the most.[13]

Sometimes, specialising in high-end low-technology products, such as top brand fashion, may well involve a high degree of technological expertise for sophisticated fabrics, marketing and branding techniques, organisation of production, etc. Still, the majority of Italian companies tend to continue to focus on low technology, with relatively low R&D content. The point is that despite considerable improvements in the past decade, Italian exports are still specialised in relatively low-tech traditional sectors. As a result, they still have a hard time competing with low-cost countries upgrading their technological expertise, especially in Asia and Eastern Europe.

Two items in our Table 6.1 confirm the considerations highlighted at the beginning of this chapter: the index of Export quality, a composite measure based on both value and quantity of bilateral trades (produced by the IMF) and the index of Economic complexity, a composite measure of the productive capabilities of large economic systems, based on both (a) the diversification of export markets and (b) the ubiquity of products exported.[14] Italy has an intermediate ranking on both items, not at the bottom, but not among the best performers as sometimes thought.

6.7 The drama of the North–South divide

Italy's most severe problem is the historical and unresolved North–South divide. The South (Mezzogiorno) has the same problems as the rest of the country, just magnified. Connections rather than merit are more important than in the rest of the country for a young person to find a job, a young researcher to become a professor, a civil servant to get a promotion, etc.

After the war, almost every conceivable policy tool was tried in repeated and massive attempts to solve the problem, but with modest results.[15] Table 6.3 shows some basic numbers for the seven decades since WWII. The South has now around 34 per cent of the Italian population, down from 37 per cent in the 1950s.[16] Emigration has reduced the population of the South, as millions left their land, especially in the 1950s, in the hope of finding

---

[13] See Mayer-Ottaviano (2008) and Galli-Paganetto (2002).

[14] This index is constructed by the Observatory on Economic Complexity, a project started at MIT. URL: https://oec.world/en.

[15] For a review see: Chenery (1962), Lutz (1963), Saraceno (1980), Faini et al. (1993), Graziani (2020), Scotti-Zoppi (2020).

[16] Here the period after WWII is considered, but the problem was already a matter of concern after Italy's unification and has been the subject of a vast literature. See among others: Nitti (1900), Fortunato (1911), Gramsci (1916), Croce (1925), Salvemini (1955), Villari (1981), Ciocca (2013), and Toniolo (2013b).

Table 6.3 The North–South divide

	1951 1960	1961 1970	1971 1980	1981 1990	1991 2000	2001 2010	2011 2017
Mezzogiorno: GDP (as a share of Italy)	23.9	24.0	24.0	24.6	24.4	23.7	22.7
Mezzogiorno: population (as a share of Italy)	37.2	36.2	35.1	35.8	36.3	35.4	34.5
Mezzogiorno: GDP per capita (index, Centre-North = 100)	53.2	55.9	58.5	58.3	56.7	56.9	55.9
Consumption (as a share of area's GDP)							
Mezzogiorno	98.6	96.2	94.9	97.4	98.4	102.5	102.6
Centre-North	71.7	70.5	70.7	72.6	72.6	73.0	75.0
Italy	78.1	76.7	76.5	78.7	78.9	79.9	81.2
Net Exports (as a share of area's GDP)							
Mezzogiorno	−28.1	−31.4	−30.5	−28.1	−21.1	−24.3	−19.5
Centre-North	+4.7	+6.6	+7.3	+7.2	+8.3	+6.0	+6.9
Italy	−3.2	−2.5	−1.8	−1.5	+1.1	−1.1	+1.0
Investment (as a share of area's GDP)							
Mezzogiorno	29.5	35.2	35.6	30.7	22.7	21.4	16.8
Centre-North	23.7	22.9	22.0	20.2	19.1	20.8	17.9
Italy	25.1	25.9	25.2	22.8	20.0	21.0	17.6

Source: Galli-Gottardo (2020b), and authors' calculations on ISTAT and Bank of Italy data, averages for selected periods.

a better life either in the industrial North, around Milan and Turin, or abroad, in Germany, Belgium, and the USA.

The share of southern GDP is now around 23 per cent, more or less the same as in the 1950s. Since the population has decreased, the gap in terms of GDP per capita is now slightly lower than in the 1950s. However, changes in this crucial variable are minimal: GDP per capita in the South is still 55 per cent of that in the Centre-North; in other words, average production per capita is a little more than half that of the Centre-North. In the 1970s, after two decades of massive public investment and incentives to private investment, the gap was slightly reduced so that GDP per capita of the South reached a peak of 58.5 per cent. This was primarily the effect of support to domestic demand, since rather little changed in terms of the endogenous productive capacity of the South.

To be sure, the South today displays a very different landscape compared to the 1950s. The gap in GDP per capita has not fallen, but nor has it risen, which means that the South's growth rate has been more or less the same as that of the rest of Italy. The population now lives mainly in cities, and the service sector, mainly in government and tourism, employs many more people than agriculture. Running water, electricity, health services, public schools, universities, public transport, airports were rarely available 70 years ago and now are almost always the norm.

Nonetheless, the gaps are evident in many areas of the economy and society. Unemployment was 17.6 per cent before the pandemic, while it was only 6.1 per cent in the Centre-North. The female employment rate was a meagre 32.5 per cent against a (very unsatisfactory) 57.8 per cent in the rest of Italy. Youth employment (15–34) was 28 per cent (46.8 per cent in the rest of Italy). Income inequality is considerably higher, productivity per worker is some 30 per cent lower. Civil proceedings require almost twice as much time. According to official estimates, the shadow economy is 19.4 per cent of the entire economy, and nearly 40 per cent of households have at least one member employed irregularly.[17] The gap also shows up in social engagement measures: participation in the latest European elections was 44.7 per cent against 62.4 per cent in the Centre-North.

Despite all the massive policy efforts displayed after WWII, the South never managed to develop an industrial fabric capable of sustaining an autonomous growth process. The result is that the South is the largest subsidised area of Europe. It can best be seen from the data on consumption and net exports. In the past two decades, consumption (of private and public goods) has been higher than GDP, which occurs in very few of the world's most impoverished areas. Consumption in the South is 102 per cent of GDP, while in the Centre-North, it is at 75 per cent, a relatively normal ratio by international standards. Consumption can be higher than local production because massive government transfers provide additional support.

Net exports (exports minus imports in the national accounts definition) convey the same message. The South has always had a deficit in its trade balance of between 20 and 30 per cent of its GDP. The rest of the country has always run a surplus that has kept Italy not too far from balancing. Such large deficits could be sustained for so many decades because of transfers via the public sector.

Reconstruction of the public sector accounts prepared by the Bank of Italy shows that in the period 2014–16 the ratio of total primary spending (by national and local governments) to GDP is 39.5 per cent in the Centre-North and 65 per cent in the South. In the region of Calabria (the tip of Italy's geographical boot), public spending over GDP reaches 81 per cent, meaning that GDP is almost entirely made up of public spending.[18]

---

[17] ISTAT (2020a).
[18] Galli-Gottardo (2020a).

It is helpful to look at Figures 6.3 and 6.4 to better grasp the nature of the problem. The first displays total investment (private and public) as a share of GDP in the South and the Centre-North. Until the mid-1990s, investment was much higher in the South because of higher public sector resources and

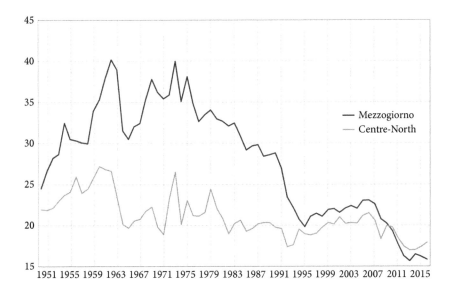

Fig. 6.3 Investment/GDP ratio
Source: Galli-Gottardo (2020b), and authors' calculations on ISTAT data.

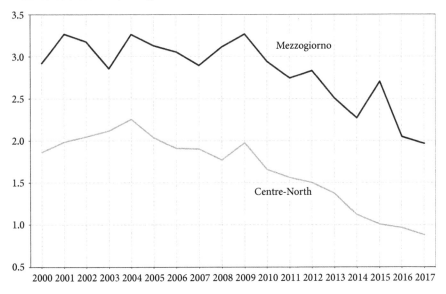

Fig. 6.4 Public investment/GDP ratio'
Source: Galli-Gottardo (2020b), and authors' calculations on Bank of Italy data, general government as a % of GDP.

very generous incentives to private investment. The latter included, among others, zero social security contributions on all firms established in the South, whether local or not, a ten-year total exemption from corporate taxes, and special subsidies given to large firms investing in the South. Most of these incentives ended in the first half of the 1990s because they were considered illegitimate state aid by the EC.

In any case, for as much as four decades, the investment ratio was much higher in the South; at times, it was almost twice as large. But productivity from investment was considerably lower. According to a study published by the Bank of Italy,[19] the gap in GDP per capita would have virtually disappeared by the late 1970s had investment efficiency been in line with that of the rest of the country.

Figure 6.4 shows that even in the past two decades, despite Italy's major budgetary problems, public sector effort for the South did not vanish; public investment fell in Italy, but in the South, it remained higher than in the Centre-North by about 1 per cent of GDP.

These data should convince anyone that the problems of the South are the same as those of Italy. They cannot be solved with public investment unless such investment is instrumental in bringing about radical changes in the quality of institutions, the business environment, and the incentive structure: competition, merit, and talents must substitute for patronage, bosses, and lobbies. As argued by Coco and De Vincenti (2020), this conclusion is far from being generally accepted in the current Italian debate. A lobby for the South asks for more money from Rome and is one of the most powerful in the country, made up of local politicians, entrepreneurs, and intellectuals. It is not organised into a political party. Still, it is probably more effective than the lobby for the North, even though in the latter there is a relatively important political party, i.e. the League (which used to be the Northern League).

6.8 Quality of government in the regions of Italy

The most comprehensive dataset on the quality of government across European regions is the EQI (environmental quality index) compiled by Charron et al. (2021) at the University of Gothenburg, funded by the EC. The 2021 survey includes 17 questions for a large sample of European Union residents (more than 129,000) in 27 countries and 208 regions.

---

[19] Galli-Onado (1990).

The index looks at three aspects: quality (public services perceived quality), impartiality (fair treatment for all citizens irrespective of their characteristics or connections), and corruption (no abuse of public offices for private gain). Quality is measured through questions focused on education, health care, and the police. Seven different questions try to assess if respondents feel that there are privileges in accessing certain vital public services to capture the more complex issue of impartiality. Finally, corruption is an average of perception and experience.

Nordic countries are typically at the top of this ranking, while Eastern European countries are towards the bottom. The best Italian region (Trentino) is in 100th position, meaning that it is around the median of the 208 European regions: while 99 regions do better than Trentino, 108 do worse (Table 6.4 and Figure 6.5).

Table 6.4 Quality of government: EQI index

Macro Region	Region	Rank/208			
		Index	Quality	Impartiality	Corruption
North	Trentino	100	62	122	113
North	Friuli-VG	104	89	127	103
North	Veneto	109	86	137	106
North	Bolzano	117	94	142	115
Centre	Toscana	126	106	136	123
North	Emilia-Romagna	127	91	161	136
North	Piemonte	132	130	153	119
North	Valle d'Aosta	133	108	148	155
North	Liguria	142	142	154	130
Centre	Umbria	148	133	173	149
Centre	Marche	149	148	169	138
North	Lombardia	156	127	177	168
South	Abruzzo	173	165	180	173
Centre	Lazio	181	170	179	182
South	Molise	182	186	184	170
South	Sardegna	186	177	201	172
South	Puglia	190	189	194	180
South	Sicilia	191	172	198	191
South	Basilicata	196	187	203	184
South	Campania	206	203	200	206
South	Calabria	207	205	208	200

Source: Charron et al. (2021), and authors' calculations, EQI index 2021, 208 EU regions.

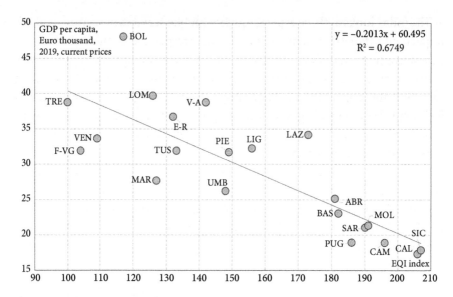

Fig. 6.5 EQI index vs GDP per capita of Italian regions

Note: TRE=Trento, BOL=Bolzano.

Source: Charron at al. (2021), authors' calculations.

Trentino is also the best region in Italy for the three components of the index: Quality of public services (62nd), Impartiality (122nd), and Corruption (113th). At the other extreme, there is Calabria, which is at the bottom of the ranking for all categories.

All southern regions are at the bottom of the table. Note that there is typically a considerable distance between the North and the South. Most northern regions are between 100th and 140th, while most southern regions are between 180th and the bottom of the ranking. The best southern region (Abruzzo, which geographically is in the centre of Italy but is usually classified as part of the South) is a little below Lombardy, the region that ranks lowest among northern regions.

These are, of course, subjective rankings since they are based on survey questions that reflect residents' views about their own government. To find more objective government quality measures, one can look at the May 2021 update of the IQI index (Index of Institutional Quality), based on Nifo-Vecchioni (2015).

Table 6.5 and Figure 6.6 display such IQI indices of institutional quality that are entirely based on objective measures. These indices range from zero (lowest quality) to 100 (highest quality). The overall index (IQI), displayed in the first column, is a weighted average of the other four indices.

Southern regions are again at the bottom of the table. Of the four components of the index, the one that probably adds more value relative to the EQI

Table 6.5 Institutional quality index: IQI index

Macro region	Region	IQI Index	Government Effectiveness	Regulatory Quality	Rule of law	Corruption	Voice and Accountability
North	Trent-A.A.	89	44	84	91	97	83
North	Friuli V.G.	85	60	56	84	83	67
North	Veneto	84	55	59	85	92	67
North	Lombardia	79	57	61	66	87	77
Centre	Marche	79	53	61	75	93	66
North	Emilia R.	77	56	66	67	91	65
Centre	Toscana	73	53	70	63	90	58
North	Valle d'Aosta	72	13	80	100	88	64
Centre	Umbria	71	47	51	65	95	66
North	Piemonte	69	41	49	72	94	58
North	Liguria	60	50	56	48	81	53
Centre	Lazio	58	50	65	41	79	53
South	Abruzzo	53	37	45	57	65	51
South	Basilicata	43	25	35	50	57	55
South	Puglia	39	31	24	41	72	39
South	Molise	33	3	33	56	42	55
South	Sardegna	31	16	41	28	63	39
South	Campania	25	45	23	21	24	23
South	Calabria	19	31	9	15	53	21
South	Sicilia	19	19	22	23	59	20

Source: Nifo-Vecchioni (2015), updated to 2019, IQI in Italian regions, range between 0 (worst) and 100 (best).

index is Government effectiveness because it evaluates many public outputs and is based entirely on official sources.[20] In particular, it considers social services, such as education and health care, economic services (e.g. infrastructure, ICT, banks), environment (recycling, air quality, etc.). With few notable exceptions, southern regions are at the bottom also for this indicator.

The low ranking of the South in The rule of law reflects the presence of mafia organisations, as measured by crimes against properties and persons. The presence of mafias is also captured by the indicator on Corruption, where southern regions are particularly low. The indicator is based on objective measures such as the number of municipalities placed under the control of an

---

[20] See Osservatorio sui Conti Pubblici Italiani (2021).

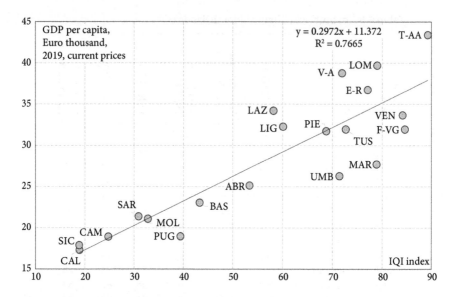

Fig. 6.6 IQI index vs GDP per capita of Italian regions

Source: ISTAT, IQI dataset of Italian regions and provinces, Nifo-Vecchioni (2015), updated to 2019, authors' calculations.

external commissioner due to mafia infiltration, crimes against public properties, and the difference between existing infrastructure and the amounts spent to build it.[21]

Almost 30 years ago, Ignazio Visco, a Neapolitan and later a governor of the Bank of Italy, wrote:

> the problems of this land are intertwined with a reality in which the use of intimidation, violence and collusion prevents individuals and firms from fulfilling their opportunities and competing in the market. [. . .] Without a minimum government, the honest earning of a salary or a profit by new entrants may require acts of civic heroism.

In 2010, he added:

> [. . .] Still today, it is necessary to be aware of the costs that organised criminality imposes on economic as well as social development of the large area of the Mezzogiorno.[22]

Since then, many bosses of the various mafia organisations have been arrested and convicted. But the situation has hardly improved.

---

[21] This is a measure proposed in Golden-Picci (2005).
[22] Barca-Visco (1993) and Visco (2010).

In light of these considerations, Robert Putnam (1993) was certainly not wrong in arguing that history matters, though his theory does not seem to fit the data for each and every region of Italy. He suggested that what may have played a role is that the South has always had an essentially feudal and autocratic system, based on the property of land, with a king endowed with absolute powers. In addition, its more feudal nature has caused the region to be the origin of the mafia and has created a less prosperous area; the mafia's hierarchical structure is very similar to southern Italy's feudal roots. In contrast, there had been several centuries of flourishing independent municipalities in the North and the Centre, based on rewarding the entrepreneurship of the class of merchants and bankers, as occurred in Genoa, Venice, Florence, Milan, and other cities.

In addition, it should be added that the unification of Italy in 1861 was widely perceived as a conquest by the northern Kingdom of Savoy. For about a decade, the new Kingdom of Italy had to fight against 'brigandage', a widespread and ancient phenomenon of criminals, which had some support from the formerly ruling Bourbon family in the hope of restoring its power.

Putnam's ideas were perhaps new for political scientists and economists but were almost obvious for historians. In 1916, Antonio Gramsci, an intellectual who eventually became one of the founding fathers of the Italian Communist Party, wrote that the origin of the divide should be placed as far back as the Longobards' occupation of northern Italy (in the sixth century A.D.) because it ended political unity in the Italian peninsula, as the Romans had shaped it. Gramsci then wrote that

> in the North the Municipalities had given rise [. . .] to a courageous bourgeoisie filled with entrepreneurial initiatives and there was an economic organisation similar to that of other European nations, which favoured the development of capitalism and industry. [In the South] the kingdoms of the Swabians, the Anjou, the Spaniards and the Bourbons [. . .] created nothing; there was no bourgeoisie, agriculture was primitive and was not even enough to satisfy the local market.[23]

Finally, let's restate that, as for the rest of Italy, history is not destiny. Destiny can be changed. It depends on the willingness of the citizens to start rewarding entrepreneurship rather than connections, scientific research rather than loyalty to a baron, good politicians rather than bosses. To sum up, the South needs to put merit at centre stage, at least as much as the rest of Italy.

[23] Gramsci (1916).

6.9 Inequality and social mobility

One of the key objectives of any egalitarian culture is, of course, that of reducing inequality and providing equal opportunities for children coming from wealthy and low-income families. None of these objectives has been achieved. Income inequality, as measured by the Gini coefficient,[24] is at 0.32 (Figure 6.7), which is slightly higher than the OECD average (0.30) and is higher than in all Nordic countries, Germany (0.29), France (0.28), and Japan (0.30). Korea, Spain, Estonia, and Portugal are more or less at the same level as Italy.[25] Turkey, Chile, the USA, Israel, and mainland China have much higher inequality.

In large part, however, the inequality level of Italy is but a reflection of the North–South divide. In the North and the Centre, inequality is lower and more or less at the same level as in Germany (30 and 29 respectively); in the South, it is higher (34). The key point is that aggregating regions with very different income levels results in an increase in overall measured inequality.[26]

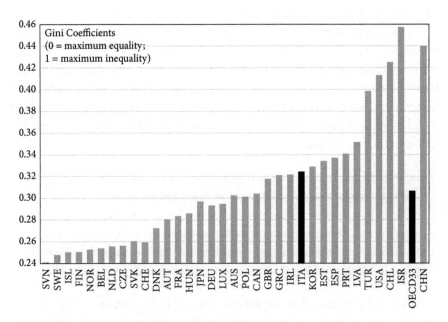

Fig. 6.7 Income inequality in 33 OECD countries and China
Source: OECD (2018), and authors' calculations.

---

[24] See OECD (2018).
[25] Italy's Gini coefficient may indeed be perceived as high given that the distribution of values is skewed towards countries with very high inequality, with the median value being below the OECD average.
[26] Ciani-Torrini (2019).

Over time, inequality has not increased. The Bank of Italy has stated this point several times in research papers and its Annual Report.[27] Inequality—writes the Bank of Italy—did not increase after the GFC of 2008 or after the recession due to the European sovereign debt crisis. 'Overall, inequality stabilised at levels close to those of the end of the 1970s'.[28] No progress, but also no worsening.

A recent OECD report highlights that there is an important gap between income inequality and the perception of inequality. For Italy, this gap is particularly sizeable. The fraction of people who believe it is the responsibility of the government to reduce income differences, among those who think that such disparities are too large, shows Italy at the top of the list, second only to Portugal. Interestingly, people who believe that hard work matters more than luck or other circumstances beyond an individual's control, such as parental wealth, for getting ahead in life are also more accepting of income inequality, because they believe that high earning disparities are the reward for differences in individual effort. Italy is again at the bottom of OECD reporting countries, and this is especially true for the young between 18 and 34 years. The effectiveness of individual effort may also be thought of as a measure of how the broad concept of meritocracy is perceived as a powerful tool for social mobility. In Italy, it is not, and thus disillusioned people tend to ask the government for income redistribution.

As with income distribution, not much progress has been achieved in terms of equality of opportunity. The OECD (2018) is the most comprehensive and compelling comparative study on this issue; we quote it with a few comments. Italy is one of the countries that has achieved the least progress in education for all. Indeed, as we have seen in Chapter 5, only a very small share of the population has a university degree.

Even more importantly, Italy is one of the OECD countries where educational attainment is more problematic across generations. Table 6.6 shows the educational accomplishments of the offspring of families in which neither parent has an upper secondary degree: these boys and girls can attain a university degree only with 6 per cent probability, which is one of the lowest in the OECD, together with the Czech and Slovak Republics. Note that this number is 11 per cent in Germany, 13 per cent in the much-criticised US system, and above 20 per cent in the UK and most Nordic countries.

Furthermore, the probability that such girls and boys will attain only a degree in lower secondary or less (the same as their parents) is 64 per cent,

---

[27] Bank of Italy (2016), Brandolini et al. (2018), and Cannari-D'Alessio (2018).
[28] Metrics depicting inequality should not be confused with poverty. Due to the pandemic, the poverty risk measure of the Italian Statistical Office shows an increase from 16.2% in 2019 to 19.1% in 2020.

Table 6.6 Likelihood of educational attainment if neither parent has attained upper secondary education

Country	Lower secondary or less	Tertiary
Slovak Republic	0.38	0.05
Czechia	0.29	0.06
Italy	**0.64**	**0.06**
Austria	0.35	0.08
Turkey	0.73	0.09
Slovenia	0.37	0.09
Poland	0.23	0.10
Germany	0.32	0.11
USA	0.28	0.13
Chile	0.46	0.13
Greece	0.42	0.15
France	0.37	0.17
Ireland	0.39	0.19
Sweden	0.28	0.20
Belgium	0.28	0.20
Netherlands	0.40	0.21
UK	0.41	0.21
Spain	0.56	0.22
Norway	0.36	0.24
Japan	0.22	0.24
Denmark	0.33	0.25
Korea	0.27	0.25
Estonia	0.21	0.26
Israel	0.23	0.27
Finland	0.20	0.32
Canada	0.20	0.33
New Zealand	0.31	0.35
OECD27	0.42	0.13

Source: OECD (2018), and authors' calculations.

which is one of the highest in the OECD; only Turkey, with 73 per cent, fares worse. This number is 28 per cent in the USA and 41 per cent in the UK. These numbers unambiguously show that Italy has little intergenerational mobility.

Another useful indicator computed by the OECD is the number of people who belong to a social class that is higher or lower than that of their parents (Figure 6.8). In Italy, those in a higher class than their parents are 30.9 per cent of the total population aged 25 to 64. It is the lowest value in OECD26, except for Austria (22.5), an outlier—probably due to differences in measurement—and Portugal (29.2). This number is around 42 per cent in Germany and the

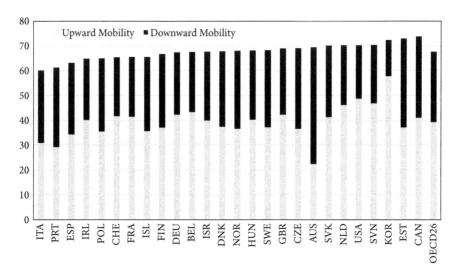

Fig. 6.8 Absolute social class mobility

Note: Percentage of 25–64 year-olds whose social class is higher or lower than that of their parents, 2002–14. Social class is based on the nine European Socio-Economic Classification (ESEC) categories constructed based on occupation.

Source: OECD calculations based on all seven European Social Surveys (ESS) for European countries (2002–14), the Panel Study of Income Dynamics (PSID) for the United States (1999–2013), the Cross-National Equivalent Files (CNEF) for Australia and Korea (2000–14), the General Social Survey (GSS, cycle 15) for Canada, and authors' calculations. The classes are defined as: 1 Higher Managerial and Professional Workers; 2 Lower Managerial and Professional Workers; 3 Routine Clerical Work; 4 Routine Service and Sales Work; 5 Small Self-Employed with Employees; 6 Small Self-Employed without Employees; 7 Manual Supervisors; 8 Skilled Manual Workers; 9 Semi- and Unskilled Manual Workers.

UK and reaches 49 per cent in the USA and 58 per cent in South Korea. Furthermore, a large body of literature confirms that professions have typically been transferred from parents to children with little competition and little social mobility relative to most western countries.[29]

Italy is also the country in the OECD in which the sum of upward and downward mobility is lowest. Hence, it is not much of a surprise that relative class mobility is very low (Figure 6.9). Indeed, it is the lowest among the twenty-five countries analysed by the OECD, except for Korea.

Data are normalised so that the average country (which happens to be Belgium) is equal to 1. So if we compare Italy (with a value of 2) with the US (0.7), we can tell that persistence in a given social class (among those considered by the OECD) is almost three times higher in Italy.

The finding that Italy has low relative mobility is a strong indictment that opportunities are unequal among individuals of different social origins. It is helpful to resort to the same metaphor used in OECD (2018) to

---

[29] Galli (1996), Schizzerotto-Bison (1996), Faini et al. (1997), and Schizzerotto (2011).

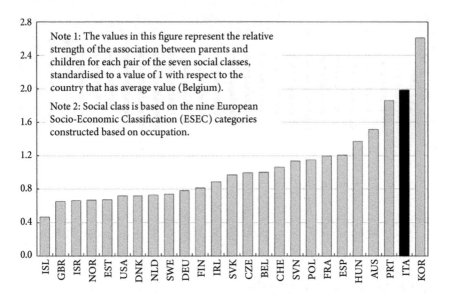

Fig. 6.9 Relative persistence in social class, 25 OECD countries

Source: OECD calculations based on all seven ESS surveys for European countries (2002–14), the PSID for the United States (1999–2013), the CNEF for Australia and Korea (2000–14), and authors' calculations.

explain the difference between absolute and relative mobility. Metaphorically speaking, mobility acts as a set of escalators: most people go up as long as there is aggregate growth, but some groups move faster than others. Therefore, their relative positions vary upward or downward over time. Absolute mobility measures by how much individuals have gone up (or down). In contrast, relative mobility tells us how the relative positions have changed, thus abstracting from the effects of aggregate growth.

We conclude with a technical remark that has interesting implications. In light of the numbers displayed so far, it may seem difficult to understand why, in the same OECD data, earnings mobility (both intra- and infra-generational) for Italy is not particularly low, being around the OECD average. The OECD notes that earnings mobility is higher than class or educational mobility in most Southern European countries. It attributes this fact to the prevalence of very small companies 'where there is an important intergenerational transmission of professions, but where the earnings dispersion can be large'. We believe that this is a correct intuition and indeed an interesting one. As we will see in Chapter 9, Southern European countries, particularly Italy, have a substantial—anomalous—share of self-employed and irregular workers.

The rigid regulation of the labour market is largely circumvented through outsourcing to very small companies, the self-employed, and irregular workers. For these workers, it may be challenging, though not impossible, to attain a better education and higher social class than their parents. Still, they may well improve their income. Society is rigid and does not reward merit. But the market takes its revenge and makes it possible for many people without any social protection to improve their earnings.

6.10 Gerontocracy

Given this overall picture, it is no surprise that the young suffer from high unemployment and low wages. Nor it is a surprise to find that many of the most talented youth leave the country to study and work abroad.[30]

According to the national statistical office, 899,000 Italians have cancelled their residence in Italy over the past ten years. Their average age was 33, and 208,000 had a university degree.[31] However, this figure likely underestimates the actual size of the brain drain because migration has been rising, and many people change their residence status only many years after they have actually moved out.

The low return to higher education (see Chapter 5) is only one possible reason behind the emigration of young Italians. Other reasons are low wages, the concentration of unemployment among the young, including those with a tertiary degree, and the very slow increase in earnings during their professional life.

The last two features are some of the main manifestations of gerontocracy. In turn, this is one of the most odious symptoms of a non-meritocratic society: young men and women must wait in line, no matter their talents. Often, they must wait until those before them either retire or die. The idea of letting a young talented person jump the social queue is almost absent from Italian culture.

We start with wages and focus on the most relevant to young adults: net wages of singles with no children (see Table 6.7). Italy is one of the European countries with lower than average wages, even considering the correction for differences in the cost of living. It is one of the most dramatic consequences of no growth for a quarter of a century.

Next we look at employment for the young. Figure 6.10 shows that the employment rate among young Italians (age 15–24) is among the lowest

---

[30] This paragraph draws on Galli et al. (2021b).
[31] ISTAT (2021a).

Table 6.7 Average net wages[*]

Countries	(Values in euro)	(Values in euro PPA)
Austria	32,810	28,830
Belgium	29,389	25,523
France	27,768	24,477
Germany	31,831	29,653
Italy	**21,463**	**21,103**
Luxemberg	41,239	31,247
Nordic countries	36,455	27,830
Portugal	14,148	16,156
UK	36,045	30,287
Spain	21,241	22,060
EU27	**24,005**	**23,522**

[*] Single with no children, 2020 data.
Source: Eurostat databank, and authors' calculations.

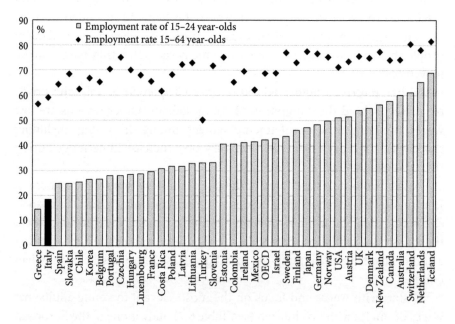

Fig. 6.10 Employment rate by age group
Source: OECD Databank and authors' calculations, % of the population in same age group, 2019.

in the OECD, below that of Spain. Moreover, Italy is one of the countries with the most remarkable difference between the overall employment rate (age 15–64) and that of the young.

Table 6.8 Wage gaps by age group

	25–54/ 15–24	55–64/ 25–54	55–64/ 15–24
	Percentage increase or decrease		
Ireland	88	7	101
USA	87	9	103
Netherlands	82	15	109
Greece	77	28	127
UK	70	−2	67
Korea	70	−7	59
Luxembourg	69	26	113
Denmark	69	2	73
Germany	68	10	85
Canada	67	0	67
Japan	65	2	68
Colombia	64	20	97
Norway	64	10	81
Australia	60	1	62
Switzerland	59	13	80
Turkey	57	19	88
Iceland	56	7	68
Portugal	53	20	84
Spain	53	14	74
Finland	53	3	58
Costa Rica	52	21	83
France	49	17	75
Austria	48	20	78
Hungary	48	−3	44
Slovenia	47	12	64
Belgium	47	24	81
Sweden	45	8	56
New Zealand	43	−1	41
Slovakia	40	−8	28
Czechia	38	−4	32
Mexico	37	−1	36
Poland	35	−6	27
Italy	34	19	59
Estonia	33	−20	6
Lithuania	33	−15	12
Latvia	32	−24	0

Source: Authors' calculations on OECD databank, data on 2019.

This means that on top of Italy's general employment problem, there is a specific intergenerational dimension. The message is that the young can wait. Of course, if they have the opportunity and the attitude, they go abroad.

Slow-moving careers is another manifestation of gerontocracy or lack of meritocracy and can explain why young people go abroad. Table 6.8 displays wage gaps by selected age groups. The first column displays the percentage difference between average earnings at age 25–54 and 15–24. In Ireland, a young person can expect to improve by 88 per cent. In Italy, the improvement is only 34 per cent. Italy is at the bottom of the OECD group along with the three Baltic countries. Again, the young can wait.

Column 2 displays the increase or, if negative, the decrease in earnings between age 55–64 and age 25–54. Here the rise in Italy is 19 per cent, around the OECD average. Note that in some countries, seniors' wages decrease. The increase over the entire working life (59 per cent, in the third column) is rather low, but not very far from the OECD average (66 per cent).

These data tell us that wages increase very late in the professional lives of individuals in Italy. So, again, the message is that the young can wait.

To identify the specific prospects for young graduates, we look at their employment rate a few years after graduation.

In Figure 6.11, histograms display the employment rate for 25–34 year-olds with tertiary education. Italy has the lowest number (67.8 per cent) in the entire OECD, considerably below Turkey (72.3), Greece (72.8), and Spain

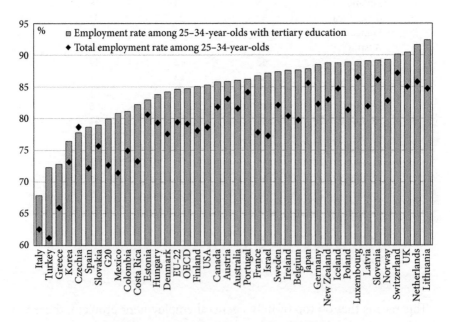

Fig. 6.11 Employment rate for 25–34 year-olds with tertiary education
Source: OECD Databank and authors' calculations, % of the population of same age group, 2019.

(78.6). The EU22 (members of the EU that are part of the OECD), the OECD average, and the USA are all around 80 per cent. In many countries, the numbers are around 90 per cent. Note there is a relationship with the employment rate for the entire population in the age group 25–34 (the black squares), but it is not an automatic one. For instance, Italy is last for employment of persons with tertiary education, but Turkey is below Italy for the entire population of the same age group.

This indicates a specific problem for young graduates (especially those majoring in humanities) on top of the general employment issue for the young. Attaining a tertiary degree does not pay much in terms of the probability of finding a job. It may be a consequence of the small size and rudimentary organisation of most Italian firms. But whatever the reason, the point is, once again, that merit is weakly rewarded. Those who make the effort (and sometimes the sacrifices) necessary to attain a tertiary degree do not see their efforts rewarded.

In conclusion, the primary employment problems concern women, the South, and the young, including those with high educational attainment. A young woman from the South who wants to work typically leaves her land. Moreover, most temporary contracts are concentrated in these three categories. Chapter 8 will discuss labour market conditions in an effort to understand these conditions and the discrimination between insiders and outsiders. Many trades union policies aimed at protecting union members rather than the generality of workers are at the root of discrimination.

But in any case, it is an additional element indicating that society does not recognise merit. If it did, we would not find that women, the young, and residents in particular areas are so much more disadvantaged than in most other countries.

7

Competitiveness

*Low foreign direct investment—Connections and corporate governance—
Relationship finance—The burden of regulation—Lobbying by tax evaders—
The rage of taxpayers*

7.1 Low foreign direct investment

So far in the book, we have seen the general environment in which companies operate in Italy. The key points that have emerged from that analysis are
low social capital, poor governance, lack of reward for merit. These points,
in turn, imply the quality of regulation is lacking, whether it concerns the
environment or enterprises. In the following pages, we look at how such poor
regulatory quality affects the life of companies and their appetite for investing
in the country.

Table 7.1 provides the overall picture. Italy's ranking is particularly low
in labour market areas, burden of regulation, the financing ecosystem, contract enforcement, property rights, and investor protection. All these factors
impinge on the competitiveness of Italian companies, making it difficult to
do business in Italy.

A manifestation of these problems is the low foreign investment into Italy.
In the past twenty years, on average, foreign direct investment (FDI) into Italy
(including the participation of only 10 per cent of voting stock) has been only
1.2 per cent of GDP, which compares with 2.1 per cent in France, 2.6 per cent
in Germany, and 3.1 per cent in Spain.[1]

These data suggest that, despite being on paper an open economy, Italy
is not very attractive, essentially because the business environment is rather
hostile and has substantial adverse effects on competitiveness.

In addition, as we saw in Chapter 2, high unit labour costs have reduced
price competitiveness. Wages are not high relative to most other similar countries, but labour productivity has stalled for a quarter of a century. The result
has been a massive loss of cost competitiveness, especially in the first decade

---

[1] Source: World Bank's database.

Meritocracy, Growth, and Lessons from Italy's Economic Decline. Lorenzo Codogno and Giampaolo Galli,
Oxford University Press. © Lorenzo Codogno and Giampaolo Galli (2022). DOI: 10.1093/oso/9780192866806.003.0008

Table 7.1 Enterprise conditions and the investment environment

Pillar	Element	Italy/ 167	Italy/ 34	Top Country /167
Enterprise Conditions	Labour market flexibility	165	34	Singapore
Enterprise Conditions	Burden of regulation	126	34	Singapore
Enterprise Conditions	Price distortions	43	25	Finland
Enterprise Conditions	Environment for business creation	9	8	Taiwan, China
Enterprise Conditions	Domestic market contestability	1	1	Multiple—3
Investment Environment	Financing ecosystem	74	32	USA
Investment Environment	Contract enforcement	57	30	Singapore
Investment Environment	Restrictions on international investment	55	29	Singapore
Investment Environment	Investor protection	41	28	Finland
Investment Environment	Property rights	31	27	Singapore

The notation 'Multiple—n' indicates that n countries are in the top position.
Source: Legatum Institute (2020), authors' calculations.

of the century. From 1995 to 2008, the loss relative to Germany was more than 30 percentage points (Figure 7.1). Among the major Eurozone countries, only Spain had a greater loss. In the subsequent decade, both Spain and Italy had a long period of wage moderation, which made it possible to recoup part of the gap. However, Italy's cumulated loss is still relevant (17 per cent) and is slightly greater than that of Spain (14 per cent). Also, France and Belgium recorded a loss of competitiveness from 1995 to 2008. However, it was much smaller than Italy's and Spain's, and entirely recovered during the past decade. Overall, during the first ten years after the introduction of the euro, several countries did not adapt to the new reality in terms of wage dynamics and productivity. The impact emerged on Italy's external position in the balance of payments. It worsened vis-à-vis Germany and other smaller Eurozone countries and, through reduced net export contribution, it also reduced GDP growth. The current account balance of Germany, which was in deficit until 2001, turned positive after that and continued to improve until a peak of 8.6 per cent of GDP in 2015. It then slowly declined, but in 2020 it was still a sizeable 7.1 per cent of GDP. Italy's current account was balanced at the launch of the euro and turned negative afterwards reaching 3.3 per cent of GDP in 2010. Since then, it has steadily improved to 3.8 per cent of GDP by 2020.

The no-euro camp has used these numbers to show that the single currency was the by-product of German mercantilism, meaning its vocation to dominate Europe through beggar-thy-neighbour policies. While Germany,

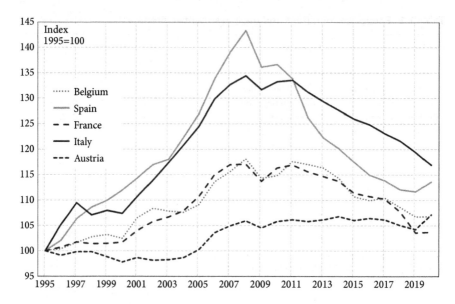

Fig. 7.1 Unit labour costs per person relative to Germany
Source: Eurostat, authors' calculations.

indeed, did nothing to stimulate its domestic demand and reduce its current account surplus, the Eurozone periphery did not manage to preserve its price competitiveness. Italian firms and institutions, like those of other countries, failed to withstand the challenges of the euro, as well as those stemming from technological innovation and competition from emerging economies.[2]

In any case, the costs of such failure were considerable. One of these costs was a long period of forced wage moderation in the following decade; this fact, together with the innovative capacity of exporting manufacturers, and their ability to partly compensate their loss in price with non-price competitiveness, was sufficient to fix the external account but not to restore economic growth. Restoring growth would also have required adapting the institutional framework in which business operates.

In the following pages, we look in greater detail into the major institutional factors that impede competitiveness. However, before doing that, it is worth looking at these same problems from the point of view of a multinational corporation that considers investing in Italy (Table 7.2). In addition to the issues highlighted above, a multinational corporation is likely to examine whether there are capital controls, restrictions to holding foreign currencies, and the

---

[2] On the issue of external disequilibria in the Eurozone there is a large literature. A good synthesis can be found in de Guindos (2019). This issue is also central to the volumes edited by Baldwin and Giavazzi (2015) and by Campos et al. (2020).

Table 7.2 Investing in Italy

Element	Indicator	Italy/ 167	Italy/ 34	Top Country
Investor Protection	Auditing and reporting standards	88	32	Finland
Investor Protection	Conflict of interest regulation	74	23	Multiple—2
Investor Protection	Extent of shareholder governance	68	24	Norway
Investor Protection	Insolvency recovery rate	33	24	Multiple—8
Investor Protection	Strength of insolvency framework	15	6	Multiple—2
Restrictions on International Investment	Prevalence of foreign ownership of companies	134	34	UK
Restrictions on International Investment	Business impact of rules on FDI	116	31	Singapore
Restrictions on International Investment	Freedom of foreigners to visit	57	6	Multiple—2
Restrictions on International Investment	Capital controls	16	5	Multiple—2
Restrictions on International Investment	Freedom to own foreign currency bank accounts	1	1	Multiple—33
Restrictions on International Investment	Restrictions on financial transactions	1	1	Multiple—28

The notation 'Multiple—n' indicates that n countries are in the top position.
Source: Legatum Institute (2020), authors' calculations.

free movement of people. Italy has no such limitations as they were abolished in the 1990s in the run-up to the European single currency.

However, the situation is quite different when looking at such items as Business impact of rules on foreign investment and Prevalence of foreign ownership of companies.

Such items are pretty negative and contrast sharply with the prevalent view in Italy that there have been fire sales of 'national jewellery' to foreigners. This is obviously not true, in light of the data shown above, demonstrating that FDI into Italy is minimal.

In addition, foreign companies are not very welcome, despite Domestic market contestability being high (Table 7.1). Occasionally, governments take some initiatives to encourage foreign companies to invest in Italy, usually through the Ministry of Economic Development, the Foreign Office, or by such agencies as the Italian Trade Agency (ICE). But the reality is that Italians are rather unhappy with foreign companies because—so goes the mantra— 'they are outside the range of democratic control'. In some cases, it may be accurate, but otherwise, it simply means that they can close their shop if it is no longer profitable. For Italian entrepreneurs, this is more difficult because if they close a factory or reduce the labour force, they may have a hard time with other activities. Connections with politics are essential for Italian companies so that they try to avoid creating tension with the political establishment. A foreign-owned company is freer to act in the interest of its shareholders.

7.2 Connections and corporate governance

Shareholders of a multinational company are also more likely than those of an Italian company to look at such items as Auditing and reporting standards, Conflict of interest regulation, and Extent of shareholders' governance. In Italy, they are more important than elsewhere, as most companies are non-listed and strictly controlled by a family group. In addition, a foreign company wants to make sure that the firms with which it does business have high reporting standards and serious internal controls to avoid conflicts of interest, all aspects for which Italy's ranking is low.

The first of these three indicators comes from the WEF survey, while the second and third are from the World Bank. The conflict of interest indicator is a composite measure of the protection of shareholders against directors' misuse of corporate assets for personal gain: (a) transparency of related-party transactions; (b) shareholders' ability to sue and hold directors liable for self-dealing; and (c) access to evidence and allocation of legal expenses in shareholder litigation.

The Extent of shareholder governance is also a composite measure that deals with the rights of shareholders in corporate governance. It is formed of: (a) shareholders' rights and role in major corporate decisions; (b) governance safeguards protecting shareholders from undue board control and entrenchment; and (c) transparency on ownership stakes, compensation, audits, and financial prospects.

So, both items deal with how well shareholders are protected from abuses coming from directors or the controlling shareholder.

Various studies have established that, in the Italian case, the problem is not the state of the legislation.[3] After a long process that started at the beginning of the 1990s, a comprehensive legislative text was approved in 1998 (called TUF or Draghi Law, from the then Director of the Treasury), which regulates finance and corporate governance according to best foreign practice. On paper, Italy has some of the most advanced legislation for the protection of minority shareholders. Even in the Anglo-Saxon world, requirements

---

[3] Roe (2000) and Bianchi-Bianco (2006).

and corporate control to protect minorities are not as stringent as in Italy; for instance, the guaranteeing role of the president, actions of the board of auditors, voting by list, and the requirement of having at least one independent director on the majority list. However, there is a gap between the rules and their application. The institution responsible for ensuring rules enforcement (CONSOB, the National Commission for Companies and the Stock Exchange, i.e. Italy's watchdog) is too often absent.

So, the problem is not corporate governance law. Instead, it stems from the fact that most Italian companies, including those listed, are strictly controlled by one single family group. When family members hold all the key positions in a company, it is improbable that one can have the sort of checks and balances that are crucial for good corporate governance and are indeed prescribed by the law. So, for instance, most delicate decisions must be approved by the Committee for transactions with related parties, which must be formed by independent members of the board. The problem is that this committee is usually not given the basic set of information needed to evaluate the transactions.[4]

Historically, the mass of small domestic investors with minority interests in Italian companies, the so-called 'oxen park', was regularly the victim of predatory behaviours. Although, things have improved somewhat over the years, this situation is a severe problem for the small investor, but it may become a fatal one for the country if it wants to attract foreign investment. This is because investors manage their international allocation not only with risk and reward in mind but also considering the level of the legal protection of minority interests. Their interests are very much aligned with those of small domestic investors.

Some financial market events highlighted the problem of minority shareholders' protection and that CONSOB did not enforce the rules.

Mistakes can occur, but what happened with Monte dei Paschi, the banks in the Veneto region, and several other cases goes beyond ordinary mistakes. In the eyes of foreign investors, what was most striking was the lack of public explanation about the authorities' action or inaction.

In January 2017, an international investment fund, frustrated by the lack of response from the Italian watchdog, decided to put all the documentation of controversy on its website:[5] all the letters sent to CONSOB, the information collected, etc., related to the sale of a listed company. The evidence appears

---

[4] Enriques (2018).

[5] 'The fund Elliott puts online Hitachi's sins on Ansaldo' (La Stampa), 'Elliott vs Hitachi, the fund online the secrets of IPO on Ansaldo Sts' (Milano Finanza), 'Online the accusations of Elliott against Hitachi' (Il Secolo XIX), 'The war between Elliott and Hitachi is also decided on the web' (Il Giornale), 18 January 2017.

to suggest that there was a deliberate action to the detriment of minority shareholders, into which CONSOB only partly intervened. The majority shareholders voted in favour of removing an independent director accused of 'excessive diligence', who had dared to raise the issue. The so-called 'action of responsibility', i.e. an effective means of protecting all shareholders, was instrumentally used by the majority shareholder to eject a particularly diligent director appointed by the minority on the board. CONSOB remained silent.

A large body of research shows that countries with an effective legal framework to protect minorities tend to have more robust markets because investors are more willing to take risks.[6] But the law itself is not enough; what matters is enforcement and the administrative ability to implement rules. In Italy, the mirror effect of this phenomenon is the relatively high value of the private benefits of control. The next section will explain why Italy's equity investment culture is still underdeveloped. Still, the problem of enforcement is undoubtedly part of the story since minority shareholders' protection is central.

The conclusion of this (very short) discussion is that in a system in which relations are more important than merit, it is challenging to have a sound corporate governance system.

7.3 Relationship finance

One of the main casualties of low social capital is the financial system. Lending money requires trust. The bank must be reassured that the borrower will make good use of the money and do her/his best to pay interest and capital back to the bank. Much more trust is required for equity financing because monitoring the company is very difficult, especially with many small dispersed shareholders. When trust and merit are missing, the result is relationship finance, i.e. finance based on personal connections.

Venture capital is a case where trust is of the essence since very little is known ex ante about a newly created company and, as Table 7.3 shows, Italy's

---

[6] See, for instance, Capron-Guillén (2009).

Table 7.3 Finance

Indicator	Italy/ 167	Italy/ 34	Top Country
Venture capital availability	153	33	Multiple—2
Financing of SMEs	143	33	Multiple—5
Soundness of banks	120	31	Finland
Access to finance	68	30	Israel
Depth of credit information	51	11	Multiple—10
Commercial bank branches	8	4	Luxembourg
Quality of banking system and capital markets*	1	1	Multiple—29

* The top score in the last item is due to the fact that the Bertelsmann Stiftung Index deals only with developing countries. Developed countries are missing. As stated in Legatum (2019), '[i]n this case, [the Prosperity Index] gives these countries the highest possible score, based on our assessment that this is the score they would receive if they were included'.
The notation 'Multiple—n' indicates that n countries are in the top position.
Source: Legatum Institute (2020), authors' calculations.

Table 7.4 Venture capital investment*

	2019	2020
USA	135,649	. . .
UK	3,350	3,193
Canada	3,287	3,009
Korea	2,708	2,582
Japan	2,503	. . .
Germany	2,380	2,219
France	2,165	2,327
Netherlands	702	1,030
Spain	655	918
Switzerland	554	624
Australia	487	. . .
South Africa	482	. . .
Sweden	403	526
Belgium	396	432
Denmark	352	284
Finland	322	564
Italy	**261**	**386**
Ireland	185	388
Norway	158	118
Hungary	155	143

* By country of destination, million US dollars.
Source: OECD database, and authors' calculations.

ranking on this item is quite low.[7] This is confirmed by the latest available data on total venture capital investment (from seed capital to start-ups and later stages), which show two facts. The first is that venture capital is essentially a US phenomenon. In that country, total investment is in the order of forty times the level of the second country, the UK. The second fact is that in Italy, venture capital is about one-tenth the size of that in Germany or France, and half the size of that in Spain (Table 7.4).

As we document in Chapter 6, this is one of the reasons why many graduates from Italian universities leave the country and go abroad to set up their own companies. The oft-heard story is that they do so because if in London you present a good idea, you may find someone who will finance it, while in Italy potential investors tend to appropriate it. Also, as we have seen in Chapter 6, innovation, particularly in high tech, is not vibrant.

Once again, trust is of the essence. But here again, merit is important because if one finds young graduates with brilliant ideas, it would be smart to encourage them to develop their potential. This is the best way to make money, at least in the long run.

The most obvious and striking fact about finance is that the Milan stock exchange is tiny relative to the size of the economy. According to the latest comparative data by the World Bank,[8] Italy has only 4.8 listed companies per million inhabitants. The corresponding numbers for Germany, France, and Belgium are 7.3, 7.5, and 10.1.

Forbes 2000 is a list of the top 2,000 companies of the world ranked on mixed criteria that use data on sales, profits, total assets, and market capitalisation. In this list, Italy ranks thirty-fourth with a market capitalisation of only 15 per cent of GDP.[9] The point is that most of the (few) companies listed on the Milan stock exchange are relatively small and do not appear in the Forbes 2000 list. As a result, Italy is far behind the USA, the UK, and other Western European countries (see Table 7.5).

Looking at the list of the companies that make up this 15 per cent of GDP (Table 7.6), it is apparent that most of them are either financial (Intesa, Generali, Unicredit, Mediolanum, Mediobanca, Cattolica, Bper, Ubi, MPS, Fineco, Credito Emiliano, Banca Popolare di Sondrio), are controlled by the government (Enel, Eni, Leonardo, Snam, Poste Italiane, Saipem, Terna, MPS), or are former government monopolies that have been privatised (Telecom, and Autostrade, which was renationalised in 2021). Of the very few remaining companies, some are Italian only by residence but are controlled by foreign

---

[7] This is the answer to the WEF survey question: 'In your country, how easy is it for start-up entrepreneurs with innovative but risky projects to obtain equity funding, from extremely difficult, to extremely easy?'

[8] World Bank, Global Financial Development database.

[9] Note that this is not the Milan stock exchange market capitalisation, which is around 30 per cent of GDP.

Table 7.5 Ranking of countries in the Forbes 2000 list

Rank	Country	Market capitalisation* $US million	% of GDP
1	Hong Kong	1,061,401	290
2	Saudi Arabia	1,970,800	249
3	Switzerland	1,527,466	217
4	Ireland	588,900	152
5	USA	25,911,617	121
6	Luxembourg	70,200	99
7	Denmark	342,400	98
8	Netherlands	753,551	83
9	Sweden	401,700	76
10	Canada	1,297,960	75
11	Finland	173,300	64
12	Japan	3,176,497	63
13	UK	1,731,729	61
14	France	1,609,760	59
15	Austria	220,400	50
16	Australia	690,600	49
17	Singapore	177,129	48
18	Qatar	83,400	47
19	South Korea	710,764	43
20	China	5,979,200	42
21	South Africa	115,200	33
22	Belgium	171,300	32
23	Germany	1,239,144	32
24	Thailand	174,400	32
25	Norway	122,200	30
26	UAE	127,000	30
27	Spain	416,177	30
28	India	847,522	30
29	Russia	437,300	26
30	Malaysia	91,300	25
31	Israel	64,281	16
32	Portugal	37,200	16
33	Brazil	285,200	16
34	**Italy**	**303,235**	**15**

* Market capitalisation of companies included in the Forbes 2000 list.
Source: Authors' calculations on Forbes 2000 databank.

entities. Single-family groups control most Italian companies, and in general, the family is not happy about letting strangers look into what is considered a family affair.

A few years ago, in a meeting of the top forty or fifty Italian entrepreneurs, one of the most respected members of the group monopolised the discussion by stating that listing his company on the stock exchange was the worst

Table 7.6 Italian companies in the Forbes 2000 list

Rank 2000	Company Name	Sales (US$m)	Profits (US$m)	Assets (US$m)	Market Value (US$m)
97	Enel	86,600	2,400	192,400	69,400
125	Intesa Sanpaolo	41,300	4,700	916,100	27,300
140	Generali Group	91,900	3,000	578,600	22,500
202	UniCredit	28,800	3,600	960,500	17,200
315	Poste Italiane	36,700	1,500	267,400	11,000
468	Eni	72,500	−4,300	131,700	34,100
520	Atlantia	10,400	1,200	91,100	13,300
546	Telecom Italia	20,100	1,000	78,700	8,300
683	Unipol Gruppo	17,600	1,000	84,300	2,500
861	Leonardo	15,400	919	30,200	4,000
880	Snam	2,900	1,200	26,700	14,800
941	Banco BPM	5,800	888	187,500	1,800
1075	Mediobanca	3,400	940	92,600	5,000
1080	Terna	2,600	848	20,300	12,600
1149	Ferrari	4,200	779	6,100	27,700
1275	Banca Mediolanum	4,300	633	59,900	4,500
1445	BPER Banca	3,000	425	88,700	1,300
1474	Cattolica Assicurazioni	8,300	84	41,200	922
1493	UBI Banca	5,300	281	142,000	3,200
1569	Banca MPS	4,700	−1,100	148,500	1,300
1800	FinecoBank	769	323	31,500	6,800
1813	Credito Emiliano	2,100	225	53,500	1,500
1891	Pirelli	6,000	490	15,600	3,900
1895	Banca Popolare di Sondrio	1,200	154	46,200	713
1933	Saipem	10,200	13	14,700	2,600
1963	Prysmian	12,900	327	11,800	5,000

Source: Authors' calculations on Forbes 2000 databank.

mistake he had ever made. The reasons stated were the excessive paperwork imposed by the financial market authority and the need to disclose family affairs to financial markets, where short-term profits are more important than the company's long-term perspective.

As documented in Chapter 9, a company is considered a family affair, and connections are more important than accountability to the financial markets.

Large organisations require trust. The person or family who controls the firm must be willing to delegate powers to managers at various levels. Starting with the seminal work of Jensen and Meckling (1976), a large body of literature has dealt with the principal–agent problem—how shareholders can control managers. Managers would like to build empires for their own glory, while shareholders are interested in results. Many solutions have been devised concerning compensation for managers (e.g. stock options) and the financial structure of firms. For instance, bank debt turns out to be a rather effective way of monitoring managers. Banks have professional employees assigned to that specific task. They can monitor the trends of debt and deposits almost in real-time, know if there are any arrears, and at any moment convene the company to explain what is happening. Financial market investors are essentially precluded from these actions; at best they can only monitor the company from the outside.

Mark Roe (2003) has a convincing explanation of why not only in Italy but also in most of continental Europe, public companies have so little success. His answer is also helpful in understanding why Italy has smaller companies than most other European countries. Roe starts by observing that in continental Europe, control 'is concentrated in no small measure because the delicate threads that tie managers to shareholders in the public firm fray easily in common political environments, such as those in [the] continental European social democracies'.

It is helpful to explain what Franco Debenedetti (2004) has written in his introduction to the Italian translation of the book: Mark Roe's notion of 'Social Democracy' has little in common with the use that Europeans make of this term. Indeed, many of the features that Roe puts under the label of Social Democracy can nowadays be easily recognised as more typical of most populist parties (right or left) than of traditional social democratic parties, such as, for instance, the SPD in Germany.

In Roe's own words, 'social democracies press managers to stabilise employment, to forego some profit-maximising risks with the firm, and to use up capital in place rather than to downsize when markets no longer are aligned with the firm's production capabilities'.

In addition, 'since managers must have discretion in the public firm, how they use that discretion is crucial to stockholders, and social democratic pressures induce managers to stray farther than otherwise from their shareholders' profit-maximising goals'.

Moreover, 'the means that align managers with diffuse stockholders in the USA—incentive compensation, hostile takeovers, and strong shareholder-wealth maximisation norms—are weaker and sometimes denigrated in continental social democracies'.

For all these reasons, 'public firms there have higher managerial agency costs, and large-block shareholding has persisted as shareholders' best remaining way to control those costs'.

The critical point, for our purposes, is that in continental Europe, typically managers are considered successful when they do the sort of things that public opinion and politicians like: increase employment and never decrease it, undertake new investment, and never downsize, etc.

In addition, nowadays, a manager receives high consideration when she/he manages to pursue stakeholder value, a vague expression by which is probably meant that she/he should contribute to the SDGs (Sustainable Development Goals), approved by the General Assembly of the United Nations in September 2015. The concept of 'stakeholder value' has also become important in the USA as it has been formally embraced by the influential Business Round Table and has become the dominant concept in the high-level Davos WEF talks.[10]

It may well be that the public company will lose its appeal in the USA in the future. Still, shareholders have the problem of preventing managers from undertaking actions that may damage their value and are more successful in doing so in the USA than in Europe.

The above data suggest that these problems are more critical in Italy than in other European countries. This may be due to historical reasons and to the traditionally strong presence of trades union and politicians who are very likely to impose the sort of things that appeal to their general egalitarian values. They are unlikely to care much about a company's financial viability, and in general, they are unlikely to understand why financial statements are important.

7.4 The burden of regulation

Table 7.7 reports the items concerning the burden of regulation. Italy's ranking is among the lowest across advanced countries in nearly all these indicators. These indicators are taken from the World Bank databank, except for the first question that comes from the executives' survey of the WEF.

Consider, for instance, the third item: 'Time spent filing taxes'. This variable comes from a company's case study during the second year of operation and measures the time required to prepare, file, and pay corporate income tax, value added or sales tax, and labour taxes, including payroll taxes and social contributions. It takes a typical firm 238 hours on average per year in Italy, which means about 30 days. Instead, it takes half that time or less in Norway, Switzerland, or the Netherlands (Table 7.8). Why are there such significant differences? The answer is far from easy, also because countries like Germany and the USA are not so very different from Italy.

---

[10] Debenedetti (2021).

Table 7.7 Burden of regulation

Indicator	Italy/167	Italy/34	Top Country
Burden of government regulation	164	34	Singapore
Time spent complying with regulations	117	32	South Korea
Time spent filing taxes	102	32	Estonia
Burden of obtaining a building permit	89	28	Denmark
Building quality control index	75	20	Multiple—2
Number of tax payments	74	30	Multiple—2

The notation 'Multiple—n' indicates that n countries are in the top position.
Source: Legatum Institute (2020), authors' calculations.

Table 7.8 Time spent filing taxes

Country	Hours
Luxembourg	55
Switzerland	63
Norway	79
Ireland	81
Finland	90
UK	105
Netherlands	119
Sweden	122
Cyprus	123
Austria	131
Canada	131
Denmark	132
Belgium	136
France	139
Malta	139
Iceland	140
Spain	148
USA	175
Greece	193
Germany	218
Italy	**238**
Portugal	243

Source: Authors' calculations on World Bank 'Doing Business' (2020).

The extreme severity of US tax laws and related penalties is essential. Maybe the same is true for Germany. But why does it take only 15 days in the Netherlands, which is not a low tax country?

Most probably, the answer comes in two parts.

The first part has to do with the fact that in Italy almost all laws are complex to read and hard to interpret, as we have already seen. At the origin of this phenomenon, we have indicated the low level of social capital, i.e. the mutual lack of trust between institutions and people. The second part has to do specifically with taxes and is probably a magnified image of the lack of social trust. We cannot escape the reality that tax evasion is very high in Italy. Obliging people to spend a lot of time filing tax returns does not help contain evasion. However, the tax authority has an incentive to make sure that the rules are written so that no one can accuse it of being in some sense responsible for some episodes of evasion. In contrast, the incentive to reduce the administrative burden is weaker. The complexity and hard-to-interpret legislation and regulation could also be perceived as a powerful entry barrier for foreign companies in Italy, and in general, for open competition from abroad.

7.5 Lobbying by tax evaders

How much do we know about tax evasion in Italy? The EC has recently produced one of the few available international comparisons on value added tax (VAT).[11]

This study confirms that, among Western European countries, Italy has a higher VAT gap, i.e. the difference between what taxpayers should pay according to the tax rules and what they actually pay. These calculations are made with a considerable degree of accuracy, because VAT revenue is also the basis for part of the contribution that member states owe to the EU budget. Table 7.9 shows that in Italy, VAT revenues were only 109.3 billion euros in 2018, while they should have been 144.3 billion euros (theoretical liability). Hence, the gap is 35 billion euros, which corresponds to 24.5 per cent. Except for Greece, no other Western European country has such a large gap. With few exceptions, even Eastern European countries have a lower tax gap than Italy. The average for the entire EU is 11 per cent.

Evasion by micro-firms and the self-employed accounts for two-thirds of the total. As for this latter, ISTAT estimates that undeclared VAT amounts to 11.9 per cent of construction activities, 13.2 per cent of trade, transport, accommodation, and food, and 11.3 per cent of professional activities. Undeclared work comprises 22.7 per cent of services to households. In these sectors, competition is distorted, as well as the allocation of resources.

According to official documents, total evasion of taxes and social security contributions amount to more than 100 billion euros or 6.2 per cent of GDP (Table 7.10). Most likely, this underestimates actual evasion.[12]

[11] European Commission (2020b).
[12] This is Vincenzo Visco's claim—he should be credited for having been the only person who really reduced tax evasion when he was a member of government (1996–2001 and 2006–08).

Table 7.9 VAT gap as percentage of theoretical liability

	Revenue (billion euro)	VAT gap (%)
Romania	12.9	33.8
Greece	15.3	30.1
Lithuania	3.5	25.9
Italy	**109.3**	**24.5**
Slovakia	6.3	20.0
Belgium	31.1	19.4
Malta	0.9	15.1
UK	168.7	12.2
Czechia	16.1	12.0
Bulgaria	5.1	10.8
Ireland	14.2	10.6
Poland	40.4	9.9
Portugal	17.9	9.6
Latvia	2.4	9.5
Austria	29.3	9.0
Germany	235.1	8.6
Hungary	13.0	8.4
Denmark	29.1	7.2
France	167.6	7.1
Spain	77.6	6.0
Estonia	2.3	5.2
Luxemburg	3.7	5.1
Netherland	52.6	4.2
Cyprus	2.0	3.8
Slovenia	3.8	3.8
Finland	21.4	3.6
Croatia	6.9	3.5
Sweden	43.4	0.7

Source: Authors' calculations on European Commission (2020b).

The main tax underpayments for the government (at all levels, national and local) concern VAT and personal income tax that micro-firms (de facto self-employed) pay. Corporation tax includes all companies that pay corporate income tax which comprise different legal entities that may also be very small.

Who evades taxes? To better understand who evades taxes, it is useful to examine the evasion of direct taxes by companies (Table 7.11). Micro-companies and self-employed evade a stunning 70 per cent of what they ought to pay as direct taxes, which amounts to 32.3 billion euros of lost revenue for the government (1.9 per cent of GDP). This is the big lobby of tax evaders. It moves millions of votes and is quite powerful in parliament.

Table 7.10 Who evades taxes?

Gap between what is paid what should be paid; billion euro

Personal income tax on (irregular) dependent workers	4.3
Personal tax micro-firms	32.3
Corporate tax	9.0
VAT	36.8
Rents	0.7
Real estate tax (IMU)	4.9
Social security contributions owed by employers	2.9
Social security contributions owed by employees	8.8
Other taxes	8.3
Total	108.1
Total (% GDP)	6.2%

Source: Authors' calculations on Ministry of Economics and Finance (2020), 2017 data.

Table 7.11 Evasion of direct taxes by companies

	Micro-companies and self-employed	Corporations
Tax due, € billion	46.2	36.6
Tax not paid € billion	32.3	9.0
% of the amount due	69.9	24.6
% of GDP	1.9	0.5

Source: Authors' calculations on Ministry of Economy and Finance (2020) Report on Non-Observed Economy; 2017 data.

Tax evasion by corporations is also very substantial (24.6 per cent of what they ought to pay) but much less than micro-companies. Among incorporated entities, the very small ones are those that evade tax. Very little is evaded by large companies or by listed companies. The latter often manage to pay very little tax through their international operations, but they usually do it legally.

Note that a company that does not pay direct taxes is also more likely to evade VAT and social security contributions for its employees.

Why is there so much evasion? The answer is far from simple. There are some features that are common to all countries with high evasion. One has to do with the share of self-employed in the economy, which in Italy is very high. A rather rigid labour market has induced companies to resort to using self-employed staff. This is a way around the stringent labour laws and may be perfectly legal in some cases or illegal in others. The self-employed can more easily pay fewer taxes than they should according to the formal rules of taxation.

Another aspect of the problem is the level of the tax burden: when it is high, people feel more justified in paying less than they should. In response, it is often objected that there is a high level of tax compliance in Nordic countries, which typically have high levels of tax; in these countries, people pay because they see and appreciate the services that the government provides and funds with the proceeds of those taxes. We have no way of making sure that this argument stands up to scientific scrutiny, but it is certainly reasonable. In the end, compliance is high when the government is efficient, and there is mutual trust between citizens and public institutions. Social capital, good governance, merit seem to be keywords in understanding the degree of compliance.

Another critical factor is what people perceive as the risk they incur if they get caught by the tax authorities. This is very important. In Italy, most political leaders think it does not make much sense to persecute millions of people who survive because they escape taxes. This is why the lobby of tax evaders is so powerful.

Even several foreign observers of Italian affairs believe that a large shadow economy is one of Italy's strengths. It allows many people to make a living, especially in the South. According to ISTAT, the Italian statistical office, the shadow economy—a concept that is different from tax evasion—is as large as 11.3 per cent of GDP. It involves as many as 3.6 million workers.[13]

The idea that the shadow economy is one of Italy's strengths is twin to the notion that 'small is beautiful'. According to some, small or very small companies should be helped to survive, and thus they should not be persecuted as tax evaders. However, the informal economy reduces technical efficiency and productivity.

There is thus a vicious circle that is difficult to break. Tax authorities are asked not to be too harsh on people surviving in the shadow economy.[14] Those who survive thanks to tax evasion have no reason to become honest because they lose the competitive edge relative to their peers or larger companies if they do.

Another factor that may be at play is the idea that sinners should be pardoned or, in any case, should be given a chance. As we already mentioned, in 2013, Silvio Berlusconi, the former prime minister, was condemned by the third and last-resort-tier tribunal (*Cassazione*) to four years of jail for tax evasion. In the USA, he would probably have spent four years in prison, but not in Italy. Due to several generous provisions of the tax rules, he only spent less

---

[13] ISTAT's Report on Non-Observed Economy, year 2016–2019, 18 October 2021.
[14] See Vincenzo Visco (2017).

than one year doing community service, which in practice meant that he had to go to a clinic for elderly citizens, very near to his home villa, once a week. Intelligently, he used this period of community service to prop up his image as a model citizen, ready to help others. After one year, he was 'rehabilitated' by the Milan tribunal and his passport returned. In the European elections of May 2019, he was elected a member of the European Parliament. Some analysts have doubts about the sentence that condemned him since it was based on a presumed crime that is very difficult to prove: manipulation of international transfer prices on such intangible goods as media rights, his company's main business, Mediaset. Whatever the merits of the sentence, once the tribunal of last instance, after three tiers of judgement, condemns a person to four years of jail, it should be presumed that the person serves the sentence. But not in Italy.

Given precedents like this, the vicious circle described above becomes almost untouchable. A solid iron shield defends it. In the end, the ordinary person who struggles to survive in the shadow economy has reason to ask: why should I be the one who pays taxes?

7.6 The rage of taxpayers

Many self-employed and many small companies do not pay taxes as they should. This is a reason for deep resentment among most workers who are employees and are subject to a withholding tax levied by the employer and have no way to escape. Until 2012, the Ministry of Finance had regularly published a report detailing the average taxes paid by employers and employees in each economic sector. The result was that employers typically paid less tax than their employees. The report was very detailed since it was used to establish a presumption of evasion in each sector. Tax paid, for instance, by jewellers, a category that is considered to have high turnover, was less than that of their employees. In the last year for which data are available (2011), the average income of a dependent worker was 20,020 euros. At the same time, as the national press reported, beauty salons declared an average income of 7,200 euros, coffee shops 17,800 euros, and taxi drivers 15,600 euros. Jewellers declared 17,300 euros, hotels 18,300 euros, car dealers 10,100 euros, and hairdressers 13,200 euros.[15] There were then many economic activities that declared zero income or losses, and hence paid no tax: discos, night clubs, health resorts, sports facilities, etc.

---

[15] Source: 'Il Fatto Quotidiano', 31 May 2013.

So the question became: why don't they pay tax? This issue has been aggravated enormously during the past few years. People became aware that large international companies also manage to pay very little tax, though generally through means that are not illegal. Moreover, some scandals, such as the findings of the Panama papers, aggravated the perception of a highly unfair system.

To sum up, the lack of trust between institutions—in this case, tax authorities—and citizens creates a vicious circle that perpetuates a system perceived as highly unfair. This lack of trust (or social capital) is aggravated every day.

One of the consequences of this state of affairs is that the tax legislation is very complex. Companies have a tough time figuring out the best course to (legally) minimise the tax burden and, in any case, spend a lot of time and energy performing their duty as taxpayers. The complexity of the tax rules discourages investment in Italy even more than the level of the tax burden.

8
Egalitarianism and labour

Reforms and Penelope's shroud—Merit does not belong here—No active labour policies—The unions' lobby: protection for the lucky few—Few stable jobs—Many irregular jobs—The camouflage of false self-employed and false cooperatives

8.1 Reforms and Penelope's shroud

One of the worse indicators of Italy's economic environment relates to the labour market. As shown in Table 7.1, Italy ranks 165th out of 167 countries in terms of labour market flexibility and is at the bottom of the list of 34 advanced countries we are considering. However strange as it may appear, Italy's ranking is below that of Spain and Greece, which have record numbers of unemployment and temporary contracts.

Individual indicators that contribute to this overall ranking are shown in Table 8.1. Indicators of flexibility are responsible for Italy's low ranking in the labour market: wage determination, hiring practices, employment contracts. There is also a very unsatisfactory degree of cooperation between workers and employers. Most of these items are taken from the WEF executives' survey, except Flexibility of employment contract. This is a World Bank composite measure of how flexible are employment contracts, based on (a) maximum length of a single fixed-term contract, (b) restrictions on overtime work, and (c) whether there are fixed-term contracts prohibited for permanent tasks.[1]

It may seem strange that Italy's ranking on labour issues is so low. It is often argued that Italy has considerable flexibility at the margin because there are several ways to circumvent a rigid regulation. Some are perfectly legal ways (although inefficient, such as very short-term contracts or extreme outsourcing), some are outright illegal (irregular workers), others lie in a grey area (e.g. false self-employed, fake workers' cooperatives, wages below contractual

---

[1] The inclusion of this indicator in the World Bank Doing Business Ranking has been criticised, particularly by the International Confederation of Trade Unions, on the basis that it encourages countries to excessively relax labour protection regulation. In response, in 2009 the World Bank excluded the indicator from the overall country ranking, but kept it and its component items in the report as well as in its publicly available databank.

Meritocracy, Growth, and Lessons from Italy's Economic Decline. Lorenzo Codogno and Giampaolo Galli, Oxford University Press. © Lorenzo Codogno and Giampaolo Galli (2022). DOI: 10.1093/oso/9780192866806.003.0009

Table 8.1 Labour market

Indicator	Italy/167	Italy/34	Top Country/167
Flexibility of wage determination	161	32	Estonia
Flexibility of hiring practices	154	33	Multiple—2
Flexibility of employment contracts	139	29	Multiple—3
Cooperation in labour–employer relations	137	33	Multiple—6
Availability of skilled workers	66	25	USA
Labour skill a business constraint	38	5	South Korea
Redundancy costs	14	7	Multiple—3
Youth unemployment	145	32	Japan
Capacity to attract talented people	130	29	Switzerland
Labour force participation	113	34	Switzerland
Female labour force participation	105	34	Sweden
Waged and salaried workers	56	32	USA

The notation 'Multiple—n' indicates that n countries are in the top position.
Source: Legatum Institute (2020), authors' calculations.

minimum). These arguments contain more than a grain of truth. We hence interpret the low ranking as reflecting the evaluation of a company that does not want to resort to inefficient expedients and normally wants to hire workers with regular open-ended contracts.

Another set of arguments points to the many reforms introduced since 1996 aiming to increase flexibility in a very rigid market. In particular, in 2012 and 2015, two crucial reforms were introduced that relaxed the very rigid set of norms inherited from the 1970s, which made it almost impossible for companies to dismiss workers.[2] We believe that there are good reasons for such a low score, particularly on Flexibility in Hiring practices and Labour contracts. Companies do not care much about what is in the law but how the law is applied in practice by judges. Besides, when they hire somebody, they have to try to guess how legislation is likely to change in the future. In the two reforms of 2012 and 2015, neither many of the political class nor many judges ever accepted the reforms. In the end, two Constitutional Courts' sentences very much reduced the scope of the reforms in practice.[3] A 2018 ruling deemed unconstitutional a crucial article of a 2015 law (so-called 'Jobs Act') that determines the amount an employer has to pay when firing workers, based on their seniority.[4] The underlying idea was that the relevant judge

[2] See, in English, Boeri-Garibaldi (2018), Leonardi-Nannicini (2018), Sestito-Viviano (2018); in Italian, Sestito (2002), Dell'Aringa et al. (2017). For a broad view on the legal aspects of the labour market see Prosperetti (2019).
[3] There were probably good legal reasons for the court's decisions; the problem is that governments did not take the decisions that were necessary to remedy the situation to avoid a freezing of the labour market.
[4] Sentence n. 194, 8 December 2018.

must evaluate the decision on the amount to be paid on a case-by-case basis. In practice, this means that, after firing, the company still does not know if it has to pay six months' or three years' salary.[5] There is also evidence that judges decide whether a contract resolution is legitimate depending on the specific labour market environment. For example, judges are much more likely to side with workers in the South, mainly because it is more difficult to find a new job there than in the rest of the country.[6]

A further recent ruling by the Constitutional Court has reintroduced the obligation to reinstate a worker in her/his job if hired before the reform of 2012 when the judge decided that dismissing was illegitimate.[7] The courts' decisions reflect a general opinion among most political parties and public opinion that tends to view dismissal as a despicable action, which should be a last resort in absolutely exceptional cases.

There are many occasions in which a worker has been reinstated in the job by the courts, despite having committed rather severe crimes inside the company, such as stealing company assets or showing false sickness certificates for long periods of absence. For example, the tribunal of Rome reinstated a professional nurse who had been fired because he had thrown to the floor a patient with severe mental illness and repeatedly kicked him in the stomach and chest.[8] The tribunal did not deny the facts. The motivation for the sentence was that 'it was an isolated and exceptional fact, related to a particular type of patient, which does not have the legal characteristics necessary to define it a serious infringement [...] and justify what should remain an *extrema ratio*'.[9] This is not an isolated anecdote: it is the very reason why Italy's ranking is so low in terms of flexibility of both 'Hiring practices' and 'Employment contracts'.

Italy has a good score on redundancy costs, but this is not relevant for various reasons. First, as the International Labour Organization (ILO) notes, although redundancy costs and severance payments *strictu sensu* are low, when a worker leaves, for whatever reason, the company must pay 'an end-of-employment contract indemnity [TFR] calculated according to the formula of a year's overall salary divided by 13.5, plus 1.5 per cent for each year of service plus compensation for inflation'.[10] Second, and most importantly, the real problem from the employer's viewpoint is the risk of the worker asking

[5] Ichino, P. (2018).
[6] Ichino, P. (2005).
[7] Sentenza n. 59, 1 April 2021.
[8] This case reported in Ichino, P. (2015).
[9] Tribunal of Rome, 19 October 2001.
[10] See ILO at the link https://eplex.ilo.org/country-detail/?code=ITA&yr=2017. The cost of TFR is also incurred when the worker retires or quits the company.

the judge to reinstate her/him in the job on grounds that the dismissal was not justified.[11]

Reinstatement in the job has severe implications. Since the dismissal was 'illegitimate', legally, it is 'as if it never happened', which in turn means that the company must pay salaries and social security contributions for the entire interim period. If the sentence of the tribunal occurs ten years after the fact, which is often the case, the interim period is ten years. This is the main reason for Italy's low score in hiring practices. As we said above, various reform attempts have been enacted (notably in 2012 and 2015), but it is as yet unclear whether the system has really changed for the better.

8.2 Merit does not belong here

The low score for 'flexibility in wage determination' results from a powerful egalitarian drive by the trades union, which obviously is the opposite of meritocracy. Two factors are particularly important.

First, nationwide collective contracts in each sector account for the bulk of the average wage and do not allow for differential productivity in different companies or territories: national agreements do not even distinguish between North and South. In most cases, specific company-level contracts are not used, except for a few medium to large companies, usually accounting for a relatively small proportion of wages. In practice, they can only add to national contracts and never derogate from them.

Second, collective contracts, whether national or local, do not only fix a minimum wage, but they also fix the wage for all categories of workers, whether blue or white collared.

In the last two decades, various laws have been put in place that give fiscal incentives to firms and workers which agreed to set up company-level contracts to increase productivity instead of only relying on national contracts. This has helped create some differentiation, especially between regions of the country. Even so, results have been disappointing so far, and the portion of productivity-related add-ons is relatively tiny. Some argue that poor economic development since the introduction of the law has not provided

[11] As explained by ILO: '[According to Italian laws] a dismissal is unfair unless it is for a just cause (no notice required) or a justified motive. "Just cause", in broad terms, requires very grave conduct which, when evaluated both subjectively and objectively, constitutes a serious and irremediable reason that prevents the parties to continue the employment relationship even on an interim basis. Whether such a breach has occurred would normally have to be determined ultimately by a court, taking all relevant factors into account. Justified reason is defined as a very significant breach of contract made on the side of the employee (subjective justified reason) a reason inherent in the production process, the organisation of work or the smooth running of the undertaking (objective justified reason)' (ILO, link as in n. 10).

many opportunities for add-ons to the contractual pay. However, in reality, some degree of differentiation exists. At least in small or medium enterprises (SMEs), the primary source of differentiation is the so-called *fuori busta* (literally 'outside the envelope' pay). They are add-ons to wages given at the full discretion of the company; they are typically not disclosed because they are not part of the union agreement, and they are irregular because no taxes or social security contributions are paid on them.

All this has critical implications: companies have little margin for legally rewarding more productive workers and almost no possibility of punishing unproductive workers. This system could perhaps have worked in the Taylorist factory of the 1970s, when mass production of identical products was the key characteristic of the production system. However, it is now obsolete in facing the challenges of a knowledge economy. In such an economy, differences in productivity among apparently similar workers can be enormous: one worker might be very creative and find new and better ways to produce or sell and should be incentivised and rewarded for that.[12] On the other hand, another worker might do her/his fair share of the job and deserve the average wage.

On the opposite side of the spectrum, a negative worker can do much more damage today than on the typical 1970s production line, when it was relatively easy to monitor and control her/his productivity. The pandemic has made this point even more evident, as more people have resorted to 'remote working'. Those who work from their homes cannot be controlled while working in the same way as in the office. The whole process is harder to control, but their work results can be measured or, at any rate, evaluated. Thus, it is becoming clear that paying everybody the same is highly inefficient and may be perceived as unfair.

One of the consequences of this system is that there is no relation between wages and productivity across regions of Italy. Boeri et al. (2021b) have compared the Italian situation with that of Germany, where local and company-level bargaining is much more important. They show in a rather definitive way that the Italian system is one of the causes of high non-employment (not officially employed, but not unemployed either) in the South because both productivity and the cost of living are lower in that area.

This egalitarian culture explains why the 'Cooperation in labour–employer relations' index is a dismal 137th ranking globally. This is probably the deep root of all other problems, as it is challenging for a company to

---

[12] Ichino, P. (2005).

cooperate with organised labour unions with low consideration for productivity and company results. On the other hand, companies have never
convincingly challenged the status quo through their associations. Thus,
despite considerable progress relative to previous decades, the situation is still
substantially below the standards of other advanced countries.

8.3 No active labour policies

As shown, among others, by Pirrone-Sestito (2006), cooperation is also made
more difficult by very inefficient, or almost non-existent, active labour market policies. This situation is largely due to the fact that trade unions have
always defended existing jobs which fall under their control, rather than
helping workers improve their skills to better navigate a rapidly changing
job market. This creates a vicious circle because workers are induced to fear
change and defend existing jobs in the absence of active labour market policies. This is one of the reasons—though probably not the main one—why
Italy ranks so low in terms of innovation.

To better understand the underlying causes of the present situation, one
must go back to the post-war period and the extreme egalitarian culture that
had prevailed since the 1970s. From the very beginning, largely as a heritage of the pre-war period, the purpose of Public Placement Offices (*Uffici
di Collocamento*), as they were called, was not to help workers find a new job
through counselling and training. Nor was it to assess and classify their qualifications and then offer a valuable service to companies. By oversimplifying,
their job was just that of placing workers in a queue, based on arrival date.

The first in line was first to be served. And companies could not hire anyone else; they had to pick the first in the line.[13] The system was made more
stringent in the 1960s and 1970s, with the prohibition of private recruitment
agencies to intermediate labour, and rigid listing by the 'Statute of Workers'
(Law 30 of 1970) of the few specific reasons that could allow an employer to
bypass the compulsory system.

Hence, an employer was not allowed to hire outside such lists, with very
few exceptions. This unbelievable system was relaxed in 1991 with a law that
allowed an employer to choose a worker (*chiamata nominativa*).[14] It was not
completely abolished until 1996 when some space was given to placement
services run by private companies.[15]

---

[13] See Ichino, P. (1982), Pirrone-Sestito (2006), and Panci (2014).
[14] Law 223/1991.
[15] Law 608/1996.

Since then, public offices have often changed their names and institutional rank (run by state, regions, or provinces); but they have not yet learned how to provide valuable services to help workers find jobs. Bureaucratic inertia is enormous. Except perhaps in Milan and a few other locations, the old placement offices could not face new challenges.

The results of this system can be summarised in a few numbers. Only 2.1 per cent of those who found a job in the private sector have succeeded in doing so thanks to the intermediation of public placement offices. This amounted to 23,000 persons in 2018. It reflected not only the limited number of those who contacted those offices but also offices' inefficiency: they found a job for only 7 per cent of those who had contacted them in the previous 12 months.[16] As a result, the percentage of unemployed who contact a public placement office to find a job is 18 per cent, the lowest in Europe (see Figure 8.1).

On the other hand, more than 80 per cent of those who search for a job do so mainly by asking 'friends, relatives and trades union'. As shown in Figure 8.2, this is the highest number in Europe except for some Eastern European countries (and Turkey). Even today, people often still ask for

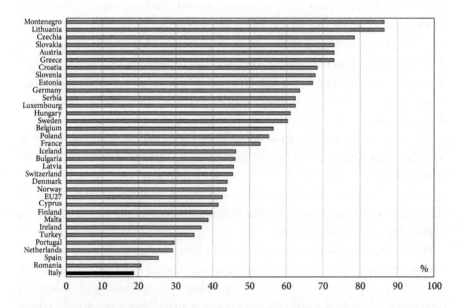

Fig. 8.1 Unemployed who contacted a public placement office

Source: Authors' calculations on Eurostat, percentage of unemployed who declare they have contacted a public placement office seeking work, 2019.

[16] Bank of Italy (2019).

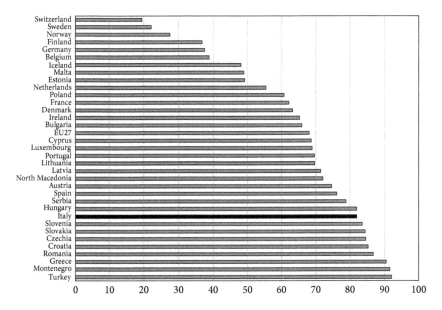

Fig. 8.2 Unemployed who contacted friends, relatives, and trades union

Source: Authors' calculations on Eurostat, percentage of unemployed who declare they have contacted friends, relatives, and trades union for seeking work, 2019 data.

recommendations, which are not the formal recommendation of a famous professor as in the US or UK. Instead, they are informal interactions that influential acquaintances can make favouring the person who is searching. And, of course, they are to be kept strictly confidential.

Placement offices do very little in terms of counselling and virtually nothing in terms of skilling or upskilling, which would be badly needed in the current rapidly changing economic environment. This situation contributes to a huge mismatch between the supply and demand of labour, especially in the South. According to a recent official survey, about one million positions were defined as 'hard to fill vacancies' even during the pandemic.[17] As a result, companies complain that they cannot find ICT engineers, qualified nurses, or blue-collar workers for the mechatronics industry, as well as tailors, plumbers, electricians, and carpenters.[18]

It is unclear whether the situation will improve with the ongoing reforms of labour offices. Yet what is clear is that the bureaucratic inertia of the egalitarian culture and praxis has done enormous damage to millions of persons looking for a job over several decades.

[17] ANPAL (2021). The number reported by ANPAL is much larger than that reported by Eurostat (only 0.8 vacancy rate). The difference is probably due to the fact that small companies tend to use informal channels to search for workers and their vacancies are not considered as such, according to the standards adopted by Euroststat.
[18] Ichino, P. (2020).

8.4 The unions' lobby: protection for the lucky few

The consequences of rigidities and inefficiencies in the labour market are many. Very few people work; many of those who do work are either self-employed or irregular, often those who have a job have a short-term contract or work part-time. Only a small minority works in structured companies, innovating and competing in international markets. Indeed, Italy has very few large private companies. Those companies are typically former public monopolies or financial institutions induced by the authorities to increase their size and consolidate. In part, these are the unintended consequences of many trades union battles since the 1970s. These battles were undertaken with good intentions to protect the weak side of the labour contract. However, after so many decades of the labour market's miserable performance, it is questionable if trades union still represent the interests of the majority of workers. Union action has been the main force resisting any change aimed at increasing participation in the labour market.

The most eloquent indicator of the present situation is the full-time-equivalent (fte) employment rate, i.e. the ratio of the working population over those aged 15–64; part-time workers are counted as a portion of a worker who performs the standard number of hours (Table 8.2). By this metric, only 54.8

Table 8.2   Full-time-equivalent employment rate by gender

Country	Total	Males	Females	Country	Total	Males	Females
Italy	**54.8**	**68.4**	**41.3**	Mexico	67.2	91.4	45.0
Turkey	57.2	81.1	33.0	Slovakia	68.5	76.3	60.5
Greece	58.9	72.3	45.8	Poland	68.8	78.8	58.9
Netherlands	59.6	71.6	47.3	USA	68.9	77.4	60.8
Spain	60.3	69.7	50.9	Korea	69.0	82.6	55.2
Belgium	60.8	69.6	51.8	Hungary	69.3	77.6	61.1
France	61.3	68.7	54.3	UK	69.3	81.1	57.6
Denmark	62.3	68.5	55.9	Switzerland	69.5	82.9	55.7
Norway	63.4	69.4	57.1	Latvia	69.8	72.8	66.9
Ireland	63.6	75.7	51.6	Israel	70.0	78.9	61.3
Chile	64.2	77.5	50.7	Portugal	70.1	76.4	64.3
Luxembourg	64.3	72.2	56.2	Sweden	70.3	74.7	65.6
Costa Rica	64.6	85.1	43.6	Lithuania	70.8	72.3	69.5
OECD	65.5	76.4	54.7	Slovenia	71.0	76.0	65.7
Australia	65.8	77.7	54.1	Estonia	71.6	77.4	66.0
Finland	66.9	71.6	62.0	New Zealand	73.5	85.4	61.9
Germany	66.9	77.9	55.6	Czechia	75.2	84.9	65.0
Austria	67.1	79.1	55.2	Iceland	82.2	91.8	71.6

Source: Authors' calculations on OECD database, % population between 15 and 64, 2019 data.

per cent of Italians aged 15–64 do work.[19] The situation is worse for women (only 41.1 per cent), in part because women more often have part-time contracts. But Italy also ranks last in the OECD in terms of employment rates for men. The difference between Italy and, for instance, Sweden is abysmal: 55 per cent against 70 per cent. Both Spain and Greece and even Turkey perform a little better than Italy.

If by the stroke of a pen it were possible to put to work as many people as in Sweden, at unchanged productivity, Italy's GDP per capita would be 27 per cent higher and one of the highest in the world. But of course, this is not possible because no single reform can perform such a fairytale transformation.[20]

Table 8.3 displays the official statistics of the labour force and shows that only 22.7 million people work, out of a population of 60 million. Close to 13.6 million are over 64, a large number due to the progress of medicine and the increase in life expectancy. Almost all of these people have the right to a pension, as do many workers who are younger than 64. In any case, excluding the relatively small portion below the age of 15 (7.9 million), the population between 15 and 64—which is still considered the working-age population in most official statistics—is 38.4 million. Those who work are 22.7 million because the others are either officially unemployed (2.6 million) or inactive (13.2 million), which means they are not counted in the labour force. Some

Table 8.3 From population to employment

A	**Population**	59.9
B	Population over 64	13.6
C	Population below 15	7.9
D=A-B-C	Population 15–64	38.4
	of which	
E	Inactive	13.2
	of which	
	Not looking for a job	10.2
	Grey area(discouraged)	2.9
F=G+H	Labour force	25.3
	of which	
G	Unemployed	2.6
H	Employed	22.7

Source: Authors' calculations on ISTAT database, million of people, 2019 data.

[19] The official employment rate is 59 per cent, a number that does not account for part-time jobs.

[20] If more workers were employed, GDP per worker would diminish because those without a job are endowed with lower productivity than those who have a job. Instead, the opposite configuration (the jobless being those with higher productivity) appears very unlikely.

are not interested in a job—usually students until they finish their studies. Many are counted as inactive because they are not actively looking for a job, but they might look for one if there were an interesting opportunity. Many people below age 64 are retired and receive a pension from the government: they are unlikely to declare that they are looking for a job. The national statistical office (ISTAT) counts 2.9 million people in the 'grey area' between inactivity and unemployment. In a more dynamic economy, probably these people would be working or searching for a job.

Overall, 22.7 million workers support a population of 60 million. The ratio is 38 per cent, which means that each worker maintains almost three persons, either through intra-family transfers or taxes.

This is one of the lowest values in Europe and compares with 53 per cent in Switzerland, 50 per cent in the Netherlands, and 49.5 per cent in Germany (Figure 8.3). Almost all Nordic countries are close to 50 per cent. France, with 40.1 per cent, is rather close to Italy. Spain, whose labour market is often considered rather inefficient, is in a better position than Italy and France. Japan, the most rapidly ageing society in the advanced world, is also above 50 per cent (not shown in Figure 8.3). The USA is at 49 per cent.

Some political forces have been arguing for a long while that immigrants are 'stealing jobs' from native workers, making political fortunes out of this

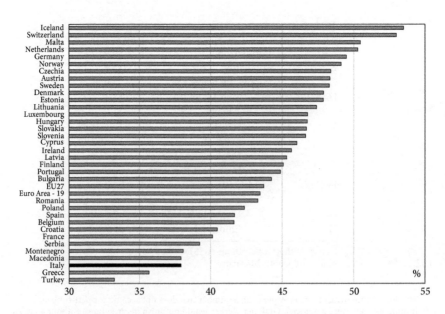

Fig. 8.3 Employment (age 15–64) over total population in Europe
Source: Authors' calculations on Istat, 2021a.

simplistic anti-immigration stance. As a matter of fact, in 2021, the government, which does also include some anti-immigration politicians, was forced to double the number of annual work permits for immigrant workers under the pressure of employers who could not find domestic workers willing to undertake some strenuous hard jobs, such as working in steel blast furnaces. These are regular job positions, fully paying social contributions and taxes, usually including training and are better paid than typical unskilled jobs. With Italy's poor demographic trends, it has become essential to rely on immigrant workers in some sectors, and there is evidence that they do not increase native unemployment.

A recent empirical paper suggests that immigration positively affects growth and eventually even unemployment in peripheral Eurozone countries.[21] This is due to complementarity with native workers, as the employment rate of migrant workers is high where there is no supply of native workers, and to the flexibility of the economy in integrating migrants and letting them generate positive externalities. Such positive externalities depend on the characteristics of domestic labour markets and are lower in countries such as Italy, with high employment protection and low activity rates. These findings confirm that migrant workers mitigate the negative consequences of the ageing population and skills mismatches, and they are crucial to improving the country's long-run growth prospects. They also confirm that labour market flexibility is essential to allow immigration to become a pro-growth phenomenon, which is another reason why reforms are needed.

8.5 Few stable jobs

Table 8.4 displays employment by firm's size in the private non-agricultural sector. The total number of people employed is 17.1 million. Of these, 4.7

Table 8.4 Employment by size of firm

Size of firm by number of people employed	Number of active firms (thousand)	Number of people employed (thousand)	Self-employed (thousand)	Employees (thousand)	Fixed-term contracts (thousand)	Open-ended contracts (thousand)	Per cent
0–9	4,180	7,592	4,585	3,007	474	2,533	24.6
10–49	191	3,409	252	3,157	501	2,656	25.7
50–249	23	2,225	26	2,199	323	1,876	18.2
>250	4	3,834	4	3,830	580	3,250	31.5
Total	4,398	17,059	4,866	12,193	1,878	10,315	100.0

Source: Authors' calculations on ISTAT database 2017 data.

---

[21] Esposito et al. (2020).

million are self-employed. It is a record number, at least in the advanced world. Of the remaining 12.2 million, almost two million have a fixed-term contract.[22]

We are then left with 10.3 million employees with open-ended contracts, most of whom work in very small companies. Around 5.1 million are employed in companies with fewer than 50 employees.

Only 3.2 million work for companies with more than 250 employees. These are the companies that carry the burden of making Italy a modern and competitive economy. Some of these companies compete successfully in international markets. Still, they are too few to make a real difference in the growth rate of an economy of 60 million people. Besides, many of these 3.2 million workers are either in the financial sector or in recently privatised or semi-privatised public monopolies.

In any case, only those 3.2 million workers can be considered to have 'a stable job'. Other jobs, especially the 5 million in companies with fewer than 50 employees, are typically much less stable because the life of these companies is more exposed to the alternate vicissitudes of the markets.

8.6 Many irregular jobs

To this picture many people who work in the shadow economy must be added (NOE, non-observed economy, as it is officially called). Table 8.5 shows the official estimate of the number of people working in the informal sector: a stunning 3.6 million. Note that these workers are counted in the 17.1 million people in Table 8.5.[23] We do not know how many of them work in the various typologies of firms, but most likely, they work in very small firms with fewer than ten employees.

As shown in the table, there are irregular workers among both employees not declared by the employer and the self-employed. The share of irregular workers is amazingly high in some sectors. Among dependent workers in agriculture, it reaches almost 40 per cent. In the subsector Services to the person, it is above 50 per cent. In the South, all these percentages are considerably higher.

---

[22] In Table 8.4 we use 2017 data as they are the latest available.

[23] However, there are various methodological differences between this table, which is part of the national accounts, and that on the labour force. The main differences with respect to the labour force survey are that (a) it includes non-residents working in Italy and excludes residents working abroad, (b) it includes inmates and people working in religious or similar establishments, (c) it includes those criminal activities that are included in the national accounts. These differences explain why the total number of workers is higher in this table than in Table 8.2.

Table 8.5 Irregular jobs

Thousand AWUs*	Total	Irregular	%
	Dependent		
Agriculture	434	164	37.7
Industry	4,091	378	9.2
Services	12,629	2,041	16.2
Total dependent	17,154	2,583	15.1
	Self-employed		
Agriculture	815	71	8.7
Industry	1,159	133	11.5
Services	5,007	800	16.0
Total self-employed	6,980	1,004	14.4
	Total		
Agriculture	1,248	234	18.8
Industry	5,250	511	9.7
Services	17,636	2,840	16.1
Total	24,134	3,586	14.9

* AWUs = number of full-time-equivalent jobs; national accounts definition.

Source: Authors' calculations on ISTAT database 2019 data.

Note that irregular work is just one component of the NOE. The others are under-declaration of profits and other sources of income, such as rents, to evade taxes. Also, there are criminal activities, e.g. activities that are illegal per se (drug dealers, for instance) or are carried out without authorisation. According to official statistics, irregular work represents about half of the total NOE. Their contribution to the value added of the entire economy is estimated at a meagre 5.2 per cent, which suggests that irregular workers are much less productive than regular workers. Thus, their contribution to the nation's economic well-being is very low.

The picture that emerges is a highly segmented economy, with many people who declare themselves unemployed or inactive, many self-employed, and most dependent workers employed in very small companies or working in the irregular economy.

Of course, the reality is always more complex than statistics. Those who declare themselves unemployed may well be working in the irregular economy or engaging in criminal activities.[24] According to the magistrates in charge of contrasting the various mafias in Sicily, Calabria, and Campania, criminal activities are much more widespread than these statistics suggest.

---

[24] The relevance of the parallel economy in the South may explain why many unemployed declare that they are not available for a job outside their own town. See Faini et al. (1993, 1997).

Quite clearly, the labour market is sick. A misguided incentive structure has caused the most unjust of all possible conditions.

Women, the young, and many middle-aged males are left out of the official labour market. The great majority of those who do work are either self-employed or work in very small companies or the irregular economy. The protection that results from the trades union battles of the past several decades—protection from unfair firing, right to a fair salary, maternity leave, right of assembly, etc.—apply to a minority of workers.

8.7 The camouflage of false self-employed and false cooperatives

There are stringent laws that punish employers who impose on the self-employed the same obligations that apply to employees, such as a certain number of working hours per day, the physical presence in the workplace, the lack of autonomy in the organisation of single tasks, etc. However, these laws are empty gestures, like shouting in the desert. For labour inspectors, it is almost impossible to distinguish between a genuinely independent entrepreneur and a dependent worker camouflaged as self-employed.

The result is that in Italy, dependent workers (those who receive a wage or salary) are 77 per cent of total workers, well below almost all other western countries (Figure 8.4). For many countries, the analogue value is at or above

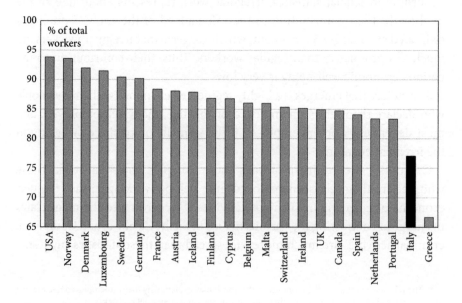

Fig. 8.4 Waged and salaried
Source: Eurostat database, and authors' calculations.

90 per cent, not only in the USA, which is known for having a flexible labour market, but also in other countries, such as Norway, Denmark, Sweden, and Germany. These numbers should convince anyone that the egalitarian values that have inspired labour market legislation and low collaboration with employers have created a severe problem. Of course, the self-employed have no protection whatsoever.[25] In particular, they can be fired at any moment, just by not renewing a collaboration or an order. It is like dismissing a worker, but it does not appear as dismissal. Simply put, a fired self-employed is a small entrepreneur who has lost an order, as often happens in a firm's life.

Similarly, the self-employed have no right to a vacation, sickness, or maternity leave. In principle, they could organise a union; but in practice, they do not even know who are the other workers with whom they should join forces, and no unions exist to protect these workers.[26] Often camouflage takes the form of false cooperative companies.[27]

The worker becomes a recorded member of the cooperative, such as an 'owner' or partner, and is registered as a worker–entrepreneur. Usually, such cooperatives have a very short life—two years or fewer—so as to elude control. In this way, labour laws, collective contracts, and payment of social security contributions are eluded, and people are paid very low wages. This type of camouflage is widespread for workers who perform very humble tasks, such as cleaning offices, taking care of illegal immigrants, doing unpleasant care tasks in hospitals. Often, such workers are recent immigrants. These cooperatives work for the private sector as well as for the public administration, at central and local level. Everybody knows the reality, but it is convenient to let things go as if there was nothing irregular. Not the best of all possible worlds!

---

[25] During the pandemic, the government introduced a subsidy for the self-employed (so-called ISCRO), which is also part of the government's plan for the reform of safety nets. For now, it is only a one-off.

[26] For a different view on the relation between self-employment and labour protection legislation, see Torrini (2005).

[27] See Regione Emilia-Romagna (2019).

9

Why are companies so small?

Small firms, pocket multinationals, and government-controlled enterprises—Small is not beautiful—Tax evasion and more—Labour market rigidities—Bureaucracy, connections, and rents—External pressures and political suspicion

9.1 Small firms, pocket multinationals, and government-controlled enterprises

The low growth of the Italian economy has many causes, as is argued in this book. Still, in the end, they all boil down to the unique characteristics of Italian companies. An old catch-phrase says: 'Growth is brought by firms, not by the stork'. True, but the reverse is also true. If there is no growth, there must be a problem within firms.

As seen in Chapter 7, there are very few large listed companies in Italy, except in the banking and insurance sector. The very few that exist are typically controlled by the state or were privatised in the 1990s. In Chapter 8, we added that the vast majority of Italian companies are very small: to recall, 50 per cent of stable employees work in companies with fewer than fifty persons and 25 per cent in companies with fewer than ten. Only 31 per cent work in companies with more than 250 persons.

This reality is rather exceptional in the international context and has been the object of many studies over a long period.[1] In the post-war period, the average size of companies was small. It increased until the beginning of the 1970s, partly because of the role of state-owned companies. Since then, there has been a continuous reduction in the average size, partly due to factors common to most advanced countries, such as increased uncertainty linked to the fall of the Bretton Woods system and the oil shocks. Such an increase in uncertainty required more flexibility for firms when workers demanded more protection and the legislation became more rigid.

[1] See Traù (2003).

Meritocracy, Growth, and Lessons from Italy's Economic Decline. Lorenzo Codogno and Giampaolo Galli, Oxford University Press. © Lorenzo Codogno and Giampaolo Galli (2022). DOI: 10.1093/oso/9780192866806.003.0010

The reaction to this scenario was outsourcing and de-verticalisation of firms, which results in lower average sizes.

In Italy, these processes were particularly relevant. The latest comparative data available from Eurostat (which has a different methodology compared to national sources) show that the share of persons employed in micro-firms (0–9 employees) in Italy is the largest in the EU (43 per cent) except for Greece (47 per cent). In the entire EU27, this share is 29 per cent, and in Germany, it is 19 per cent (see Figure 9.1).

However, to give a balanced view, it must be said that Italy has a rather solid industrial base and a group of small multinationals, which are labelled 'pocket multinationals'. These firms have managed to be successful in international markets.[2] In Europe, Italy is second only to Germany in terms of manufacturing value added (241 billion euros in 2019) and is slightly above France (240 billion euros) and the UK (194 billion euros). This manufacturing base allows Italy to be a rather good, though not excellent, exporter: its share in world trade of goods, at 2.8 per cent, is the same as that of France and higher than that of the UK (2.3 per cent). It has proved rather resilient in the

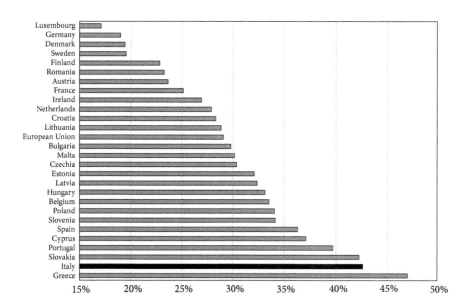

Fig. 9.1 Share of persons employed in micro-companies
Source: Eurostat databank, and authors' calculations.
Note: Micro-companies = 0–9 employees.

[2] See Coltorti (2016).

last ten years, despite fierce competition from China and Eastern Europe.[3] Italy's main exports no longer belong only to traditional sectors: they are machinery (15 per cent of total exports in 2019), mostly capital goods for industrial use; pharmaceutical products (6.2 per cent); transport equipment (4.4 per cent); fashion (4.1 per cent); and chemical products (3 per cent).[4] Federico-Giordano (2021) found that about 40 per cent of Italian industries recorded a broadly unchanged market share over the period 2010–19, suggesting a broad-based resilience by the Italian economy. The sectors that gained market share over this period are mainly agri-food products, fashion articles, and pharmaceuticals. Using the five-digit classification, they also find that twelve sectors (of which the most successful are ceramic tiles and leather goods) have maintained a share of world trade above 10 per cent over the period 2010–19.

In 2020, the national statistical office recorded 126,275 exporters out of 372,343 manufacturers. Yet, for a vast number of them (72,571) exports were worth less than 75,000 euros.[5] Exporting firms with a staff of more than 250 persons numbered 1,996 and accounted for 49 per cent of total exports, corresponding to about 15 per cent of GDP.

As seen in Chapter 8, there are 3,830,000 people working in companies with more than 250 employees in the entire economy. But since Italy's exports are almost exclusively composed of manufacturing products, we have to consider only manufacturers with more than 250, thus reducing the number of engaged persons to 919,874. The difference (almost 3 million people) is accounted for by service sector companies mainly working for the domestic market: financial services, tourism, production and distribution of water, electricity, gas, etc.

The small scale of Italian companies can be seen especially in accommodation, food, transportation, and trade, which represent a significant share of gross value added in Italy. These are also among the low productivity growth subsectors.[6]

Public authorities at central or local levels have stakes in many utility companies and often control them. According to the latest available data, relative to 2018, these companies number 8,510 and employ 924,068 persons.[7] About half of them are controlled by central government. They are active mainly in

---

[3] See Federico-Giordano (2021). The numbers for export shares are taken from UNCTAD, at: https://unctad.org/topic/trade-analysis/chart-10-may-2021.
[4] Osservatorio Economico Ministero degli Esteri e della Cooperazione Internazionale. For an account of what Italy does, see Giunta-Rossi (2017).
[5] ISTAT (2021b).
[6] European Commission (2020c).
[7] ISTAT (2021b). See also Casamonti-Gottardo (2020).

professional, scientific and technical activities, distribution of water, sewage, waste management, transport, and storage. These companies are very heterogeneous in terms of activity, management styles, and efficiency, but one thing is true for all of them. Politicians make appointments at central or local level: connections are the obvious channel for reaching top-level positions and often also for internal promotion and hiring.

Overall, as we saw in Chapter 8, the problem is that successful companies, those that compete in international markets, are not sufficient—in terms of number and size—to make a real difference to the aggregate performance of the economy.

9.2 Small is not beautiful

The most peculiar feature of Italian companies is that they are usually controlled by a single family and family members hold key positions inside the firm and not just on the board. A recent research paper from the Bank of Italy found that most Italian companies are owned by one single family and that in these companies the entire management is an expression of the owner family. These firms are two-thirds of the total in Italy, compared with a third in Spain, about a quarter in France and Germany, and only 10 per cent in the UK. The conclusion is that 'family-owned firms, particularly Italian ones, tend to prefer an executive selection process based on closeness and loyalty to the owners, rather than on specific expertise with regard to the company's business sector and strategies'.[8]

Quite clearly, merit is not at centre stage. It is therefore not surprising to find that firms entirely managed by members of the owner's family are less successful in innovation.[9] The propensity to spend on R&D is 14.4 percentage points lower in such firms than others; the propensity to innovate is 4.3 percentage points lower.[10] Another study shows that social connections and family background appear to be the primary determinant of entrepreneurship. At the same time, the level of talent, skills, and education is less relevant.[11] Several studies show that a founder's characteristics,

---

[8] Bugamelli-Lotti (2018). See also Lippi-Schivardi (2014), Bandiera et al. (2015), and Baltrunaite et al. (2019).
[9] Brandolini- Bugamelli (2009).
[10] Andretta et al. (2021) show that 'family ownership and the coincidence of management with ownership are negatively related with firm productivity'.
[11] Micozzi (2013).

particularly pre-entry work experience, impact firms' dynamics in the long run while her or his education does not appear to have any significant effect.[12]

If one family controls all aspects of the company, then the company is unlikely to grow. It usually takes professional managers to grow the business, as these families are more preoccupied with retaining control than growing.

Until the 1960s and 1970s, many commentators thought that small was beautiful. Many small companies materialised from excellent entrepreneurship and were the basis of a dynamic and growing economy. No longer. Now it is clear that Italy's problem is that the many small companies that have been set up in the three decades since the war were unable to grow and remained very small.

It is equally evident, at least to most analysts, that these small companies are not up to the challenges of the knowledge economy, are run in a very rudimentary fashion, and know very little about technological progress and modern managerial organisations. They depend on banks for their financing and are unable to become international companies or have a significant share of export over total sales.

These companies are not beautiful. Instead, we should say that they are rather ugly. According to the last survey of SMEs carried out by the EC, productivity of Italian micro-firms was 31,000 euros per person employed, which is below the productivity of EU's micro-firms of 37,000 euros. More importantly, their productivity is a fraction of that of larger modern firms.

Unfortunately, these companies are the ones whose associations are best organised and most influential. They move millions of votes, hence are rather influential on policy decisions. They often defend anti-competitive arrangements—for instance, in retail trade, against large-scale distribution—and do very little to help the government combat tax evasion and corruption.

9.3 Tax evasion and more

Some commentators have pointed the finger at Italian entrepreneurs.[13] This is partly right, but we believe only partly.

As seen in Chapter 7, micro-companies manage to evade an incredible 70 per cent of the amount they ought to pay in income tax. A company that evades income tax must also avoid other taxes. Certainly, it bypasses VAT because it needs to display low revenue. It may also show higher costs, for

---

[12] Grilli et al. (2014).
[13] Pellegrino-Zingales (2017) and Ciccarone et al. (2010).

instance, by attributing to the company what are in reality costs borne for personal or family reasons. These companies often use irregular workers, which means that they evade social security contributions and often do not recognise workers' rights and do not abide by the regulations concerning safety and security on the job. As is stated in the 2020 ILO annual report, although there are no official statistical sources on the proportion of occupational accidents in micro-enterprises, several empirical studies show that they are more prone to higher occupational injury and fatality rates.[14] Figures for the EU indicate that the fatal accident rate in micro- and small enterprises is nearly double that of larger companies.[15] It is, of course, valid for Italy as well. Given the structure of Italian companies, it is probably truer in Italy than in most other European countries.

However, we believe that there are more profound structural causes of this problem, and it is helpful to use an anecdote to illustrate our point.

Confindustria—the leading organisation of Italian industrial companies—has a special, very active section for small companies, comprising about 98 per cent of total members—showing again how large is the number of small companies. In 2011, Confindustria[16] organised a meeting between its small business section and researchers at the Bank of Italy who had carried out a study showing that managers of Italian companies are typically members of the owner's family. Almost a thousand entrepreneurs showed up at this meeting, turning the discussion into a major event.

Entrepreneurs showed full awareness that their companies were too small and that this was an obstacle to making their companies more capable of carrying out R&D, selling in international markets, and becoming more competitive. Criticism of Italian dwarfism was so widespread that they could not hide their awareness of the problem.

However, they were not happy about the discussion. At one point, an entrepreneur—let's call her Anna—stood up and said: 'In my company, we hired a professional CEO. It cost us one million euros: half as yearly salary and another half to get rid of him after one year of disasters'. This statement was cheered with much applause from the audience. Quite clearly, this was the prevailing sentiment.

Given the crucial importance of the issue of company size, we now try to provide our best explanation as to why entrepreneurs do not want their companies to grow. We see three possible factors, which may all play a role: (a) rigidities in the labour market; (b) complex bureaucracy and political

---

[14] ILO (2020).
[15] European Agency for Safety and Health at Work (2005).
[16] At the time, one of the authors of this book was managing director of Confindustria.

connections; (c) external pressures on companies and a general suspicion of public opinion against large companies.

9.4 Labour market rigidities

The relation between labour market rigidities and company size is often misunderstood. Regulation for very small companies is less strict or more generous than for larger companies; most rules imposed on companies have exceptions for small or very small companies, including rules on firing personnel or accounting standards. But this is not the critical point.

The obvious response to a rigid labour market is outsourcing all possible non-essential functions. If a task—say, maintenance or legal advice—is performed by another company rather than by employees, it is easy to change supplier if the service is unsatisfactorily performed or becomes too expensive. Instead, if employees perform the function inside the firm, any change is difficult to carry out.

For the same reason, companies have de-verticalised as much as possible. This is, of course, a general trend everywhere and is partly the reason behind the success of so-called global value chains. But in Italy, this process has been pushed to the extreme.

A move entirely away from a vertical structure may work as in the following example of a relatively successful shoe producer—let's again call it Anna's firm. It has a large warehouse in which for most of the time there are neither machines nor people. Periodically, the company receives semi-finished shoes from China that are stored in the warehouse. Afterwards, a few hundred self-employed artisans come to the warehouse, load those shoes onto their own trucks, and carry them to their factories, which are usually the basements of their homes. They transform the Chinese shoes into fashion products, using the design and machinery that Anna's company has provided for them. They then bring the finished product back to the warehouse, from where the shoes start their journey to their final markets.

Many people work for Anna's company: several hundred workers in China and several hundred self-employed in Italy. But the trick is that the firm has only five dependent workers: an accountant, a driver, and some fashion designers. The workers may or may not pay taxes, may or may not abide by the work health and safety regulations, or may have irregular workers helping them. Anna cannot be held responsible for what may happen in someone else's basement. She is proud of her organisation of labour, which makes her company flexible and low cost. Her only complaint is that she has to spend some considerable time in China. But with this organisation, she can easily accommodate changes in tastes, fashion, etc. Workers are as flexible as one can imagine.

With this approach and organisation, Anna can hardly become the patron of a large modern international company, but she does not care. Anna is the daughter of poor peasants and could not study after elementary school. She can now afford to send her sons to the best universities and have a beautiful home and a luxury car. She is a respectable person in her local community, and she can easily lobby the mayor to organise better roads for the trucks carrying her company's products.

Thousands of small companies work like Anna's, but often with one additional feature. Usually, they specialise in tiny niche markets. For example, no one produces bicycles, but one can find producers of bicycle saddles or brakes. Much of the Italian metallurgic industry makes parts for German manufacturers, primarily for cars and specialised pieces of machinery. Italy's mechanical sector accounts for one-third of Italy's exports. Italy used to have an important car manufacturer (Fiat). However, after mergers with Chrysler and more recently with Peugeot, it has become an international company with tax residence in the Netherlands. It is listed in Milan, Paris, and Wall Street.

The Edison Foundation tracks the 1,400 products in which Italy is one of the top five exporters in the world.[17] The first ones are: 'Handbags with outer surface of leather', 'Packing or wrapping machinery', 'Sunglasses', 'Footwear with outer soles and uppers of leather', 'Cruise ships', 'Ceramic flags and paving, unglazed', 'Uncooked pasta, not stuffed or prepared, not containing eggs'. Some of these products are rather general, like 'Sunglasses' and 'Cruise ships', which correspond to two of the very few large companies, Luxottica and Fincantieri. Most other products are very narrowly defined, and the more narrow the definition becomes, the more likely it is that one can find a top producer.

Italy is good at producing niche products, and niches have to be very narrowly defined. This extreme specialisation is a direct consequence of the owners' choice to let companies remain small. Despite these top niche products, as we have seen, the performance of Italian exports is not very satisfactory. It is less brilliant than that of France or Spain, not to mention Germany.

---

[17] Fondazione Edison (2019).

9.5 Bureaucracy, connections, and rents

Another reason why firms remain small is that owners do not want an external professional manager. Owners often have connections or are part of lobbies that they want to hide from strangers, and thus they only trust family members. Often these are connected with political figures at the local or national level. They may also be connected to key figures in bureaucracy, the judiciary, or some authorities. Connections are perhaps more important in Italy than in other countries because, as argued above, bureaucracy is very complicated, and the laws must be interpreted.

An entrepreneur like Anna would say that bureaucracy is one of the main evils for a company that wants to be competitive, together with high taxes and rigid labour. Still, she would also tell you that the public employees with whom she usually deals are excellent people.

A successful entrepreneur such as Anna often has connections. Such connections allow her to survive and even prosper by capitalising on an advantage over possible competitors. The connected company enjoys a rent which is the direct consequence of the complexity of the bureaucratic machine.

This system impedes free competition much more than anti-competitive behaviours that are under the vigilant eye of the antitrust authority.

These points and their logic emerge very clearly in a recent paper.[18] We think that there is some truth in what these researchers find through a sophisticated statistical methodology that involves observations of more than 4 million firms from 1993 to 2014. In their own words, they find that:

a. Politically connected firms grow in employment and revenue, survive longer in the market, and have lower productivity growth. This finding is consistent with the view that political connections help firms remove particular market frictions or block competition instead of assisting them in pushing the productivity and technology frontiers.
b. Political connections might alleviate certain market frictions, such as regulatory barriers or bureaucratic burdens. However, giving incumbents a decisive advantage over new entrants negatively impacts market competition and creative destruction.

For our purposes, point (b) is the crucial one. Firms resort to political connections because this is how they can alleviate what the authors, somewhat euphemistically, call 'certain market frictions', which are very real regulatory and bureaucratic barriers. Once they overcome such obstacles, they have a

---

[18] Akcigit et al. (2018a). See also Cingano-Pinotti (2013).

decisive advantage over their potential competitors and earn what can be called incumbent rent.

From a societal perspective, this mechanism is detrimental because it impedes open competition and Schumpeterian creative destruction, which is the main engine of economic growth. But from the point of view of the individual firm, what is described is a pragmatic and balanced solution. It requires connections with politicians but may also involve public officials, members of authorities, and judges.

Such connections are often vital for the firm. In most cases, it may have a hard time surviving without them. At the same time, it is quite understandable that the controlling family does not want to share such connections with people who are, to some extent, strangers, such as professional managers. In some cases, the connection may imply illegal dealings, in which case it is clear that certain secrets must remain within a strict circle, but this is more the exception than the rule.

We thus have a second explanation of why firms remain small: connections must be kept within small family circles.

The question is how important is this explanation. Based on our experience, we do not share the view emerging from some of the literature that we have cited so far, for two reasons. The first is that, as already argued, we do not believe that the Italian elite, including the corporate elite, can be characterised as corrupt, a suggestion conveyed by several papers.[19] The second reason is that Italy has several companies that manage to be successful in international markets. For the sake of precision, we can say that these are a large proportion of the 1996 exporting companies with more than 250 employed persons, making up some 49 per cent of exports.

These companies may or may not have domestic connections, but they certainly strive in open international markets. They do not receive much help when they export or decide to trade internationally. Indeed, instruments that can help companies sell or produce abroad (export credit, financing of internationalisation, country marketing, etc.) seem to have fewer resources and be less effective than in most other competing nations.

In conclusion, it seems fair to say that many Italian companies survive and perhaps prosper because of their connections, but this is only part of the story. Some other companies compete with their own forces, and for these companies, merit is probably more important than connections.

---

[19] Akcigit et al. (2018a) cite a statement from Carmelo Zuccaro, chief prosecutor of Catania, which we find definitely excessive: 'There are public officials who, instead of serving the interests of the community, put themselves at the service of private individuals. It is a devastating situation: those firms that have political and administrative support, thanks to the "good friend", manage to obtain illicit benefits, while honest companies look on, astonished at what happens'.

9.6 External pressures and political suspicion

Mark Roe's explanation of why public companies in continental Europe are comparatively fewer may also help explain why companies remain small in Italy. Let us recall the central message of Roe's research. According to the egalitarian values that tend to prevail in continental Europe, managers are under intense pressure to stabilise employment and forego some profit-maximising risks.[20] They also tend to use up capital instead of downsizing when markets are no longer aligned with their production capabilities. In essence, managers are considered successful when they do what public opinion and politicians expect: increase employment and never decrease it, undertake new investment and never downsize, pursue socially important goals such as protecting the environment, etc.

Reasons why the public company does not fly in continental Europe can also explain why companies remain small in Italy. The forces that induce managers to pursue different interests from those of shareholders are powerful. With few notable exceptions, successful managers tend to please public opinion, politicians, and trades union: they are the ones who have a good press.

The problem is compounded in Italy because of a general feeling of hostility towards large companies.[21] It is generally believed that they are the ones who exploit workers, damage the environment, and evade taxes. However, the opposite is typically true: working conditions are better, and there is more attention paid to the environment in large companies than in small ones. As for taxes, the bulk of tax evasion in Italy comes from very small companies.

A company above a certain 'visibility threshold' receives attention from public opinion, the media, the environmentalists, and, in the end, from tax authorities and magistrates. At least when they are tiny, small companies can survive with some tax evasion, partial respect for environmental and worker rights, and irregular workers. Again, these are additional reasons why entrepreneurs like Anna would be reluctant to hand over the keys of their business to strangers.

And these are some of the structural reasons why merit is not highly considered even in the corporate world. For these same motives, young Italians with excellent university degrees do not find jobs, even though the number of graduates in the population is low. Typically, small Italian firms demand skilled technical workers who have completed technical high school, not those who have a university degree. Thus the most brilliant young Italians go abroad to find companies that demand masters degrees and high skills.

---

[20] Roe (2003).
[21] Debenedetti (2021).

PART IV

SUMMING UP AND LESSONS

10

Summing up on Italy

The bright spots—The problems: bureaucracy—Governance—Justice—Labour—Finance—Education—Competition policy—Public debt—Reform fatigue and the rhetoric of inequality—Italy and the EU: the Great Misunderstanding—A tale of two countries: Italy and Germany

10.1 The bright spots

We have presented Italy's problems in the book, and we will sum them up in this chapter. But this endeavour would not be very effective and credible if we did not briefly highlight some of the country's bright spots that we have already mentioned in the book.

First, as indicated in Chapter 4, Italy is a country with all the characteristics of a thriving democracy: division of powers, freedom of speech, association, and information. Sometimes this is denied because it is said that some politicians control the media or that judges act to influence politics or vice versa. There is some truth in these claims. Still, overall we think that, despite several hard vicissitudes, Italy has managed to remain a functioning liberal democracy: new political parties have often substituted for old ones, and the country is open to change. The press is free and vital. Arguments suggesting that journalists are subservient to this or that power structure has validity in some instances.[1] These relate to some self-limitations by the press in reporting on corporates, which are the primary source of their advertising revenue. Moreover, there is the well-known problem of information silos. However, new editorial initiatives are flourishing, and journalists dare to touch on all politically sensitive issues. Several independent and courageous journalists have risked their lives in reporting, for instance, about organised crime and the mafia.

Second, we have also argued that Italy is less corrupt than would appear from the most popular indices of perception of corruption. Criminality and

---

[1] The World Free Press Index places Italy in 41st position after most advanced and many developing countries. See Reporters Without Borders (2021).

Meritocracy, Growth, and Lessons from Italy's Economic Decline. Lorenzo Codogno and Giampaolo Galli, Oxford University Press. © Lorenzo Codogno and Giampaolo Galli (2022). DOI: 10.1093/oso/9780192866806.003.0011

corruption are severe problems, but not to the point of considering them the primary reason for Italy's poor economic performance. Here, we are in disagreement with some of the recent economic literature on Italy.

Third, we have documented that in times of crises, the political class has been able to appoint as prime minister persons of outstanding prestige and proven capabilities who had not been previously involved in politics. This suggests that the political system may have many problems, but it still can see its own limits and react to them. In these cases, contributions from a vital civil society, yet another bright spot, has been of paramount importance.

Fourth, we documented that Italy has a rather solid industrial base and several hundred 'small multinationals' that have successfully withstood the challenges of open international markets. In the last decade, Italy has been one of the few advanced countries to have managed to maintain its export share in world trade (2.8 per cent), despite the rising role of China and other emerging economies. These companies may or may not have domestic political connections, but certainly can distinguish between good and bad managers and know how to recognise and reward merit. They do not rely on privilege, protection, and anti-competitive behaviour. A decisive push to simplify bureaucracy and clarify laws can come from these companies. But unfortunately, they are too small and too few to make a real difference for the whole economy. That is why they do well, and the country does not.

Fifth, Italy's private sector has a high saving rate and low debt. This fact, together with the competitiveness of the manufacturing sector, contributes to a surplus in the current account, which is close to 4 per cent of GDP. As a result, the country's net financial position has turned positive after having been in negative territory for many years.

The many magistrates who have fought and are still fighting against the mafia represent another bright spot. Many of them continue to do their job despite sometimes risking their lives. It is also true for many other workers who keep doing their job with commitment and passion, despite an economic environment that is often unsupportive.

Finally, although we are critical of the Italian education system, we have listed several university departments at the top of international rankings. Although competition, merit, and meritocracy are almost absent from Italian universities, some bright spots do exist.

10.2 The problems: bureaucracy

To sum up Italy's key impediments to economic growth and competitiveness in a manageable and straightforward way, we have put together in Table 10.1

Table 10.1 Italy's low-ranking indicators

Lowest 30 indicators compared to 34 advanced countries

Topic	Indicator	Rank /167	Rank /34	Top Country /167
Beaurocracy	Burden of government regulation	164	34	Singapore
Governance	Confidence in national government	160	34	Singapore
Judiciary	Efficiency of dispute settlement	157	34	Singapore
Governance	Public trust in politicians	149	34	Singapore
Governance	Transparency of government policy	148	34	New Zealand
Investment	Prevalence of foreign ownership of companies	134	34	UK
Labour	Labour force participation	113	34	Switzerland
Labour	Female labour force participation	105	34	Sweden
Governance	Complaint mechanisms	65	34	Netherlands
Judiciary	Alternative dispute resolution mechanisms	60	34	Norway
Finance	Confidence in financial instructions and banks	164	33	Singapore
Governance	Efficiency of government spending	156	33	Singapore
Governance	Efficiency of legal framework in challenging regulations	155	33	Finland
Labour	Flexibility of hiring practices	154	33	Multiple—2
Finance	Venture capital availability	153	33	Multiple—2
Finance	Financing of SMEs	143	33	Multiple—5
Labour	Cooperation in labour–employer relations	137	33	Multiple—6
Governance	Delay in administrative proceedings	93	33	Singapore
Education	Digital skills among population	73	33	Finland
Governance	Policy coordination	67	33	Multiple—23
Judiciary	Protection of property rights	67	33	Finland
Judiciary	Civil justice	58	33	Germany
Education	Education level of adult population	53	33	South Korea
Governance	Government quality and credibility	48	33	Singapore
Governance	Efficient use of assets	45	33	Multiple—22
Governance	Enforcement of regulations	43	33	Austria
Governance	Regulatory quality	41	33	Singapore
Labour	Flexibility of wage determination	161	32	Estonia
Judiciary	Time of resolution, commercial cases	151	32	Singapore
Labour	Youth unemployment	145	32	Japan

The notation 'Multiple—n' indicates that n countries are in the top position.
Source: Prosperity Index of the Legatum Institute (2020).

the thirty individual indicators where Italy ranks lowest among the thirty-four major advanced nations.

These are problems that cry out for reform. Yet, bearers of vested interest, lobbies, and in many cases also politicians are in widespread denial.

The first item in the list is Burden of government regulation. It is the synthetic indicator of the complexity of the legal system and the inefficiency of bureaucracy. The excessive burden of regulation is widely recognised as an obstacle to economic growth and external competitiveness.

However, public employees and their unions are in widespread denial. As shown in various chapters, they have successfully buried any attempt to introduce merit in wages and promotions. Denials reappear whenever government advances simplification proposals; there are always those who protest and force the government to step back.

It has long been recognised that every bit of the bureaucracy that makes life complicated for persons and firms has some vested interest to protect.[2] It does not come from heaven. For instance, in May 2021, the government proposed to fully 'liberalise' public procurement subcontracting, as foreseen by a European directive, instead of limiting it to 30 per cent of the total, as was envisioned by the previous legislation. There were immediate protests from trades union, arguing that subcontracting can be an easy avenue for mafias and 'pirate companies' that do not respect labour contracts and legislation. The strange aspect of the story is that it seems as if mafias and pirate companies are deemed to be tolerable up to 30 per cent, but no more. The real reason behind the unions' position has to do with their under-representation in small companies and their better influence over contractors than subcontractors. Of course, the correct approach is that the law, and national labour contracts, as long as they exist, should be enforced on all firms, irrespective of whether they work with the public administration as main contractors or as subcontractors.

It is not an isolated anecdote. Almost all resistance to reforming and simplifying bureaucracy are vested in noble arguments. And at times, such arguments have a grain of truth. When the judiciary does not function efficiently and does not punish criminal behaviour in a reasonable time frame, ex-ante checks and controls become necessary.

10.3 Governance

Institutional reforms are challenging to address. The underlying issues appear in many items of the inglorious list in Table 10.1: Confidence in national government is among the lowest in the world, as are Public trust in politicians, perceived Transparency of government policy, Complaint mechanisms as an item that measures political accountability, Efficiency of government spending, Delay in administrative proceedings, Policy coordination, Government quality and credibility and, last but not least, Regulatory quality. This is a really formidable list of problems, which have deep roots in Italian history and are very difficult to solve without a strong meritocratic revolution.

Attempts to solve these problems through electoral or constitutional reforms have not succeeded. The four electoral systems that Italy has had in the past quarter of a century have changed the political panorama but

---

[2] See Galli-Cassese (1998).

have not produced tangible results for ordinary citizens in terms of less bureaucracy or more efficient public spending. Moreover, two constitutional reforms tried to give more stability to the government and clarify the power of central and regional governments. However, they were rejected in popular referenda in 2006 and 2016.

Inefficient governance and the legacy of low mutual trust help explain one of Italy's critical problems: tax evasion (Chapter 7).

Inefficient governance, together with labour rigidities and weighty bureaucracy, can go a long way in explaining why political connections are so important for private companies (Chapter 9). In turn, these factors help explain why families that control most companies, especially in the service sector, are averse to letting them grow, listing them in the stock exchange, internationalising them, and hiring professional managers. These facts partly explain why, since the 1990s, so many Italian companies did not withstand the new challenges of globalisation and a knowledge-based economy.

10.4 Justice

Italy has dismal rankings for Efficiency of dispute settlements, Alternative dispute resolutions (although some positive steps have been undertaken over the past few years), Efficiency of legal framework in challenging regulations, Protection of property rights (an item that is a precondition for the functioning of a market economy), Civil justice in general, Enforcement of regulation; and Time to resolve commercial cases.

Recent surveys show that several scandals, such as the Palamara scandal mentioned in Chapters 1 and 4, have caused a sharp fall in the degree of trust in the judiciary. But, here, denial is the norm. Magistrates do not believe in international rankings. When public opinion protests against incredibly slow justice, magistrates ask the government for more money and administrative personnel. However, as we showed in Chapter 5, the missing element in Italy's judiciary is not money; it is merit because salaries increase over time only with seniority.

The judiciary can maintain its independence, a crucial pillar of democracy, and yet evaluate its members on meritocratic criteria, as does the Bank of Italy, an institution that is proud of its independence.

Hence we want to scream—politely—that magistrates can no longer disregard international rankings and should no longer affirm that those rankings do not consider the specificities and complexities of Italian society. The problem of the judiciary is home-made. Magistrates should look inside their own ranks to understand the issues.

In any case, there is a lesson that can be drawn. A problem may be fully evident and gigantic, but interested parties may still deny it.

The evils may not be with the magistrates who defend the status quo but with politicians who do not see the problem or are too weak to address it. Nevertheless, it is challenging to introduce reforms perceived as hostile by magistrates and some voters. We regret that attempts at institutional and judicial reforms have so far failed, as an inefficient judiciary also remains a stumbling block for other reforms. It is a major impediment to FDI and domestic companies' growth and competitiveness.

10.5 Labour

Labour market problems came next in the list with items that are extremely low worldwide: Labour force participation (position 113th over the entire set of 294 countries), Female labour force participation (105th), Flexibility in hiring practices (154th), Cooperation in labour–employer relations (137th), Flexibility of wage determination (161st), Youth unemployment (145th).

There is no doubt that the labour market is in need of radical reform and that this has almost been forgotten in the public debate. Labour market problems relate to low labour force participation, low female participation—a blunder that is no longer tolerable—and high youth unemployment. Most of these critical problems are concentrated in the South.

As we argued in Chapter 8, the disconnect between wages and firm-level productivity is a genuine concern and one issue that cries out for radical change. And the (low) Flexibility in hiring practices reflects the substantial counter-reform by the judges on the Jobs Act's attempted changes. As a result, today's labour market is probably no more flexible than before the reform. It is considered by international managers to be one of the least flexible in the world. Italy's low position on Cooperation in labour–employer relations is probably the critical problem that makes it difficult to even think of modernising the system.

Labour reform is off the radar of most politicians. Of course, many people complain about unemployment, especially among the young, females, and in the South. These are indeed crucial problems. Still, very few recognise that many of them derive from the legal and contractual rigidities of the market. Trades union have always been asking for gigantic public investment plans to solve the problem. Now the massive plan, NextGenerationEU, has arrived. However, such a plan will have only transitory effects on employment through higher aggregate demand unless radical labour market reforms are enacted.

It is fair to say that trades union and much of the political class are in denial of these urgent problems. Instead, political leaders prefer to talk about redistribution (on the left) and lower taxes (on the right). Reforming the labour market is simply not perceived as a priority.

10.6 Finance

Three critical items concern finance: Confidence in financial institutions, Venture capital availability and Financing of SMEs. Despite infinite efforts by all governments, especially for the financing of SMEs, these are still matters of significant concern.

Many of the problems are related to the myth that local or cooperative banks play a positive role in local communities. It may have been true in the past. Now they are a source of problems. SMEs need the best banks to grow, not the local or cooperative banks, and this has become increasingly evident in recent years. Banks must have substantial capital and contestable governance in today's world.

It has taken spectacular failures and dramas (Monte dei Paschi di Siena, the Venetian banks, and some smaller banks) to understand that meritocracy is also a value in banking: banks' very task is to select companies and projects that are creditworthy, thereby allowing financial resources to be properly allocated within the economy. Being creditworthy means having merit and therefore deserving credit. Merit, not connections, should be at the heart of banking business.

10.7 Education

As we have already seen in Chapter 5, Italy ranks very low on: Digital skills among population and Education level of adult population.

This is another case of denied reality. Many distinguished and respectable professors would say that Italian schools and universities were top-level once. Then, mass education came, and the level fell. Not true, or at least not in comparison to what has happened in the rest of the world. Mass education is a reality in most other advanced countries, but not in Italy, where the share of the population with tertiary education is meagre. It will remain low for a long time since the new flow of graduates is also very low. Share of population aged 25–34 with tertiary education is 27.7 per cent in Italy; only one OECD country (Mexico) fares a little worse. In many countries, the share is around or above 50 per cent; in South Korea, it is at 70 per cent. In addition, the quality is rather low, as we have argued by looking at the very low international ranking of almost all Italian universities and the PISA tests performed by the OECD on 15-year-old students' skills. In these tests, Italy is between twenty-third and twenty-ninth position.

Teachers, like magistrates, typically complain about lack of resources, which in this case is at least partly true. But money is not the only scarce resource. Merit is too. And this is in significant part a result of the absence of a widespread system to evaluate schools or teachers, and thus careers are determined mainly by seniority. Merit is much disregarded in Italian schools and universities.

10.8 Competition policy

This item is part of the inglorious list only indirectly as it is a component of the (low) 'Regulatory quality'. This is probably for good reason. Several other countries have many of the same problems. In Italy, some results have been achieved with the liberalisations of the late 1990s and in 2006–08. However, precisely because so many other things are problematic, we would argue that Italy needs a very robust competition policy.

According to the Antitrust Authority, pro-competition reforms in the service sector can increase productivity in manufacturing by more than 25 per cent. Key sectors in need of reform are public procurement, the more than 8,000 companies held by local authorities, public transport, the exit of protected zombie firms, liberalisation of retail commerce, elimination of entry barriers for large retailers, auctions for the distribution of natural gas and hydroelectric power, and private pension funds. Quite appropriately, the authority points a finger at the 'bureaucratic burdens which represent a relevant obstacle to doing business and create barriers to entry in the markets'. As we have argued in the book, the combination of obscure bureaucracy and a complex legal system is a critical obstacle to competition in domestic markets. It is why, even in the corporate sector, connections are more important than merit, which is itself a major obstacle to economic growth. According to the European Commission (2021a), 'the length, complexity and unpredictability of administrative procedures, remaining restrictions to competition, and some sectoral overregulation weigh on firms' productivity and competitiveness, discouraging investment'.

10.9 Public debt

A further challenge, which might well become the first one, is high public debt. The debt-to-GDP ratio reached 155.6 per cent in 2020 and is projected to return to pre-pandemic levels only very gradually, if at all. So far, this has not been a problem because the European Central Bank has kept interest rates extremely low and has bought vast amounts of government securities.

It also helps that, so far, the prevailing narrative in financial markets seems to be that interest rates will remain low for a long time, despite the recent rise in inflation. This narrative has found authoritative supporters among economists such as Olivier Blanchard, who has argued that interest rates higher than the growth rate of the economy are the exception to the rule.[3]

It is generally agreed that Italy's debt will be sustainable if there is a resumption of economic growth. What is rarely acknowledged is that growth per se is not sufficient. It is also necessary that the resulting higher revenues be used to reduce the deficit.[4] This, in turn, implies that they cannot be used to increase spending or lower taxes, which most of the time has not happened in the past. A radical change in approach and mentality is hence required. Using tax revenues to reduce the deficit is generally considered a deplorable action. *Far cassa* (collecting money) is the expression that is used to stigmatise such a despicable act. The most successful lobbying in Italy is by those who want more government spending, resulting in higher public debt. This is true more or less everywhere, but the figures show that in very few countries such lobbying has been as successful as in Italy.

10.10 Reform fatigue and the rhetoric of inequality

The enormous reform fatigue in the country is another big challenge. The prevailing mood appears to indicate that the priority must be fighting social inequality instead of promoting merit and growth.[5]

---

[3] See Summers (2020) and Blanchard (2019).
[4] Brugnara-Paudice (2021).
[5] Some protagonists of the liberalisation process implemented by centre-left governments seem to back this mood. See, for instance, Letta (2021) and Prodi (2021). See also Boitani (2021).

In many countries, inequalities are a critical problem, and the emphasis on this issue is justified. But, as we have seen in Chapter 6, inequality has not increased in Italy, a point that has been stated several times by the Bank of Italy in research papers and its Annual Report,[6] following the GFC and the sovereign debt crisis. It has now stabilised at levels close to those at the end of the 1970s.[7]

We have dealt with inequalities at lengths in this book: the North–South divide, the male–female divide, the lack of equal opportunities, and geron-tocracy. In our view, it would be a mistake to think that the problems of Italy can be solved through special provisions for the South, for women, or for the young. Such provisions may have merit in their own right, but growth and productivity are stalled everywhere in the country, in the South, and the traditionally more dynamic North. In the ranking of GDP per capita at purchasing power standards of the 280 European regions, Piedmont, Lombardy and Veneto, which were near the top twenty years ago, had lost forty-nine, twenty-two, and thirty-seven positions (to eighty-fourth, thirty-sixth, and sixty-eighth respectively) by 2019. The loss has been similar for regions of the South: Campania (−35 to 191st), Sicily (−38 to 197th), Sardinia (−21 to 169th), and Calabria (−31 to 202nd).[8]

The emphasis on inequality misses the critical problem of generalised misconceived incentives for rewarding merit and entrepreneurship. Serious measures to liberalise labour and goods markets, especially in services, and to improve the efficiency of the justice system and public administration are far more critical than measures to address specific inequalities.

In the prevailing narrative, another critical problem is the high unemployment rate among young people: this is also described in terms of inequality between the young and older generations. Some politicians and economists proposed a fixed quota in hiring by private companies. For instance, it could be no less than 30 per cent of young people.[9] But this approach is erroneous. Companies typically prefer to hire young people anyway, and the most severe social problem is unemployment among people aged 30 to 65 who have the burden of sustaining a family. Intergenerational injustice exists, and it is the public debt burden. The best way to reduce this injustice is to reduce debt. It is also crucial for schools, companies, and public administrations to identify and reward young persons with talent and determination.

---

[6] Banca d'Italia (2016), Brandolini et al. (2018), Cannari-D'Alessio (2018).

[7] They can still be perceived as elevated, although they are certainly not extreme by international standards.

[8] Svimez (2021) on Eurostat data. The 280 regions include the UK.

[9] A similar provision for young workers and women is indeed to be included in the tenders for public works under NGEU.

Those who prioritise inequalities are also generally keen to see higher taxes on the rich and companies that have 'profited' during the pandemic: essentially big tech companies and big pharma. As the EC argued, there may be good reasons for strengthening regulation on tech companies and finding ways to stop (legal) tax avoidance by multinationals; recent progress by the G20 is welcome. Still, it makes little sense to 'punish' companies that have provided beneficial services to the community during the pandemic or any other form of 'punishment' for those who do well.

The egalitarian culture, so far prevalent in Italy, also produces a typically suspicious attitude towards private enterprise. For example, in 2020, two bridges collapsed: one was on a highway crossing the city of Genoa and run by a private company (Autostrade per l'Italia) and the other on a road run by the public road company (Anas) in Northern Tuscany. After the first accident, there was a wave of anger against private companies for whom profits are more important than human lives. After the second accident, no such indignation was seen against a government that could not control the safety of its roads; in the latter case, there were no casualties, but it was pure luck.

10.11 Italy and the EU: the Great Misunderstanding

Among the major problem facing Italy today, we must mention what we call 'The Great Misunderstanding' between Italy and much of the rest of the European Union.

The pandemic and the following deep economic crisis have induced the European Union to take bold decisions, unprecedented by their nature and size. Essentially, the EU issues its own debt for up to 750 billion euros, more than 5 per cent of its GDP, under the umbrella of NGEU. These funds are given to member states partly in the form of grants (390 billion euros) and partly in the form of loans (360 billion euros). For a country like Italy, loans are convenient because the EU can borrow at lower rates than Italy's Treasury; in practice, these are subsided loans, as correctly defined in the Italian Recovery and Resilience Plan.[10]

The central part of the plan is the Recovery and Resilience Facility (RRF) which amounts to 672.5 billion euros (2018 prices). The grant component of the RRF amounts to 312.5 billion euros, and up to a maximum of 360 billion euros is available in loans.

---

[10] See Italian government (2021) at page 10.

It is evident that the formula used to allocate the funds favours two countries, Spain and Italy, and, to a smaller extent, France. According to current estimates,[11] the share of grants that Italy and Spain will get is 20.8 per cent and 21.0 per cent of the total, respectively, much higher than their share in EU27 GDP (12.8 per cent for Italy, 8.9 per cent for Spain).

As for the loans, each country can borrow up to a limit of 6.8 per cent of its 2019 gross national income (GNI). Based on current information, some countries initially decided not to take the loans they were entitled to (notably Spain) or only partly (Portugal, Slovenia, Cyprus), at least for now. As some countries decided not to take up their loans, Italy has the lion's share of financial resources.

Germany and France conceived the entire NGEU plan to help countries of the South (mainly Italy, Spain, Portugal, and Greece) and those of the East. Italy is the country most under observation for both economic and political reasons.

Italy has very high public debt, and it seems incapable of producing economic growth. Given its economic weakness, Italy is the one country that might derail the entire EU/Eurozone project, as it was already threatening to do both in 2011 and 2019.[12] The announcement of the NGEU plan with a substantial amount of funding (more than the Marshall Plan) flowing to Italy is one reason why the anti-European populist sentiment has abated, and a government of national unity has become possible. All political parties (except Brothers of Italy) wanted to be on board and have a say on the distribution of these resources.

However, it would be a mistake to conclude that the long-standing conflicting views between the North and South of Europe have ended. The South—and Italy in particular—has a very different vision of Europe from the North. Italians generally think that funds they are receiving from Europe are somehow due. It was the duty of the EU (often mentioned as an outside entity) to respond to the pandemic with a significant spending plan. After all, NGEU is much smaller than the stimulus plans introduced in the USA.

More to the point, many believe that Italy had the right to receive the money because it had suffered so much from the pandemic and, in previous years, from the EU's many alleged mistakes: too much austerity imposed on Italy

---

[11] The allocation of funds is based on a complex formula which also takes into account the GDP and unemployment performance in 2020 and 2021.

[12] As Bastasin and Toniolo (2020) wrote, 'the success of NG-EU and RRF has an existential significance for future European prospects; and this success depends, to a large extent, on Italy's ability to use the financial resources (transfers and loans) efficiently, through the definition and implementation of the so-called National Recovery and Resilience Plan'.

and inefficient decision-making on the redistribution of migrants arriving from the southern Mediterranean.[13]

Seventy years ago, Italians were thankful to the USA for aid provided through the Marshall Plan. Today, Italians are hardly grateful to Germany or France and the other EU countries for NGEU help. If anything, the EU should spend more, and the issuance of common debt should become a permanent feature of the EU. The notion that permanent common debt requires a transfer of power and responsibility from member states to the Union—hence giving up sovereignty and changing the Treaties—is not a topic for discussion, except in very restricted circles. For northern countries, it is clear that the debt issued for the NGEU plan is of a temporary nature and should be wholly amortised in the next few decades (by 2058).

The misunderstanding between Italy and the North extends to other important economic policy areas and especially budgetary policy. Once in a while, the EU Commission warns that high debt countries should be careful. In 2023, fiscal rules that were suspended for the pandemic will be reintroduced, although probably with some adaptations to the new reality. However, most Italians do not seem to care about their high public debt: somehow, the problem will be solved, as Europe cannot afford to let Italy go bust.

The misunderstanding extends to monetary policy. Italians tend to think that the European Central Bank (ECB) has a duty to bail out a country with problems on its sovereign debt. This is the position of the politicians that were part of the populist yellow–green coalition. But it tends to find broader support in other political parties as well. After all—so goes the story—nobody told Italians that the central bank would no longer rescue their sovereign debt after the launch of the euro. In Italy, soft budget constraints are the norm: central government intermittently bails out municipalities or regions. Why shouldn't the same apply to member states in the EU/Eurozone? This appears to be the prevailing attitude in Italy.

The misunderstanding also extends to state aid. Italian politicians tend to see European rules on state aid and competition as a sort of perversion of euro-bureaucracy. And no government so far has dared to let Alitalia or Monte dei Paschi go bust. However, most other countries want the rules to be reintroduced after the partial suspension decided in the wake of the pandemic. At most, some changes are considered necessary for geopolitical

---

[13] In effect, Italy was one of the countries that suffered most from the pandemic; see Cottarelli-Paudice (2021).

reasons to face challenges coming from the giant companies of China and the USA.

We conclude this paragraph by pitilessly stating that Italy has behaved towards the EU like the South of Italy has often behaved towards Italy in recent years: asking and pretending. The conflict with the North is dormant but still very much alive.

10.12 A tale of two countries: Italy and Germany

Until the beginning of this century, Italy and Germany were labelled 'the two sick nations' of the advanced world because of their low growth. Both tried to face such situations with reform. Italy started promoting reforms to spur growth (and reduce the deficit) in the early 1990s, and never stopped trying. More than thirty years of attempted reforms did not produce the expected results. Growth did not materialise, and the debt-to-GDP ratio skyrocketed.

On the other hand, after the round of reforms enacted by the Schröder government, Germany in only a few years, from 2003 to 2005, made a new start. On these reforms, there is extensive literature but no consensus on their effectiveness. For instance, Burda (2007), Gros (2013), Gaskarth (2014), and others argue that the reforms were fundamentally successful. Instead, Sinn and others (2006) think they were successful but too timid. According to yet another interpretation, for instance, by Carlin and Soskice (2009), Dustmann et al. (2014), and Wolf (2014), the key factor of German success was multi-year wage moderation, which gave it a solid competitive edge in export- and import-competing sectors.[14] Despite not having a flexible labour market, Germany, like some other Northern European countries, has wage-setting institutions that enable nominal wage growth to be coordinated so as to achieve a real exchange rate target that maintains competitiveness. According to a story that is often heard in Germany, the radical reforms that the Schröder government implemented were the shock that made it clear to everybody that Germans had no choice. They had to accept sacrifices to return to growth. This factor was at the root of the long period of wage moderation and economic development that followed, although somewhat at the expense of the rest of the Eurozone due to nominal rigidity in wages in other countries.

---

[14] For many commentators, the reforms were a glass half empty and a glass half full, in that they created winners and losers: see Krebs-Scheffel (2013), Kaczorek (2019).

In 2021 Italy, many commentators believed that the tragedy of Covid was the kind of shock that made people aware of the importance of helping oneself; that is to say, taking risks and creating new activities with the same entrepreneurial spirit that animated the country in the first two decades after the war. After all, Italy is still the second industrial country in Europe. It has a few hundred 'small multinationals' that have managed to withstand the challenges of international markets and thrive. And, according to many, the new apparently calm and constructive political climate around Mario Draghi may help to introduce the reforms needed to create the right incentives for a genuinely new beginning for the country. For now, it is just hope.

11

Lessons

It could happen to you—No Silicon Valley without a Stanford—Ivy League and equal opportunities—Other causes of the decline—The merits of meritocracy and the demerits of the alternatives—Reality denied—From humility to confidence

11.1 It could happen to you

Our main take is that meritocracy is fundamental for economic prosperity, especially when a country needs to switch from imitation-led growth to endogenous frontier growth.

In the case of Italy, problems arose when, at the same time (a) the country could no longer grow by imitation, as it had done in the three decades after WWII, (b) it became fully exposed to international competition (due mainly to China's entry into the WTO, the enlargement of the EU, and the creation of the euro), and (c) it could no longer resort to low wages as it did until the 1960s, or artificial stimuli to aggregate demand with currency devaluation especially as in the 1970s, and public debt especially as in the 1980s.

As we saw in Chapter 2, TFP, a measure of innovation capacity and the efficient use of factors of production, had stalled after the 1970s, so that since then Italy had found itself in a semi-permanent state of crisis.

Italy should have replaced the triad formed by imitation, devaluation, and the accumulation of public debt with the much more virtuous one made by excellent research, technological innovation, and good governance. But all this would have required a little more foresight to create institutions capable of selecting and promoting people based on their merit rather than on their connections.

We have talked about Italy, and we have stressed the factors that caused Italy to have a worse performance than its peers. But what has happened to Italy could happen to other countries. Many other countries in the world have heavy historical legacies and low social capital, for instance due to rather

Meritocracy, Growth, and Lessons from Italy's Economic Decline. Lorenzo Codogno and Giampaolo Galli, Oxford University Press. © Lorenzo Codogno and Giampaolo Galli (2022). DOI: 10.1093/oso/9780192866806.003.0012

recent colonial history. And many other countries have to make the leap from imitation-led growth to endogenous growth. It seems that this leap has been made successfully by most countries in Asia. But this is less so in South America, and we do not yet know what will happen to the emerging nations of Africa.

11.2 No Silicon Valley without a Stanford

There is nothing new at the core of the technical argument made above about Italy, as our contribution concerns only the role of competition and meritocracy, whose rejection we view as a means of self-preservation of old elites and old and new lobbies. As shown in Chapter 1, almost the entire literature on Italy's decline is along the lines we have described: Italy's initial conditions were not up to the challenge represented by the transition to a fully open knowledge-based economy.

This basic technical argument about merit is very present in recent international literature. In particular, Aghion et al. (2021) argue that countries must go through a radical adaptation of policies and institutions to switch from imitation-driven growth to frontier innovation: 'Frontier innovation comes above all from the knowledge economy, in particular from basic research and post-graduate education: no Silicon Valley without Stanford University'.

This is a crucial point. It is very difficult to switch from imitation to endogenous frontier innovation for a country that does not have excellent research. And in Chapter 5, we saw how and why meritocracy had been kept out of Italian universities, in favour of a semi-feudal system based on personal loyalty to the 'barons' who dominate the field. The basic principle of the anti-meritocratic egalitarian culture that has prevailed, especially since the 1970s, implies that funds should not be allocated to reward the best departments but help the laggard catch up. This culture goes a long way in explaining why Italian universities are so low in all international rankings.

The core technical argument has been thoroughly analysed and made compelling by Phelps et al. (2020); they show that in the three decades after WWII, most European countries grew by imitation, i.e. importing technological innovation from the USA. The USA was, and still is, the technological leader of the world. In this context, Italy did not stand out as a major centre of what they call 'indigenous innovation', i.e. innovation produced within the country. Still, it managed to adopt American innovation quickly. In the succeeding four decades, productivity growth fell almost anywhere, including Germany and France, but Italy's decline was particularly severe. According to the estimates of Phelps et al., Italy was among the countries that did not succeed in substituting imported with indigenous innovation. While the specific estimates are fraught with technical difficulties, the intuition seems to us absolutely sound.

11.3 Ivy League and equal opportunities

Edmund Phelps is a Nobel Prize winner in economics and the author of a splendid book, *Mass Flourishing*. In his own words:

> People from all walks of life, not just scientists and lab technicians, possess inborn powers to conceive 'new things', whether or not scientists have opened up new possibilities. And a modern society allows and even encourages people to act on newly conceived things—to create and try them—which stimulates people to conceive the new. The whole nation might be on fire with new ideas.[1]

These words do not refer only to companies but to the 'whole nation'. Indeed, our book shows that all facets of society must be involved in the innovation effort. A modern dynamic economy needs efficient institutions: public administration, judiciary, educational systems, health care and, indeed, the political system.

For 'the whole nation to be on fire', a number of basic conditions must be satisfied. Phelps cites the elimination of policies, laws, and deal-making impeding or blocking new entrants bearing new ideas. In addition, 'getting rid of the close ties between powerful corporations and the government would also be helpful'. It is also necessary 'to minimise the bureaucracy involved in starting a business, registering property, or obtaining building permits'.

We agree. In addition, we would say that merit must be rewarded in the education system and on the job.

We are not searching for the moon, and we have made an example of one institution, the Bank of Italy, which is capable of selecting and promoting its employees based on their merit, a fact that explains the prestige that the bank has managed to maintain both inside the country and internationally. The Bank of Italy is one of the few meritocratic institutions in Italy. Note that the Bank of Italy is a public administration and is subject to many of the same restrictions and trades union rules as other public institutions.

---

[1] Phelps et al. (2020), page 5.

One of the strong points of the Bank of Italy is that, de facto if not *de iure*, it hires its top economists almost exclusively after they have completed at least a master degree from a foreign university, typically among the best in the USA and the UK. This fact alone goes a long way in demonstrating that, at least in the field of economics, the graduate and postgraduate programmes of most Italian universities are not considered top level.

We want to point out this fact to Daniel Markovits and the many other critics of Ivy-League-plus universities. Italy would be much better off had it many top-level universities as well.

To these critics, we point out another key fact that we demonstrated in Chapter 6 of this book: the much higher social mobility of the USA relative to Italy, measured in terms of educational attainment of children with different family backgrounds. The offspring of a family in which neither parent has attained a high-school degree has a 6 per cent probability of obtaining a university degree, one of the lowest in the OECD. Instead, they have a 64 per cent probability of attaining only a lower secondary degree or less; this number is a record, in the sense that it is the highest in the OECD, except for Turkey. In the USA, the equivalent figures are 13 per cent (more than twice as much as Italy) and 28 per cent (less than half much as Italy).

In light of this situation, it is really difficult to say that Ivy-League-plus universities are the killers of equal opportunity. By contrast, they are more likely to contribute to equal opportunity.

Beyond the specifics about the admission policies of these institutions, the general argument in favour of meritocracy in higher education is that selection is much more likely to be based on merit in the education system than on the job, where connections inevitably play a more prominent role. If the education system does not send perceptible signals about the potential of young people, connections become almost a must for evaluating people.

11.4 Other causes of the decline

To be sure, we have not 'proved' that lack of meritocracy is the cause of the decline. We cannot find a single variable measuring all the dimensions of meritocracy that can be thrown into an econometric model to explain economic growth.

However, we have provided plenty of evidence that (a) merit is disregarded while (b) it is an essential ingredient for a knowledge-based economy to be competitive and produce prosperity.

In some cases, we have quoted research that 'proves' or, to the very least, argues convincingly that connections produce inferior results. It was the case in the corporate sector, in which there is evidence that firms that are entirely managed by the owner's family tend to have mediocre performance, as they do less R&D, they are less productive, and less likely to become internationalised (see Chapter 9). Another rather convincing piece of evidence is that politically connected firms tend to have better sales and profits but are less productive and innovative than their competitors. Most importantly, such firms are likely to succeed in the domestic market but not in international markets.

Are there other explanations of the Italian decline? Undoubtedly, the answer is 'yes', and we have accounted for many of them throughout the book. We do not consider most of them as alternative explanations to the lack of meritocracy, and in many cases, we consider them an essential part of the story.

In macro-courses, we will not teach our students that the 'cause' of the decline is lack of merit or meritocracy. Instead, we will continue to tell them that the causes, in the sense in which economists use this term, are the end of the imitation era, entry into the knowledge economy, and lack of reform in the governance of the system as well as in many other areas, such as the labour market (so as to reduce its rigidities), the fiscal framework (so as to reduce evasion), the judiciary (so as to speed up processes), the universities (so as to reward the best departments), etc.

To those who want to go a little deeper, we will say that failure to address the challenges depicted above and implement the necessary reforms has a lot to do with the elites' lack of competition and meritocratic legitimacy. In turn, this is because competition and meritocracy have many enemies in elites and lobbies, like those of many professions, but also of teachers, public workers, or particular groups of companies. So far, these lobbyists have won their battles and managed to impede the dynamism of the economy.

To be sure, we have no indication that lack of meritocracy emerged only in the 1990s when the decline became apparent. Most probably, it was also present before; that is the reason why in previous decades Italy's economic growth was made possible by 'imitation' and by rather special conditions, such as low wages until the 1960s, devaluation, public debt, and major state intervention in the economy in the 1970s and 1980s. Very little frontier endogenous innovation took place in those decades.

In the Chapters 3 and 4 on Social Capital and Governance, we dealt with alternative explanations, such as the lack of trust among Italians and between Italians and all sorts of institutions: banks, government, politicians, judges.

In the chapter on Governance, we have shown that there is something fundamentally wrong in the way many entities, in both public and private sector, are run.

There are no simple reforms that can fix the legacy of low mutual trust. But we have argued that if merit is given more importance in hiring, wage increases, and promotions, top figures in public administration and the private sector would be more respected, and politicians would have stronger legitimation among voters.

As for governance, we believe that reforms can improve the system even if merit does not enter the picture. Constitutional and electoral reforms are very important in our view. The objective should be to make governments more stable and draw clear lines between the competencies of different institutions, especially between central government and the regions. From this point of view, we argued that both reforms that were unfortunately rejected by two referenda, in 2006 and 2016, would have improved the efficiency of the system.

More to the point, we used to think that the critical problem of Italy was weak and unstable government and that electoral and constitutional reforms could solve this problem. We still believe that such reforms would be important, but we cannot close our eyes to a simple fact. In the past quarter of a century, Italy has experimented with four different electoral systems which have changed the political landscape but have not been able to produce visible changes in the sort of things that matter for ordinary citizens or firms: bureaucracy has remained burdensome, laws have remained unreadable, the efficiency of the judiciary has not improved, nor has the school system, as certified by the OECD (see Chapter 5). This experience, together with the startling stalling of the economy, led us to delve deeper into the Italian problem and identify a common thread in the lack of meritocracy.

We have also shown that even politicians do not inspire much confidence in the same voters who elected them. By trying to explain this apparent paradox, we have shown that in the end, when things get tough, most people and even members of parliament are happy to choose as prime minister someone who has merit because he has proved to be very competent in other fields.

At a somewhat deeper level, we have argued that lack of mutual trust is a historical legacy that has to do with the fascist era and, more importantly, a long history in which Italians, especially in the South, have been under foreign domination.

Hierarchies, obedience, lack of freedom, lack of reward to merit, and creativity are features of Italian society inherited from the fascist regime. But, of course, this is not a surprise: what else can be expected from a dictatorship?

It is not surprising that Maria Montessori, an Italian physician and educator, was banned by Mussolini; all Montessori schools that had been rather successful in the country since the beginning of the century were closed in 1936. Her educational methods were adopted in all corners of the world, in the West and the East, but not in Italy. The Italian schools' system remained largely unchanged after the war. Teachers, not pupils, were the kings; the acquisition of ideas was centre stage, rather than what Maria Montessori called 'the liberation of the lively powers of the mind'.[2]

However, these features have much deeper roots in Italian history than in many other countries. As we argued in Chapter 3, many centuries of foreign domination had created a mental habit more prone to obedience than creativity and entrepreneurship.

This is particularly true in much of the southern regions of Italy, where obedience, sometimes to criminal organisations, nepotism, and patronage, rather than merit, are more common. As shown in Chapter 6, the North–South divide has remained unchanged since WWII, even though laws are obviously the same in all areas of the country. Central government has made massive efforts to solve the problem, mainly through public investment and very generous incentives for private investment, without much success. As we have documented, what makes the difference is the quality of public services, including schools, justice, and law enforcement.

The same problems are present in the North, but they appear more severe in the South, which is rather far from that modern society that encourages people to act on the new things that Edmund Phelps envisaged.

11.5 The merits of meritocracy and the demerits of the alternatives

In a recently published book, Adrian Wooldridge, *The Economist*'s political editor, gives a splendid account of how merit has shaped our societies for the best and is key to understanding the West's prosperity. His key points in favour of a meritocratic society are the same as ours: 'First, it prides itself on the extent to which people can get ahead in life on the basis of their natural talents. Second, it tries to secure equality of opportunity by providing education for all. Third, it forbids discrimination on the basis of race and

---

[2] Montessori (1992).

sex and other irrelevant characteristics. Fourth, it awards jobs through open competition rather than patronage and nepotism'.[3]

In other words, recalling the opening sentences of this book, meritocracy is the opposite of what Franco Modigliani saw when he came back to Italy and tried to find a position as a professor of economics. He rediscovered with enormous disgust how different were Italian from US universities. On top of the social ladders were the barons, one notch under God; underneath, a large group of 'hopeful and servile assistants'; at the bottom of the pyramid, 'the students about whom nobody cares'. His conclusion was almost without hope as he saw the deep origin of the Italian crisis in this state of affairs. As he wrote, 'a leadership that has been selected based on its ability to accept humiliation and forgo self-respect cannot rule Italy'.

The only realistic alternative to selection by merit is patronage through personal and family connections. Throughout this book, we have shown that merit has a minimal role in the careers of many Italians. The salaries of public sector employees, teachers, magistrates, and even doctors increase essentially by seniority. At top levels, promotion becomes the key to improving wages, and such advancement is often due to personal or family connections. As for the judiciary, the Palamara scandal, which we first mentioned in Chapter 1, has put this reality in front of everybody; career advancement at the top level of the judiciary is due to connections, most often with politicians.

Quite clearly, when merit is disregarded, the key to the social elevator and sometimes even to survive is loyalty to some boss, i.e. to some powerful man or woman who decides who can be promoted. In substance, as we have argued, this is a form of semi-feudal system, with strict hierarchies or castes.

Patronage is the opposite of equal opportunity. It is the main avenue through which privilege is transmitted from one generation to the next. It should be considered incompatible with liberal democracy as we have learnt to understand this term over the last couple of centuries.

We have also argued that it may be true that sometimes there is a problem with the arrogance of the meritocratic elite. Still, the arrogance of a mediocratic elite is certainly worse because it is not backed by the recognition that the elite is chosen among the best. The obvious problem is that mediocre leaders have a low level of legitimacy in the eyes of voters. Populism finds fertile ground in such situations, although it can put down roots in entirely different contexts.

---

[3] Wooldridge (2021).

Lack of meritocracy is particularly acute in Italy because the corporate world is not always a good example. As we have seen, corporate nepotism discourages professional managers and is in itself one of the critical reasons for Italy's dismal performance, as Schumpeterian creative destruction is seriously hampered.

In such a world, young people find a job not because they send round excellent CVs, but because they know someone who knows. This fact, which is ascertained by the European statistical office, is one of the most odious aspects of the system. As argued in Chapter 8, Italians learn very early in their life that patronage is more important than merit.

Likewise, women are more discriminated against on the job than in any other advanced nation; indeed, Italy ranks last among advanced nations and 105th over 167 nations in terms of female participation in the labour market. This is but the most visible aspect of the blunder of the gender gap, which is the precise opposite of equal opportunity. If merit had a greater value in hiring decisions, the gap relative to most advanced nations would not be significant.

A related problem is brain drain. Low economic growth and mediocrity discourage the best graduates to stay in the country. They decide to go abroad, deepening mediocrity and low growth. Having international experience is undoubtedly a plus, but the balance of flows is heavily skewed. Italy attracts few top-ranking students from abroad.

To be sure, in the corporate world, merit matters much more than in any other corner of society because companies are usually exposed to some competition. But merit is less important than in many other countries.

The problem of the corporate world derives largely from heavy bureaucracy and an intricate legal system. As argued in Chapter 9, companies survive because they have connections in such a system. This does not mean that Italy is a highly corrupt country (Chapter 4). Corruption is a severe problem, but the reality of corruption is less widespread than the perception, although there is always corruption and crime when mafias are part of the game.

11.6 Reality denied

Another clear lesson of this book—admittedly, not a new or surprising one—is that those who have responsibilities can do an extraordinary job defending themselves and pointing to some extraneous factors as the source of the crisis.

In the 1970s and the 1980s, the culprits were the oil price shocks and terrorism (both red and black). Of course, the oil price shocks hit all oil consuming countries more or less in the same way. Still, no other country suffered the same consequences as Italy regarding wage-price spiral, inflation, deficit in the balance of payments, public debt, and the nationalisation of zombie firms. Japan initially had a similar jump in inflation but soon found a way to return to a more stable macroeconomic environment.

Terrorism was indeed a more serious problem than in most other countries, at least in the past, but it was not a prerogative of Italy (Israel is the other obvious example).

Then comes Italy's public finance problem. The increase in public debt was essentially due to the increase in spending, as in many other countries, which was not matched by a sufficiently timely rise in taxation. In the end, politicians were not fully aware of the debt problem, or they did not really want to acknowledge or care about it. The deficit improved considerably towards the end of the 1980s; however, it was too late to make a real difference and avoid the crisis of 1992 and the ensuing devaluation of the lira.

In all his speeches throughout the 1980s, Carlo Azeglio Ciampi, governor of the Bank of Italy (later prime minister and then president of the Republic), screamed against the burgeoning public debt as loud as he could. The political class did not listen, and Italians still carry this enormous weight on their shoulders.

In most recent times, the culprits, especially for the populists, have been the euro, the EU, Germany, France, and immigration. This is recent history, well known to everybody.

Less known is that much of the country is in permanent denial about the current state of affairs, as exposed in this book. As we have seen in Chapter 10, judges and teachers, and public officials in general, do not see the problems in their own backyard and actually deny them. They are thus obliged to find culprits somewhere else, and their favourite target is actual, or more often, presumed austerity. Their highest target is to deny that public debt is a problem. Indeed, this has been one of the winning cards of the populists in the elections of 2018.

11.7 From humility to confidence

Banning any rhetoric, key recommendations for all countries in a similar situation as Italy are the same—although in reverse order and with some additions—as those indicated by Mario Draghi a few weeks before ending his mandate as President of the European Central Bank.[4] He said that to

---

[4] Draghi Mario (2019) 'Lectio Magistralis' delivered at the Catholic University of Milan in October 2019.

make good decisions, three qualities are essential: knowledge, courage, and humility.

We reverse the order because, for a country like Italy, the quality that comes first is humility; then come knowledge and courage. We also add confidence in the future, which is essential to ensuring that good decisions will contribute to a better state of affairs.

Humility means recognising that other nations might do as well as we do and perhaps better. It means that politicians and teachers, magistrates, civil servants, and managers should look carefully at what has been achieved in other countries, as we have tried to do in this book.

Unfortunately, many persons in key positions do not understand English, the language in which much of the international knowledge, from hard sciences to economics and sociology, is written. Many mistakes would be avoided if there were a bit more knowledge of the errors made abroad. With its great variety of 195 countries, the world is an immense source of examples, good and bad. Looking only in one's courtyard or at one's past is an enormous waste.

The second virtue, knowledge, should be obvious, but it is not. Today, we live in a world in which the importance of knowledge is challenged. Populists reject the idea of objective or scientific knowledge. Trust in science has diminished, as the popularity of 'no vax' positions has shown during the pandemic. If this can happen, there surely is a need to reaffirm the values and concepts that western civilisation has learnt from the Renaissance, the Enlightenment, and the Scientific Revolution.

The third virtue, courage, is necessary because political leaders must tell the truth to the voters to build the required consensus for reform. For the ideas expressed in this book, we will be accused of being anti-patriotic and not seeing all the positive aspects of Italy; we surely will. This is false: we love our homeland, we are the real patriots, and for this reason, we want Italians to see reality as it is, without the distorting lens of nationalistic rhetoric.[5] Writing a book is easy; building political consensus around the truth and then delivering is altogether a different story and requires courage.

In turn, courage requires the conviction that there is a way out. If the situation is desperate, there can be no courage because one would ask: courage for what?

History is full of examples of countries that have gone through a decline or were even destroyed by war, epidemics, or natural catastrophes and were

---

[5] As is argued by De Bortoli (2020), a renowned economic journalist, there are many things that Italians like to keep to themselves.

reconstructed and then flourished. Our memory goes to the peasants of the Venetian region, which was very poor after WWII and a land of emigration. Many had their homes destroyed by bombings. They reconstructed their homes with their own hands and made them better than before, without any aid from the government and with no one teaching them how to do it. By the 1990s, that region had become one of the richest in Europe. Very few countries in the world are in such a desperate situation. As concerns Italy, it is still the second industrial country in Europe, and it has a few hundred small multinational companies that manage to export and withstand the challenges of highly competitive international markets. These companies know the crucial role of such concepts as competition, innovation, evaluation, and merit. It should not be impossible to bring these concepts to the rest of the economy, both private and public.

We do not expect that the radical changes needed can occur in one day or even during the life span of an enlightened government. We are moderate reformists, not revolutionary, and we know that change requires time. But people must become aware that they are indeed necessary; otherwise, no transformation will be possible. As someone said, 'the elevator to success is out of order, you'll have to use the stairs . . . one step at a time.'[6] This works as long as most people know that there are stairs and that they have to climb them, step by step.

---

[6] Joe Girard, American salesman, motivational speaker, and author.

Bibliography

Abravanel, Roger. 2010. *Regole. Perché tutti gli italiani devono sviluppare quelle giuste e rispettarle per rilanciare il paese* {Rules. Why all Italians must develop the right ones and respect them to relaunch the country}. Milan: Garzanti.

Abravanel, Roger. 2021. *Aristocrazia 2.0, Una Nuova Élite per Salvare l'Italia* {Aristocracy 2.0, A New Elite to Save Italy}. Milan: RCS Media Group.

Acemoglu, Daron and James A. Robinson. 2012. *Why Nations Fail: The Origins of Power, Prosperity, and Poverty*. New York: Crown Publishers.

AGCM (Italian Competition Authority). 2021. *Proposte di riforma concorrenziale* {Proposals for pro-competition reforms}. 23 March. Available at www.agcm.it/media/comunicati-stampa/2021/3/S4143.

Aghion, Philippe and Peter Howitt. 2009. *The Economics of Growth*. Cambridge, MA: The MIT Press.

Aghion, Philippe, Céline Antonin, and Simon Bunel. 2021. *The Power of Creative Destruction*. Cambridge, MA: Harvard University Press.

Akcigit Ufuk, Salomé Baslandze, and Francesca Lotti. 2018a. Connecting to power: political connections, innovation, and firm dynamics. *NBER Working Paper*, no. 25136, October.

Akcigit, Ufuk, John Grigsby, Tom Nicholas, and Stephanie Stantcheva. 2018b. Taxation and innovation in the 20th century. *NBER Working Paper* no. 24982, September.

Alesina, Alberto. 2002. *Senso non comune. L'economia oltre ai pregiudizi* {Uncommon sense. Economics beyond prejudices}. Milan: EGEA Bocconi University Press.

Alesina, Alberto, Carlo Favero, and Francesco Giavazzi. 2019. *Austerity. When It Works and When It Doesn't*. Princeton, NJ: Princeton University Press.

Alfaro, Laura, Alan Auerbach, Mauricio Cárdenas, Takatoshi Ito, Sebnem Kalemli-Özcan, and Justin Sandefur. 2021. Doing business: external panel review. *Final Report*. 1 September.

Amato, Giuliano. 1992. Il mercato nella costituzione {The market in the constitution}. *In Quaderni Costituzionali*, no.1, pp. 7–19.

Amato, Giuliano. 1995. La tutela della concorrenza: regole, istituzioni e rapporti internazionali: conclusioni {Competition policy; rules, institutions, international relations: conclusions}. International Seminar Organized by AGCM (Italy's antitrust authority) 20 November in Rome. Available at https://www.agcm.it/dettaglio?id=eee87215-1263-4873-8190-b650ab64db6d.

Amato, Giuliano. 2015. *Le istituzioni italiane, un viaggio lungo cinquant' anni* {Italian institutions, a journey of fifty years}. Bologna: Il Mulino.

Andretta, Camilla, Irene Brunetti, and Anna Rosso. 2021. Productivity and human capital—the Italian case. *OECD Productivity Working Papers*, no. 25, July.

ANPAL (National Agency for Active Labour Policies). 2021. *I programmi occupazionali delle imprese* {Occupational programmes of the firms}. April; Rome.

Arrow, Kenneth, Samuel Bowles, and Steven N. Durlauf (eds). 2000. *Meritocracy and Economic Inequality*. Princeton, NJ: Princeton University Press.

ARWU. 2021. *Academic Ranking of World Universities*. Shanghai, China.

Baldwin, Richard and Francesco Giavazzi (eds). 2015. *The Eurozone Crisis: A Consensus View of the Causes and a Few Possibile Solutions*. London: CEPR Press. Cepr- A VoxEU.org eBook.

Baltrunaite Audinga, Elisa Brodi, and Sauro Mocetti. 2019. Assetti proprietari e di governance delle imprese italiane {Ownership and governance of Italian firms}. *Bank of Italy. Occasional Papers*, no. 512, October.

Bandiera, Oriana, Luigi Guiso, Andrea Prat, and Raffaella Sadun. 2015. Matching firms, managers, and incentives. *Journal of Labor Economics* 33(3): 623–681.

Bank of Italy. 2017. *Italy's Lost Productivity and How to Get it Back*. Riccardo Faini Memorial Conference. 13 January in Rome. Available at https://www.bancaditalia.it/pubblicazioni/altri-atti-convegni/2017-riccardo-faini-memorial/index.html.

Bank of Italy. Various months. *Statistical Bulletin*. Rome.

Bank of Italy. Various years. *Annual Reports*. Rome.

Barbieri, Giorgio and Francesco Giavazzi. 2014. *Corruzione a norma di legge. La lobby delle grandi opere che affonda l'Italia* {Corruption according to the law. The lobby of great works that sinks Italy}. Milan: RCS Rizzoli.

Barbuto, Mario, Carlo Cottarelli, Alessandro De Nicola, and Leonardo D'Urso. 2020. Come ridurre i tempi della giustizia civile {How to reduce the length of civil proceedings}. *Osservatorio sui Conti Pubblici Italiani*, 5 June. Available at https://osservatoriocpi.unicatt.it/cpi-archivio-studi-e-analisi-come-ridurre-i-tempi-della-giustizia-civile.

Barca, Fabrizio and Ignazio Visco. 1993. L'economia italiana nella prospettiva europea: terziario protetto e dinamica dei redditi nominali {The Italian economy from a European perspective: protected tertiary sector and dynamics of nominal incomes}. In Ignazio Visco and Stefano Micossi (eds) *Inflazione, concorrenza e sviluppo: l'economia italiana e la sfida dell'integrazione europea. Saggi in ricordo di Stefano Vona* {Inflation, competition and development: The Italian economy and the challenge of European integration. Essays in Memory of Stefano Vona}, pp. 21–91. Bologna: il Mulino.

Barro-Lee Dataset. 2020. *Educational Attainment*. Available at www.barrolee.com/.

Barucci, Emilio and Federico Pierobon. 2010a. *Stato e Mercato nella Seconda Repubblica, Dalle Privatizzazioni alla Crisi Finanziaria* {State and Market in the Second Republic, from Privatisation to the Financial Crisis}. Bologna: il Mulino.

Barucci, Emilio, Claudio De Vincenti, and Michele Grillo. 2010b. *Idee per l'Italia, Mercato e Stato* {Ideas for Italy, Market and State}. Milan: Francesco Brioschi Editore.

Bassanini, Franco. 2003. *Good Governance Strategies: A Prospect for Integration: Reflections from the Italian Experience*. Fifth Global Forum on Reinventing Government. 3–7 November. Mexico. Available at https://www.bassanini.it/lammodernamento-dellamministrazione-pubblica/.

Bastasin, Carlo and Gianni Toniolo. 2020. *La strada smarrita. Breve storia dell'economia italiana* {The lost way. A short history of the Italian economy}. Bari: Laterza Editore.

Bastasin, Carlo, Lorenzo Bini Smaghi, Sergio De Nardis, Claudio De Vincenti, Valeria Meliciani, Marcello Messori, Stefano Micossi, Pier Carlo Padoan, and Gianni Toniolo. 2021. Three conditions for Italian reform success. *Policy Brief 11/2021 Luiss-SEP*. 14 June.

Bauer, P., I. Fedotenkov, A. Genty, I. Hallak, P. Harasztosi, D. Martinez Turegano, D. Nguyen, N. Preziosi, A. Rincon-Aznar and M. Sanchez Martinez. 2020. *Productivity in Europe. Trends and Drivers in a Service-Based Economy*. EUR 30076 EN. Luxembourg: Publications Office of the European Union.

Beccattini, Giacomo. 1998 *Distretti industriali e made in Italy* {Industrial districts and made in italy}. Turin: Bollati Boringhieri Editore.

Begg, Iain, Annette Bongardt, Kalypso Nicolaïdis, and Francisco Torres. 2015. EMU and sustainable integration. *Journal of Europea Integration* 37(7): 803–816.

Bella, Edoardo. 2021. Un confronto tra i voti della maturità e i risultati INVALSI prima e dopo la pandemia {A comparison of graduation grades and INVALSI tests before and after the pandemic}. *Osservatorio sui Conti Pubblici Italiani*, 27 November. Available at https://osservatoriocpi.unicatt.it/ocpi-pubblicazioni-un-confronto-tra-i-voti-della-maturita-e-i-risultati-invalsi-prima-e-dopo-la-pandemia.

Bénabou, Roland. 2000. Meritocracy, redistribution, and the size of the pie. In Kenneth Arrow, Samuel Bowles, and Steven N. Durlauf (eds) *Meritocracy and Economic Inequality*, pp. 317–339. Princeton, NJ: Princeton University Press.

Bianchi, Patrizio. 2013. *La Rincorsa Frenata, l'industria italiana dall'unità alla crisi globale* {The interrupted catch-up, Italian industry from unity to the global crisis}. Bologna: il Mulino.

Bianchi, Marcello and Magda Bianco. 2006. Italian Corporate Governance in the Last 15 Years. European Corporate Governance Institute. *Working Paper* no. 144, November.

Blanchard, Olivier. 2019. Public debt and low interest rates. *American Economic Review* 109(4 April): 1197–1229.

Boeri, Tito and Pietro Garibaldi. 2011. *Le riforme a costo zero. Dieci proposte per tornare a crescere* {Reforms at zero cost. Ten proposals to return to growth}. Milan: Chiarelettere Editore.

Boeri, Tito and Pietro Garibaldi. 2018. Il Jobs Act come esperimento quasi scientifico: cosa suggeriscono i dati? {Jobs Act as a quasi-scientific experiment: what do the data suggest?}. *Economia Italiana*, 2018/2–3.

Boeri, Tito, and Roberto Perotti. 2021a. L'università italiana continua a non premiare la ricerca {Italian University continues not to reward research}. *Lavoce.info*. 17 March. Available at https://www.lavoce.info/archives/72920/luniversita-italiana-continua-a-non-premiare-la-ricerca/.

Boeri, Tito, Riccardo Faini, Andrea Ichino, Giuseppe Pisauro, and Carlo Scarpa (eds). 2005. *Oltre il Declino*. {Beyond Italy's Decline} Bologna: il Mulino.

Boeri, Tito, Moretti Enrico, Ichino Andrea, and Johanna Posch. 2021b. Wage equalization and regional misallocation: evidence from Italian and German provinces. *Journal of the European Economic Association* 19(6), December 2021: 3249–3292.

Boitani, Andrea. 2021. *L'illusione liberista* {The neo-liberal illusion}. Bari: Laterza.

Bovini, Giulia and Paolo Sestito. 2021. I divari territoriali nelle competenze degli studenti {Regional variation in students' competences}. *Bank of Italy. Occasional Papers* no. 645, October.

Brandolini, Andrea and Matteo Bugamelli (eds). 2009. Rapporto sulle tendenze nel sistema produttivo italiano {Report on trends in the Italian productive system}. *Bank of Italy. Questioni di economia e finanza*, no. 45.

Brandolini, Andrea and Roberto Torrini. 2010. Disuguaglianza dei redditi e divari territoriali: l'eccezionalità del caso italiano {Income inequalities and regional gaps: the exceptionality of the italian case}. *La Rivista delle Politiche Sociali* 3: 27–58.

Brandolini, Andrea, Romina Gambacorta, and Alfonso Rosolia. 2018. Inequality amid income stagnation: Italy over the last quarter of a century. *Bank of Italy. Occasional Papers*, no. 442, June.

Brugnara, Luca and Federica Paudice. 2021. La sostenibilità del debito pubblico non è solo una questione di crescita {Debt sustainability is not only a matter of growth}. *Osservatorio sui Conti Pubblici Italiani*, 19 May. Available at https://osservatoriocpi.unicatt.it/cpi-debpil_cpi.pdf.

Brunetta, Renato and Giuliano Cazzola. 2003. *Riformare il Welfare è possibile* {Reforming Welfare is feasible}. Rome: Ideazione Editrice.

Brusco, Sebastiano. 1990. The idea of industrial districts: Its genesis. In F. Pyke, O. Becattini, and W. Sengenberger (eds) *Industrial Districts and Inter-firm Co-operation in Italy*. Geneva: International Institute for Labour Studies.

Bugamelli, Matteo and Lotti Francesca (eds). 2018. Productivity growth in Italy: a tale of a slow-motion change. *Bank of Italy. Questioni di economia e finanza*, no. 422.

Bugamelli, Matteo, Stefania Fabiani, Stefano Federico, Alberto Felettigh, Claire Giordano, and Andrea Linarello. 2018. Back on track? A macro-micro narrative of Italian exports. *Italian Economic Journal* 4(1): 1–31.

Burda, Michael. 2007. German recovery: It's the supply side. *VoxEU*, 23 July. Available at https://voxeu.org/article/german-recovery-it-s-supply-side.

Buti, Marco (ed.). 2009. *Italy in EMU. The Challenges of Adjustment and Growth*. Basingstoke: Palgrave Macmillan.

Buti, Marco and Marcello Messori. 2021. Euro Area policy mix: from horizontal to vertical coordination, *CEPR Policy Insight* 113, October.

Buti, Marco, Alessandro Turrini, Paul Van den Noord, and Pietro Biroli. 2008. Defying the 'Juncker Curse': Can reformist governments be re-elected? *European Commission, Economic Papers 324*, May.

Buti, Marco, Alessandro Turrini, Paul van den Noord, and Pietro Biroli. 2010. Reforms and re-elections in OECD countries. *Economic Policy* 25(61): 61–116.

Cabigiosu, Anna and Anna Moretti. 2020. *Osservatorio nazionale sulle reti d'impresa 2020* {National observatory on firm networks 2020}. Venice: Edizioni Ca' Foscari. Available at www.edizionicafoscari.unive.it/media/pdf/books/978-88-6969-485-1/978-88-6969-485-1_SOfRP3b.pdf.

Campos, Nauro, Paul De Grauwe, and Yuemei Ji (eds). 2020. *Economic Growth and Structural Reforms in Europe.* Cambridge: Cambridge University Press.

Cannari, Luigi and Giovanni D'Alessio. 2018. La disuguaglianza della ricchezza in Italia {Inequality of wealth in Italy}. *Bank of Italy. Occasional Papers*, no. 428, March.

Capano, Gilberto, Marino Regini, and Matteo Turri. 2017. *Salvare l'università italiana* {Saving Italian universities}. Bologna: Il Mulino.

Capron, Laurence and Mauro F. Guillén. 2009. National corporate governance institutions and post-acquisition target reorganization. *Management Paper*, no. 8, Wharton University.

Capussela, Andrea Lorenzo. 2018. *The Political Economy of Italy's Decline.* Oxford: Oxford University Press.

Carli, Guido. 1996. *Cinquant'anni di vita italiana* {Fifty years of Italian history}. Bari: Editori Laterza.

Carli, Renato and Marcello Messori. 2020. *Italia 2030. Proposte per lo sviluppo* {Italy 2030. Proposals for growth}. Milan: La Nave di Teseo.

Carlin, Wendy and David Soskice. 2009. German economic performance disentangling the role of supply-side reforms, macroeconomic policy and coordinated economic institutions. *Socio-Economic Review* 7(1): 67–99.

Casamonti, Matilde and Giulio Gottardo. 2020. Le dimensioni dello stato imprenditore italiano {The size of the entrepreneurial state}. *Osservatorio sui conti pubblici italiani.* 24 December. Available at https://osservatoriocpi.unicatt.it/ocpi-Imprese_pubbliche.pdf.

Casavola, Paola, Piero Cipollone, and Paolo Sestito. 1999. Determinants of pay in the Italian labor market: Jobs and workers. In David Haltiwanger, Jim Spletzer, Jules Theeuwes, Julia Lane, and Kenneth Troske (eds) *The Creation and Analysis of Employer and Employee Matched Data*, pp. 25–57. Amsterdam: North Holland Elsevier.

Cascavilla, Alessandro. 2020. Le cause delle differenze dei tempi della giustizia civile nei diversi tribunali italiani {Reasons for differences in the duration of civil proceedings across different Italian tribunals}. *Osservatorio sui Conti Pubblici Italiani*, 23 July.

Cassese, Sabino. 1998. *Lo Stato Introvabile* {The state is nowhere to be found}. Rome: Donzelli Editore.

Cassese, Sabino (ed.). 2015. *Riforme istituzionali e disciplina della politica* {Institutional reforms and political discipline}. Milan: Giuffré Editore.

Cassese, Sabino. 2016. Cinque domande sulla riforma della Costituzione {Five questions on the reform of the Constitution}. *Assonime, Note e Studi*, October.

Castronovo, Valerio. 2013. *Storia economica d'Italia. Dall'Ottocento ai giorni nostri* {Economic history of Italy. From the 1800s to today}. Turin: Einaudi Editore.

Castronovo, Valerio, Renzo De Felice, and Pietro Scoppola. 1999. *La storia d'Italia del XX secolo* {History of Italy in the 20th century}. Rome: Editalia-Istituto poligrafico e Zecca dello Stato.

Castronuovo, Salvatore. 1992. Mezzogiorno: the theory of growth and the labor market. *Journal of Regional Policy* 12: 333–365.

Charron, Nicholas, Victor Lapuente, and Monika Bauhr. 2021. Sub-national quality of government in EU member states: Indicators. *QoG Working Paper Series* 2021:4, University of Gothenburg.

Chenery, B. Hollis. 1962. Development policies for Southern Italy. *Quarterly Journal of Economics* 76(4 Nov): 515–547. Oxford University Press.

Ciampi, Carlo Azeglio and Alberto Orioli. 2011. *Non è il paese che sognavo* {This is not the country I was dreaming of}. Milan: Il Saggiatore.

Ciani, Emanuele and Roberto Torrini. 2019. The geography of income inequality: recent trends and the role of unemployment. *Bank of Italy. Occasional Papers*, no. 492, April.

Ciaschini, Maurizio and Gian Cesare Romagnoli. 2011. *L'Economia Italiana: Metodi di analisi, misurazione e nodi strutturali* {The Italian economy: Methods of analysis, measurement and structural nodes}. Milan: Franco Angeli.

Ciccarone, Giuseppe, Maurizio Franzini, and Enrico Saltari (eds). 2010. *L'Italia Possibile, Equità e Crescita* {Italy, possibility of equity and growth}. Milan: Francesco Brioschi Editore.

Cingano, Federico and Paolo Pinotti. 2013. Politicians at work: the private returns and social costs of political connections. *Journal of the European Economic Association* 11(2): 433–465.

Cingolani, Stefano. 1990. *Le grandi famiglie del capitalismo italiano.* {The great families of Italian capitalism}. Bari: Laterza.

Ciocca, Pierluigi. 2013. Brigantaggio ed economia nel Mezzogiorno d'Italia, 1860–1870 {Brigandage and the economy of the Mezzogiorno of Italy, 1860–1870}. *Rivista di storia economica*, April. Bologna: il Mulino.

Cipolletta, Innocenzo. 2012. Gli anni settanta, una frattura nel processo di crescita {The 1970s, a break in the growth process}. In Francesco Silva (ed.) *Storia dell'IRI* {History of IRI}, pp. 69–112. Bari: Laterza Editore.

Cipollone, Piero and Ignazio Visco. 2007. Il merito nella società della conoscenza {Merit in a knowledge society}. *Rivista Il Mulino*, no. 1/2007. Bologna: il Mulino.

Coco, Giuseppe and Claudio De Vincenti (eds). 2020. *Una questione nazionale; il Mezzogiorno da problema a opportunità* {A national issue: The mezzogiorno from a problem to an opportunity}. Collana Astrid. Bologna: Il Mulino.

Codogno, Lorenzo. 2009. Two Italian puzzles: Are productivity growth and competitiveness really so depressed? In Marco Buti (ed.) *Italy in the EMU: The Challenges of Adjustment and Growth*, pp. 87–116. Basingstoke: Palgrave Macmillan.

Codogno, Lorenzo. 2015. Revitalising Europe's economy: Towards growth. In Luigi Paganetto (ed.) *Achieving Dynamism in an Anaemic Europe*, pp. 167–198. Switzerland: Springer International.

Codogno, Lorenzo. 2016. Italy's referendum: Renzi's gamble failed, so what's next? *EUROPP, London School of Economics and Political Science*, 6 December. Available at www.bit.ly/2g3OG25.

Codogno, Lorenzo. 2018. The economic reforms of the 17th legislature. In Andrea Goldstein (ed.) *Le riforme economiche della XVII legislature*, pp. 25–34. Bologna: Il Mulino.

Codogno, Lorenzo. 2019a. Italy: New government, same old problems. *Friends of Europe*, 26 September. Available at www.friendsofeurope.org/insights/italy-new-government-same-old-problems/.

Codogno, Lorenzo. 2019b. The euro and economic governance: National priorities and quest for stability. In Carlo Altomonte and Antonio Villafranca (eds) *Europe in Identity Crisis: The Future of the EU in the Age of Nationalism*, pp. 93–119. Milan: ISPI.

Codogno, Lorenzo. 2020. Macroeconomic imbalances procedure: Has it worked in practice to improve the resilience of the euro area? *In-Depth Analysis, European Parliament, PE 634.403*, February.

Codogno, Lorenzo. 2021. The legacy of Banca d'Italia. In Christiane Liermann Traniello, Thomas Mayer, Francesco Papadia, and Matteo Scotto (eds) *The Value of Money. Controversial Economic Cultures in Europe: Italy and Germany*, pp. 145–154. Loveno di Menaggio: Villa Vigoni Publishing.

Codogno, Lorenzo and Francesco Felici. 2008. Assessing Italy's reform challenges. *Rivista di Politica Economica* IX(X, Sep–Oct): 43–118.

Codogno, Lorenzo and Giampaolo Galli. 2017. Uscire dall'Euro: una scelta suicida {Exiting the euro: A suicidal choice}. In Marta Dassù, Stefano Micossi, and Riccardo Perissich (eds) *Europa, sfida per l'Italia*, pp. 56–61. Rome: LUISS University Press.

Codogno, Lorenzo and Giampaolo Galli. 2018a. Perché è uno scenario catastrofico per il lavoro e il risparmio {Why is it a catastrophic scenario for jobs and savings?}. In Carlo Stagnaro (ed.) *Cosa succede se usciamo dall'Euro?* {What would happen if we exited the Euro?}, pp. 105–120. Milan: IBL Libri.

Codogno, Lorenzo and Giampaolo Galli. 2018b. Populism and the broken engine of the Italian economy. *EUROPP, London School of Economics and Political Science*, 18 April. Available at http://blogs.lse.ac.uk/europpblog/2018/04/20/populism-and-the-broken-engine-of-the-italian-economy/.

Codogno, Lorenzo and Silvia Merler. 2019. Una sospensione volontaria dell'incredulità: il contratto di governo e la Legge di Bilancio {A willing suspension of disbelief: The contract for government and the budget}. In Edoardo Bressanelli and David Natali (eds) *Politica in Italia* {Politics in Italy}, pp. 151–172. Bologna: il Mulino.

Codogno, Lorenzo and Luigi Paganetto (eds). 2011. *Measuring Italy's External Competitiveness*. Soveria Mannelli (Catanzaro): Rubbettino Editore.

Codogno, Lorenzo and Paul van den Noord. 2021. *Assessing the Next Generation EU, LEQS. London School of Economics and Political Science*, no.166/2020, February.

Coltorti, Fulvio. 2016. *Le grandi imprese nello sviluppo industriale italiano* {Big companies in Italy's industrial development}. Milan: EDUCatt.

Confcommercio. 2020. *Nota sulla stima della natimortalità delle imprese nel 2020* {Note on an estimate of demography of firms in 2020}, 28 December. Available at www.confcommercio.it/-/nota-stima-nati-mortalita-imprese-2020.

Corak, Miles. 2013. Income inequality, equality of opportunity, and intergeneralional mobility. *Journal of Economic Perspectives* 27 (3, Summer): 79–102 .

Corsetti, Giancarlo, Lars Feld, Philip Lane, Lucrezia Reichlin, Hélène Rey, Dimitri Vayanos, and Beatrice Weder Di Mauro. 2015. *A New Start for the Eurozone: Dealing with Debt*. London: CEPR Press.

Costi, Renzo and Marcello Messori. 2005. *Per lo Sviluppo. Un capitalismo senza rendite e con capitale* {In favour of development. A capitalism without rents and with capital}. Bologna: il Mulino.

Cottarelli, Carlo. 2015. *La spending review, un bilancio* {Spending review: What has been achieved}. 8 February. IBL libri.

Cottarelli, Carlo. 2017. *What We Owe: Truth, Myths and Lies about the Public Debt*. Washington, DC: Brookings Institution Press.

Cottarelli, Carlo. 2019. *I sette peccati capitali dell'economia italiana* {The seven deadly sins of the Italian economy}. Milan: Feltrinelli Editore.

Cottarelli, Carlo. 2021. *All'Inferno e ritorno. Per la nostra rinascita sociale e economica* {To Hell and back. For our social and economic rebirth}. Milan: Feltrinelli.

Cottarelli, Carlo and Alessandro De Nicola. 2019. *I dieci comandamenti dell'economia italiana* {The ten commandments of the Italian economy}. Catanzaro: Rubbettino Editore.

Cottarelli, Carlo and Giulio Gottardo. 2021. Previsioni su deficit, debito pubblico e aiuti europei nel 2021 {Forecasts on deficit, debt and European aid in 2021}. *Osservatorio sui Conti Pubblici Italiani*, 26 March. Available at www.osservatoriocpi.unicatt.it/cpi-Finanza_pubb_2021.pdf.

Cottarelli, Carlo and Federica Paudice. 2021. Perché il Covid-19 non è uguale per tutti {Why is Covid not the same for all countries?}. *Lavoce.info*, 27 April.

Council of Europe. 2020. *European Judicial Systems CEPEJ Report*. Available at www.rm.coe.int/evaluation-report-part-2-english/16809fc059.

Croce, Benedetto. 1925. *Storia del Regno di Napoli* {History of the Kingdom of Naples}. Bari: Laterza. Republished by Giuseppe Galasso (ed.). 1992. Milan: Adelphi.

Leiden CWTS (Centre for Science and Technology Studies). 2021. *Methodology*. Available at https://www.leidenranking.com/.

D'Alimonte, Roberto. 2021. Serve una legge elettorale per garantire governabilità senza tradire chi vota {A new electoral law is necessary to guarantee stability without betraying the voters}. *Il Sole 24 Ore*. 24 March.

D'Andrea, Silvia and Maria Rita Ebano. 2019. La competitività del sistema Italia secondo gli indicatori più noti di business climate {Competitiveness of Italy, according to the most well-known indicators of business climate}. *Ministero dell'Economia e delle Finanze. Note tematiche*, no.1, September.

Dasgupta, Dipankar. 2005. *Growth Theory, Solow and His Modern Exponents*. New Delhi: Oxford University Press.

Daveri, Francesco. 2006. *Innovazione cercasi. Il problema italiano* {Innovation wanted. The Italian problem}. Bari: Laterza.

De Blasio, Guido and Giorgio Nuzzo. 2006. The legacy of history for economic development: the case of Putnam's social capital. *Bank of Italy. Occasional Papers*, no. 116, May.

De Bortoli, Ferruccio. 2020. *Le cose che non ci diciamo (fino in fondo)* {The things we don't tell each other (all the way through)}. Milan: Garzanti.

De Giorgi, Fulvio, Angelo Gaudio, and Fabio Pruneri (eds). 2019. *Manuale di storia della scuola italiana* {Handbook of history of the Italian school}. Brescia: Scholé.

de Guindos, Luis. 2019. Growth and competitiveness in the euro area. *The European House— Ambrosetti Forum*, Cernobbio, 7 September. Available at https://www.ecb.europa.eu/press/key/date/2019/html/ecb.sp190907~81df41228e.en.html.

Debenedetti, Franco. 2004. Preface. In Mark Roe (ed.) *La public company e i suoi nemici* {The public company and its enemies}, pp. VII–XXVII. Milan: Il Sole 24 Ore.

Debenedetti, Franco. 2021. *Fare profitti. Etica dell'impresa* {Making profits. Ethics of the enterprise}. Venice: Marsilio Editore.

De Benedetti, Carlo and Federico Rampini. 2008. *Centomila punture di spillo, come l'Italia può tornare a crescere* {One hundred thousand pinpricks, how can Italy grow again}. Milan: Mondadori.

Degni, Marcello and Pasquale Ferro. 2016. *Il ritardo nei pagamenti nelle amministrazioni pubbliche* {Late payments in public administration}. Rome: Castelvecchi Lit Edizioni.

Dell'Aringa, Carlo and Paolo Guerrieri. 2019. *Inclusione, produttività, crescita. un' agenda per l'Italia* {Inclusion, productivity, growth. an agenda for italy}. Bologna: il Mulino.

Dell'Aringa, Carlo, Claudio Lucifora, and Tiziano Treu (eds). 2017. *Salari, produttività e diseguaglianze* {Wages, productivity, inequalities}. *AREL series*. Bologna: il Mulino.

Di Mascio, Fabrizio, Alessandro Natalini, and Edoardo Ongaro. 2021. Resilience without resistance: Public administration under mutating populisms in office in Italy. In Michael W. Bauer, B. Guy Peters, Jon Pierre, Kutsal Yesilkagit, and Stefan Becker (eds). *Democratic Backsliding and Public Administration: How Populists in Government Transform State Bureaucracies*, pp. 47–75. Cambridge: Cambridge University Press.

Drèze, Jean and Amartya Sen. 1995. *India: Economic Development and Social Opportunity*. Delhi: Oxford University Press.

Dustmann, Christian, Bernd Fitzenberger, Uta Schönberg, and Alexandra Spitz-Oener. 2014. From sick man of Europe to economic superstar: Germany's resurgence and the lessons for Europe. *VoxEU-CEPR*, 3 February. Available at https://voxeu.org/article/german-resurgence-it-wasn-t-hartz-reforms.

Dyson, Kenneth and Kevin Featherstone. 1999. *The Road to Maastricht: Negotiating Economic and Monetary Union*. Oxford: Oxford University Press.

Eichengreen, Barry. 2007. *The European Economy since 1945: Coordinated Capitalism and Beyond*. Princeton, NJ: Princeton University Press.

Emmott, Bill. 2013. *Good Italy, Bad Italy: Why Italy Must Conquer Its Demons to Face the Future*. New Haven, CT: Yale University Press.

Enriques, Luca. 2018. Related party transactions. In Jeffrey N. Gordon and Wolf-Georg Ringe (eds). *The Oxford Handbook of Corporate Law and Governance*, pp. 506–531. Oxford: Oxford University Press.

Ente, Einaudi. 1989. *Oltre la crisi* {Beyond the crisis}. Bologna: il Mulino.

Esposito, Piero, Stefan Collignon, and Sergio Scicchitano. 2020. The effect of immigration on unemployment in Europe: Does the core-periphery dualism matter? *Economic Modelling* 84: 249–258.

Eudoscopio. 2021. *Confronto, scelgo, studio*. Fondazione Agnelli. Available at www.eduscopio.it/.

European Agency for Safety and Health at Work. 2005. *Promoting Health and Safety in European SMEs*. Available at www.osha.europa.eu/en/publications/report-promoting-health-and-safety-european-small-and-medium-sized-enterprises-smes.

European Commission. 2008. The LIME assessment framework (LAF): A methodological tool to compare, in the context of the Lisbon Strategy, the performance of member states in terms of GDP and in terms of twenty policy areas affecting growth. *Occasional Paper 41*, October. Available at http://ec.europa.eu/economy_finance/publications/pages/publication_summary13273_en.htm.

European Commission. 2015. Completing Europe's Economic and Monetary Union [Also known as 'The Five Presidents Report']. Available at https://ec.europa.eu/info/publications/five-presidents-report-completing-europes-economic-and-monetary-union_en.

European Commission. 2018. *Performance-Based Funding of University Research*. Available at https://eur-lex.europa.eu/legal-content/EN/TXT/PDF/?uri=CELEX:52021SC0165&from=EN.

European Commission. 2020a. *The Digital Economy and Society Index (Desi)*. Available at www.digital-strategy.ec.europa.eu/en/policies/desi.

European Commission. 2020b. *Study and Report on the VAT Gap in the EU-28 Member States*. Available at www.ec.europa.eu/taxation_customs/sites/taxation/files/vat-gap-full-report-2020_en.pdf.

European Commission. 2020c. Staff working document, *Country Report Italy* 2020. SWD (2020) 511 final. Available at https://eur-lex.europa.eu/legal-content/EN/TXT/PDF/?uri=CELEX:52020SC0511&from=EN.

European Commission. 2021a. Commission staff working document, analysis of the recovery and resilience plan of Italy. *SWD*, 165 final. Available at https://eur-lex.europa.eu/legal-content/EN/TXT/PDF/?uri=CELEX:52021SC0165&from=EN.

European Commission. 2021b. *Recovery and Resilience Plan for Italy*. Available at https://ec.europa.eu/info/business-economy-euro/recovery-coronavirus/recovery-and-resilience-facility/italys-recovery-and-resilience-plan_en.

Fabiani, Silvia, Alberto Felettigh, Claire Giordano, and Roberto Torrini. 2019. Making room for new competitors. A comparative perspective on Italy's exports in the euro-area market. *Bank of Italy. Questioni di economia e finanza*, no. 530.

Faini, Matteo. 2021. *Spies and Their Masters*. London: Routledge.

Faini, Riccardo, Giampaolo Galli, and Curzio Giannini. 1993. Finance and development: The case of Southern Italy. In Alberto Giovannini (ed.) *Finance and Development*, pp. 158–213. Cambridge, MA: Cambridge University Press.

Faini, Riccardo, Giampaolo Galli, Pietro Gennari, and Fulvio Rossi. 1997. An empirical puzzle: Falling migration and growing unemployment differentials among Italian regions. *European Economic Review* 41(3): 571–579.

Fatas, Antonio. 2018. Lost decades: Italy 3- Japan 0. *VoxEU*, 16 June.

Fauzi, Muhammad Ashraf, Christine Nya-Ling Tan, Mahyuddin Daud, and Muhammad Mukhtar Noor Awalludin. 2020. University rankings: a review of methodological flaws. *Issues in Educational Research* 30(1): 79–96.

Favero, Luca and Alessandro Stella. 2021. Valorizzazione merito docenti in Italia: il quadro attuale {Rewarding teachers on merit in Italy: The present situation}. *Osservatorio sui Conti Pubblici*. 3 December. Available at https://osservatoriocpi.unicatt.it/ocpi-Valorizzazione%20docenti-OCPI.pdf.

Featherstone, Kevin. 2001. The political dynamics of the Vincolo Esterno: The emergence of EMU and the challenge to the European Social Model. *Queen's Papers on Europeanisation no. 6/2001*.

Federico, Stefano and Claire Giordano. 2021. Beneath the surface: Investigating industry heterogeneity. *Bank of Italy. Occasional Papers* no. 641, October 2021.

Feenstra, Robert, Robert Inklaar, and Marcel P. Timmer. 2015. The next generation of the Penn World Table. *American Economic Review* 105(10): 3150–3182. Available at www.ggdc.net/pwt.

Felice, Emanuele. 2013. *Perché il Sud é rimasto indietro* {Why the South has stayed behind}. Bologna: il Mulino.

Felice, Emanuele. 2015. *Ascesa e declino. Storia economica d'Italia* {Rise and fall. Economic history of Italy}. Bologna: il Mulino.

Filosa, Renato and Ignazio Visco. 1977. L' unificazione del valore del punto di contingenza e il grado di indicizzazione delle retribuzioni {The unification of the inflation catch up and the indexation of wages}, *Moneta e Credito* 30(117): 55–83.

Fondazione Edison. 2019. *The Italian Economy in Figures.* Available at www.fondazioneedison.it/en/news/the-italian-economy-in-figures.

Fortis, Marco. 2009. *La crisi mondiale e l'Italia* {The world crisis and Italy}. Bologna: il Mulino.

Fortis, Marco and Alberto Quadrio Curzio (eds). 2006. *Industria e Distretti, un paradigma di perdurante competitività italiana* {Industry and Districts, a paradigm of enduring Italian competitiveness}. Bologna: il Mulino.

Fortunato, Giustino. 1911. *Il Mezzogiorno e lo stato italiano; discorsi politici (1880–1910)* {Mezzogiorno and the Italian state: Political speeches (1880–1910)}, Vol. 2. Bari: Laterza.

Foschi, Marta. 1996. Double standards in the evaluation of men and women. *Social Psychology Quarterly* 59 (3) Special Issue: Gender and Social Interaction: pp. 237–254, September.

Franzini, Maurizio. 2018. *Disuguaglianza economica, immobilità sociale e crescita stagnante: possibili legami tra i malesseri italiani* {Economic inequality, lack of social mobility and stagnant growth: Possible links between Italian ailments}. Milan: FrancoAngeli.

Frattola, Edoardo. 2020. La giustizia italiana è davvero sottofinanziata? {Is the Italian judiciary really underfinanced?}. *Osservatorio sui Conti Pubblici Italiani*, 18 March.

Fubini, Federico. 2014. *Recessione Italia. Come usciamo dalla crisi più lunga della storia* {Italy's Recession. how we get out of the longest crisis in history}. Bari: Laterza.

Galli, Giampaolo (ed.). 1996. *La mobilità della società italiana* {Mobility of Italian society}. Rome: SIPI.

Galli, Giampaolo. 2010. La bassa crescita: i fatti e le letture {Low growth: Facts and interpretations}. In Giuseppe Ciccarone, Maurizio Franzini, and Enrico Saltari (eds). *L'Italia possibile, equità e crescita* {Italy, possibility of equity and growth}, pp. 193–206. Milan: Francesco Brioschi Editore.

Galli, Giampaolo, Alberto Quadrio Curzio, and Marco Fortis (eds). 2002. *La competitività dell'Italia* {Italy's competitiveness}, Vol. I: *Scienza, ricerca, innovazione* {Science, research, innovation}. Milan: Il Sole 24 Ore.

Galli, Giampaolo, Luigi Paganetto (eds). 2002. *La competitività dell'Italia* {Italy's competitiveness}, Vol. II: *Le imprese.* Milan: Il Sole 24 Ore.

Galli, Giampaolo, Mario Baldassarri, and Gustavo Piga (eds). 2002. *La competitività dell'Italia* {Italy's competitiveness}, Vol. III: *Regole per il mercato* {Rules for the markets}. Milan: Il Sole 24 Ore.

Galli, Giampaolo and Jacques Pelkmans (eds). 2000. *Regulatory Reform and Competitiveness in Europe.* Edward Elgar Publishing.

Galli, Giampaolo and Sabino Cassese (eds). 1998. *L'Italia da semplificare: Le istituzioni* {Italy to be simplified: institutions}. Bologna: Il Mulino.

Galli, Giampaolo and Giulio Gottardo. 2020a. La distribuzione della spesa pubblica per macroregioni {The distribution of public expenditures among macro-regions}. *Osservatorio dei Conti Pubblici.* 26 September. Available at https://osservatoriocpi.unicatt.it/cpi-Distribuzione%20spesa.pdf.

Galli, Giampaolo and Giulio Gottardo. 2020b. La mancata convergenza del Mezzogiorno {The failed convergence of the Mezzogiorno}. *Osservatorio dei Conti Pubblici*, 10 February. Available at https://osservatoriocpi.unicatt.it/cpi-Mancata%20convergenza.pdf.

Galli, Giampaolo, and Giulio Gottardo. 2020c. Divari territoriali e conti pubblici {Regional gaps and public accounts}. *Osservatorio dei Conti Pubblici*, 27 October. Available at https://osservatoriocpi.unicatt.it/cpi-Divari_contipubb.pdf.

Galli, Giampaolo and Marco Onado (eds). 1990. *Il sistema finanzario nel Mezzogiorno* {The financial sytem in the Mezzogiorno}. *Bank of Italy. Special Issue.*

Galli, Giampaolo and Giacomo Ricciardi. 2021. Le univesità italiane nelle classifiche internazionali {Italian universities in international rankings}. *Osservatorio sui Conti Pubblici Italiani*,

17 December. Available at https://osservatoriocpi.unicatt.it/ocpi-pubblicazioni-le-universita-italiane-nelle-classifiche-internazionali.

Galli Giampaolo, Giorgio Musso, and Francesco Tucci. 2021a. Esiste un legame fra Pil e felicità? {Is there a link between GDP and happiness?}. *Osservatorio sui Conti Pubblici*. 15 June. Available at https://osservatoriocpi.unicatt.it/ocpi-pubblicazioni-esiste-un-legame-tra-pil-e-felicita.

Galli, Giampaolo, Luca Favero, and Giacomo Ricciardi. 2021b. Non è un paese per giovani {It is not a country for the young}. *Osservatorio sui Conti Pubblici*. 3 December. Available at https://osservatoriocpi.unicatt.it/ocpi-pubblicazioni-non-e-un-paese-per-giovani.

Gardner, Richard. 2005. *Mission: Italy, on the Front Lines of the Cold War*. Washington, DC: Rowman & Littlefield.

Gaskarth, Glynn. 2014. The Hartz reforms . . . and their lesson for the UK. *Centre for Policy Studies*, October. Available at https://www.bl.uk/collection-items/hartz-reforms—and-their-lessons-for-the-uk.

Gatteschi, Silvia. 2018. L'andamento del debito dopo la stretta fiscale del 2012 {The trend of debt after the fiscal restraint of 2012}. *Osservatorio sui Conti Pubblici dell'Università Cattolica*. 20 June. Available at https://osservatoriocpi.unicatt.it/.

Gavosto, Andrea. 2019. Investire in istruzione {Investing in education}. In Carlo Dell'Aringa and Paolo Guerrieri (eds). *Inclusione, produttività, crescita. un' agenda per l'Italia* {Inclusion, productivity, growth. an agenda for Italy}, pp. 567–597. Bologna: il Mulino.

Gavosto, Andrea. 2021a. Negli apprendimenti scolastici abbiamo perso tutti {In school learning we all lost out}. *Lavoce.info*. 23 February.

Gavosto, Andrea. 2021b. La paradossale vicenda della Buona Scuola {The paradoxical story of the Good School}. *Nuovi Lavori*. 1 June. Available at http://www.nuovi-lavori.it/index.php/sezioni/1248-la-paradossale-vicenda-della-buona-scuola.

Giacomelli, Silvia, Sauro Mocetti, Giuliana Palumbo, and Giacomo Rome. 2017. La giustizia civile in Italia: le recenti evoluzioni {Civil justice in Italy: Recent developments}. *Bank of Italy. Questioni di economia e finanza*, no. 401.

Giannini, Silvia and Paolo Onofri (eds). 2005. *Per lo sviluppo. Fisco e welfare* {For growth. Taxation and welfare}. Bologna: il Mulino.

Giavazzi, Francesco. 2005. *Lobby d'Italia* {Lobbies of Italy}. Milan: RCS Rizzoli.

Giavazzi, Francesco and Marco Pagano. 1988. The advantage of tying one's hands: EMS discipline and Central Bank credibility. *European Economic Review* 24: 1055–1082.

Gilardoni, Andrea, Stefano Clerici, and Alessandra Garzarella. 2011. *Infrastrutture e sviluppo* {Infrastructure and development}. Milan: Agici Finanza d'Impresa.

Giorgiantonio, Cristina, Tommaso Orlando, Giuliana Palumbo, and Lucia Rizzica. 2016. Incentivi e selezione nel pubblico impiego. {Incentives and selection in the public sector}. *Bank of Italy. Questioni di economia e finanza*, no. 342.

Giunta, Anna and Salvatore Rossi. 2017. *Che cosa sa fare l'Italia. La nostra economia dopo la grande crisi* {What Italy can do. Our economy after the great crisis}. Bari: Laterza.

Golden, A. Miriam and Lucio Picci. 2005. Proposal for a new measure of corruption, illustrated with Italian data. *Economics and Politics* 17(1). Available at www.onlinelibrary.wiley.com/doi/epdf/10.1111/j.1468-0343.2005.00146.x.

Goldstein, Andrea (ed.) 2018. *Agenda Italia 2023* {Italy's Agenda 2023}. Bologna: il Mulino.

Gramsci, Antonio. 1916. La questione meridionale e la guerra {The Southern question and the war}. In Franco De Felice and Valentino Parlato (eds). 1966. *La questione meridionale*. Rome: Editori Riuniti. Available at www.archive.org/details/AntonioGramsci LaQuestioneMeridionale/mode/2up?view=theater.

Graziani, Augusto. 2020. *Mercato, struttura, conflitto. Scritti su economia italiana e Mezzogiorno* {Markets, structure, conflict. Papers on the Italian economy and the Mezzogiorno}. *Collana Studi e Ricerche Svimez*. Bologna: il Mulino.

Grilli, Luca, Paul H. Jensen, and Samuele Murtinu. 2014. *The Imprinting of Founders' Human Capital on Entrepreneurial Venture Growth: Evidence from New Technology-based Firms*. June. Available at www.ssrn.com/abstract=2456721.

Grillo, Michele (ed.). 1996. L'autorità garante della concorrenza e del mercato tra tutela della concorrenza e politica industriale {The antitrust authority between competition and industrial policies}. *Economia e Politica Industriale* 23: 167–181.

Gros, Daniel. 2013. Learning from Germany. *Project Syndicate*. 5 March. Available at https://www.project-syndicate.org/commentary/the-limits-of-the-german-model-for-europe-s-periphery-by-daniel-gros?barrier=accesspaylog.

Guiso, Luigi, Herrera Helios, Morelli Massimo, and Sonno Tommaso. 2019. Global crises and populism: The role of Eurozone institutions. *Economic Policy* 34: 95–139.

Guiso Luigi, Paola Sapienza, and Luigi Zingales. 2004a. Does local financial development matter? *Quarterly Journal of Economics* 119(3): 929–969.

Guiso, Luigi, Paola Sapienza, and Luigi Zingales. 2004b. The role of social capital in financial development. *American Economic Review* 94(3): 526–556.

Hayek, Friedrich A. 1978. *New Studies in Philosophy, Politics, Economics and the History of Ideas.* Chicago, IL: University of Chicago Press.

Helliwell, John, Richard Layard, Jeffrey D. Sachs, Jan-Emmanuel De Neve, Lara Aknin, and Shun Wang. 2021. *World Happiness Report 2021*. Available at www.worldhappiness.report/ed/2021/.

Hildebrand, H. George. 1965. *Growth and Structure in the Economy of Modern Italy.* Cambridge, MA: Harvard University Press.

Ichino, Andrea and Guido Tabellini. 2015. Freeing the Italian school system. *Labor Economics* 30(C): 113–128.

Ichino, Andrea and Daniele Terlizzese. 2013. *Facoltà di scelta* {Free to choose a university}. Milan: Rizzoli.

Ichino, Pietro. 1982. *Il collocamento impossibile* {Impossible placemenent}. Bari: De Donato.

Ichino, Pietro. 2005. *A cosa serve il sindacato?* {What is trades union for?}. Milan: Mondadori.

Ichino, Pietro. 2015. *Il lavoro ritrovato* {Jobs rediscovered}. Milan: Mondadori Editori.

Ichino, Pietro. 2018. Lavoro: l'Italia ritorna in mezzo al guado {Labour: Italy back to square one}. *Lavoce.info*, 28 October.

Ichino, Pietro. 2020. *L'intelligenza del lavoro* {The intelligence of work}. Milan: Rizzoli.

ILO (International Labour Organization). 2020. *Improving Safety and Health in Micro, Small and Medium-Sized Enterprises.* Available at https://www.ilo.org/global/topics/safety-and-health-at-work/resources-library/publications/WCMS_740304/lang--en/index.htm.

Ingrao, Bruna and Giorgio Israel. 1990. *The Invisible Hand: Economic Equilibrium in the History of Science.* Cambridge, MA: MIT Press.

INVALSI. 2019. *Sintesi dei risultati italiani dei test Pisa 2018* {Summary of Italy's results in PISA tests}. 3 December. Available at www.invalsiopen.it/wp-content/uploads/2019/12/Sintesi-dei-risultati-italiani-OCSE-PISA-2018.pdf.

Ipsos Mori. 2019. *Trust: The Truth?* Available at https://www.ipsos.com/sites/default/files/ct/publication/documents/2019-09/ipsos-thinks-trust-the-truth.pdf.

ISTAT (Italian Statistical Office). 2020a. Rapporto Annuale 2020 {Annual report 2020}. 3 July. Available at https://www.istat.it/en/archivio/247100.

ISTAT (Italian Statistical Office). 2020b. Misure della produttività. {Measures of productivity} 4 November.

ISTAT (Italian Statistical Office). 2021a. Iscrizioni e cancellazioni anagrafiche della popolazione residente, Anno 2019 {Entries and cancellations of resident population. Year 2019}. 20 January. Available at https://www.istat.it/it/archivio/252732.

ISTAT (Italian Statistical Office). 2021b. Commercio estero e atttività internazionale delle imprese, 2021 {Foreign trade and international activities of companies, 2021}. 16 July. Available at https://annuarioistatice.istat.it/index.html.

Italian government. 2021. *Piano Nazionale di Ripresa e Resilienza* {National Recovery and Resilience Plan}. Available at https://www.governo.it/sites/governo.it/files/PNRR.pdf

Jensen, C. Michael and William H. Meckling. 1976. Theory of the firm: Managerial behavior, agency costs and ownership structure. *Journal of Financial Economics* 3/4, October: 305–360.

Jones, I. Charles. 2002. *Introduction to Economic Growth.* New York: W.W. Norton and Company.

Jones, I. Charles. 2020. *Macroeconomics* (International edn). New York: W.W. Norton and Company.

Kaczorek, Sibylle. 2019. European crisis: Germany and the role of the trade unions. *Greenleft Weekly*. 10 November. Available at https://www.greenleft.org.au/content/european-crisis-germany-and-role-trade-unions.

Keefer, Philip and Stuti Khemani. 2005. Democracy, public expenditure, and the poor: Understanding political incentives for providing public services. *The World Bank Research Observer* 20(1): 1–27, Oxford University Press.

Krebs, Toma and Martin Scheffel. 2013. German labour reforms: Unpopular success, *VOX CEPR*, 20 September. Available at https://voxeu.org/article/german-labour-reforms-unpopular-success.

Krueger, Allan. 2012. *The Rise and Consequences of Inequality in the United States*. Council of Economic Advisors, 12 January. Available at https://obamawhitehouse.archives.gov/sites/default/files/krueger_cap_speech_final_remarks.pdf.

Legatum Institute. 2019. *The Legatum Prosperity Index Methodology Report*. Available at www.prosperity.com/about/resources.

Legatum Institute. 2020. *The Legatum Prosperity Index*. Available at www.prosperity.com/about/resources.

Leo XIII. 1891. *Rerum Novarum*. Available at www.vatican.va/content/leo-xiii/en/encyclicals/documents/hf_l-xiii_enc_15051891_rerum-novarum.html.

Leonardi, Marco. 2018. *Le riforme dimezzate* {The reforms halved}. Milan: EGEA Bocconi University Press.

Leonardi, Marco and Tommaso Nannicini. 2018. I principi del Jobs Act e una breve valutazione {The principles of the Jobs Act and a brief evaluation}. *Economia Italiana* 2/3: 109–121.

Leone, Davide. 2020. *Storia delle riforme costituzionali italiane*. {History of constitutional reforms in Italy}. 7 October. Polimathes. Available at https://www.polimathes.com/caffe-lettere/storia-delle-riforme-costituzional.

Letta, Enrico. 2021. *Anima e cacciavite* {Soul and screwdriver}. Milan: Solferino.

Leythienne, Denis and Marina Pèrez-Julian. 2021. *Gender Pay Gaps in the European Union. A Statistical Analysis*. Eurostat. September.

Liaci, Salvatore. 2021. Gli stipendi e la carriera degli insegnanti: un confronto fra l'Italia e gli altri paesi {Salaries and careers of teachers: A comparison between Italy and other countries}. *Osservatorio sui Conti Pubblici*. 20 July. Available at https://osservatoriocpi.unicatt.it/ocpi-Carrierainsegnanti.pdf.

Lippi, Francesco and Fabiano Schivardi. 2014. Corporate control and executive selection. *Quantitative Economics* 5(2): 417–456.

Lotti, Francesca, and Enrico Sette. 2019. Frontier and Superstar Firms in Italy. *Bank of Italy. Questioni di economia e finanza*.

Lutz, Vera. 1963. *Italy—A Study in Economic Development*. Il Politico, Vol. 28, no. 4, December. Soveria Mannelli (Catanzaro): Rubbettino Editore.

Macchiati, Alfredo. 2016. *Perché l'Italia cresce poco* {Why italy grows slowly}. Bologna: il Mulino.

Maes, Ivo and Lucia Quaglia. 2003. The process of European Monetary Integration: A comparison of the Belgian and Italian approaches. *BNL Quarterly Review*. Banca Nazionale del Lavoro, vol. 56(227), pages 299–335.

Maltese, Curzio. 2006. *Come ti sei ridotto. Modesta proposta di sopravvivenza al declino della nazione* {How much you have declined. modest proposal to survive the nation's decline}. Milan: Feltrinelli.

Mandler, Peter. 2020. *The Crisis of Meritocracy, Britain's Transition to Mass Education since the Second World War*. Oxford: Oxford University Press.

Manzoni, Alessandro. 1984. *The Betrothed: I Promessi Sposi*. London: Penguin Classics. [First published in Italian in 1825.]

Markovits, Daniel. 2019. *The Meritocracy Trap*. London: Allen Lane.

Mayer, Thierry and Gianmarco Ottaviano. 2008. The happy few: The internationalisation of European firms. New facts based on firm-level evidence. *Intereconomics* 43. Available at www.doi.org/10.1007/s10272-008-0247-x.

Menand, Louis. *2019*. Is Meritocracy Making Everyone Miserable? *The New Yorker*, 30 September.

Merler, Silvia. 2021. *La pecora nera, l'Italia di oggi e l'Eurozona* {The black sheep, today's Italy and the Eurozone}. Milan: Bocconi University Press.

Messori, Marcello, Pier Carlo Padoan, and Nicola Rossi. 1998. *Proposte per l'Economia Italiana* {Proposals for the Italian economy}. Bari: Laterza.

Micossi, Stefano. 2016. The glass is still half-empty: Eurozone stability under threat of a 'bad shock'. *VoxEU*, 20 August. Available at https://voxeu.org/article/eurozone-stability-still-under-threat-bad-shock.

Micossi, Stefano and Paola Parascandolo. 2010. Impresa privata {Private company}. In Pinelli, Cesare and Tiziano Treu (eds). *La Costituzione economica: Italia, Europa* {The economic Constitution; Italy, Europe}. Bologna: Il Mulino.

Micozzi, Alessandra. 2013. Factors affecting the entrepreneurial dynamics in Italy: A comparison across European countries. *Economia Marche Journal of Applied Economics* 32(1): 79–94.

Mieli, Paolo. 2017. *Il caos italiano* {Italian chaos}. Milan: Rizzoli.

Mingardi, Alberto (ed.). 2008. *Cartello a perdere, assicurazioni, antitrust, e scambio d'informazioni* {Losers' cartel, insurance, antitrust, and exchange of information}. Soveria Mannelli (Catanzaro): Rubbettino Editore.

Mingardi, Alberto. 2019. *La verità, vi prego, sul neoliberismo* {The truth, please, on neoliberalism}. Venice: Marsilio.

Ministero dell'Economia e delle Finanze. various years. *Documento di economia e finanza* {Economic and financial documentation}. Available at https://www.mef.gov.it/documenti-pubblicazioni/doc-finanza-pubblica/index.html.

Ministero dell'Economia e delle Finanze. various years. *Relazione sull'economia non osservata e sull'evasione fiscale e contributiva* {Report on non-observed economy and evasion of taxes and social security contributions}. Available at https://www.mef.gov.it/ministero/commissioni/rel_ev/index.html.

Ministero dell'Istruzione. 2020. *Focus 'Esiti degli Esami di stato nella scuola secondaria di II grado' Anno Scolastico 2018–2019*. March. Available at https://www.miur.gov.it/pubblicazioni/-/asset_publisher/6Ya1FS4E4QJw/content/focus-esiti-degli-esami-di-stato-nella-scuola-secondaria-di-ii-grado--1.

Mistretta, Alessandro, and Francesco Zollino. 2018. Recent trends in economic activity and TFP in Italy with a focus on embodied technical progress. *Bank of Italy. Temi di discussione*, no. 1204. Available at https://www.bancaditalia.it/pubblicazioni/temi-discussione/2018/2018-1204/index.html?com.dotmarketing.htmlpage.language=1.

Modigliani, Franco and Tommaso Padoa-Schioppa. 1978. *The Management of an Open Economy with '100%+' Wage Indexation*. Essays in International Finance, no. 130, December. Princeton, NJ: Princeton University Press.

Modigliani, Franco and Paolo Peluffo. 1999, *Le avventure di un economista* {The adventures of an economist}. Bari: Laterza.

Mody, Ashoka and Emily Riley. 2014. *Why Does Italy Not Grow?* Bruegel Blog, 10 October. Available at https://www.bruegel.org/2014/10/why-does-italy-not-grow/.

Montessori, Maria. 1992. *Address by Dr. Maria Montessori at the First (Preliminary) Meeting of the Governing Board (Wiesbaden, 19 June 1951, translated from the German original)*, delivered at the 40th Anniversary of the UNESCO Institute for Education, pp. 49–50.

Monti, Mario. 2012. *Le parole e i fatti* {The words and the facts}. Milan: Rizzoli.

Morando, Enrico. 2010. *Riformisti e comunisti* {Reformers and communists}. Rome: Donzelli.

Moyo, Dambisa. 2018. *Edge of Chaos: Why Democracy Is Failing to Deliver Economic Growth—and How to Fix It*. New York. Basic Books.

Musso, Giorgio. 2020. Debito pubblico: quanto ne ha acquistato, quanto ne avrebbe dovuto acquistare e quanto ne acquisterà la BCE {Public debt: How much has been purchased, how much should have been purchased and how much will be purchased by the ECB}. *Osservatorio sui Conti Pubblici*. 27 November. Available at https://osservatoriocpi.unicatt.it/cpi-cpi-DebitoBCE.pdf.

Nannicini, Tommaso. 2011. *Non ci resta che crescere. Riforme: chi vince, chi perde, come farle* {We have no choice but to grow. Reform: Who wins, who loses, how to do it}. Milan: Bocconi University Press.

National Research Council. 2012. *Aging and the Macroeconomy: Long-Term Implications of an Older Population*. Washington, DC: The National Academies Press. Available at https://doi.org/10.17226/13465.

Nifo, Annamaria and Gaetano Vecchione. 2015. Measuring institutional quality in Italy. *Rivista Economica del Mezzogiorno* 1(2): 157–181. Bologna: il Mulino.

Nitti, Francesco Saverio. 1900. *Nord e sud* {North and south}. Turin/Rome: Casa Editrice Nazionale Roux e Viarengo.

North, Douglas. 1990. *Institutions, Institutional Change and Economic Performance*. Cambridge: Cambridge University Press.

Nouri, Abdul and Roland Gerard. 2020. Identity politics and populism in Europe. *Annual Review of Political Science 23*: 421–439. February.

Occhilupo, Roberta and Lucia Rizzica. 2016. Incentivi e valutazione dei dirigenti pubblici in Italia {Incentives and evaluation of public managers in Italy}. *Bank of Italy. Questioni di economia e finanza*, no. 310/16. Available at https://www.bancaditalia.it/pubblicazioni/qef/2016-0310/index.html.

OECD. 2011. *Divided We Stand: Why Inequality Keeps Rising*. Paris: OECD.

OECD. 2018. *The Role and Design of Net Wealth Taxes in the OECD*. OECD Tax Policy Studies, no. 26. Paris: OECD Publishing.

OECD. 2020 and various years. *Education at a Glance*. Paris: OECD.

OECD. 2021. *Does Inequality Matter? How People Perceive Economic Disparities and Social Mobility*. November. Available at https://www.oecd-ilibrary.org/social-issues-migration-health/does-inequality-matter_3023ed40-en.

Olensky, Marlies, Marion Schmidt, and Nees Jan Van Eck. 2016. Evaluation of the citation matching algorithms of CWTS and iFQ in comparison to Web of Science. *Journal of the Association for Information Science and Technology 67(10)*: 2550–2564.

Olson, Mancur. 1984. *The Rise and Decline of Nations: Economic Growth, Stagflation, and Social Rigidities*. New Haven, CT: Yale University Press.

Onofri, Paolo. 2001. *Un'economia sbloccata* {An unlocked economy}. Bologna: il Mulino.

Onofri, Paolo. 2016. *il grande sconvolgimento. rischi di stagnazione, tecnologia, istituzioni politiche* {The great disruption. The risks of stagnation, technology, political institutions}. Bologna: il Mulino.

Osservatorio sui Conti Pubblici Italiani. 2021. *La qualità delle istituzioni pubbliche nelle province italiane* {The quality of public institutions in Italian provinces}. Available at https://www.provinceditalia.it/wp-content/uploads/2021/06/cpi-IQI_OCPI.pdf.

Padoa Schioppa Kostoris, Fiorella. 1993. *Italy, the Sheltered Economy, Structural Problems in the Italian Economy*. New York: Clarendon Press.

Padoa-Schioppa, Tommaso. 2007. *Italia, una ambizione timida. Classe dirigente e rischi di declino* {Italy, a timid ambition. Leadership and risks of decline}. Milan: RCS Rizzoli.

Padoan, Piercarlo. 2019. *Il sentiero stretto . . . e oltre* {The narrow path . . . and beyond}. Bologna: il Mulino.

Paganetto, Luigi (ed.). 2011. *Ripresa dopo la crisi?* {Recovery after the crisis?} Rome: Eurilink Edizioni.

Paganetto, Luigi (ed.). 2014. *Report of the Group of 20. Revitalizing Anaemic Europe*. Rome: Eurilink Edizioni.

Pammolli, Fabio, Carlo Cambini, and Andrea Giannaccari (eds). 2007. *Politiche di liberalizzazione e concorrenza in Italia* {Policies of liberalisation and competition in Italy}. Bologna: il Mulino.

Panci, Massimiliano. 2014. Collocamento {Placement}. *Istituto Treccani*. Available at www.treccani.it/enciclopedia/collocamento_(Diritto-on-line)/.

Panebianco, Angelo and Sergio Belardinelli. 2019. *All' alba di un nuovo mondo* {At the start of a new world}. Bologna: il Mulino.

Parlamento Italiano. 2021. *La costituzione: riforme* {The constitution: Reforms}. Available at https://piattaformacostituzione.camera.it/4?scheda_contenuto=7.

Pavone, Claudio. 1995. *Alle origini della Repubblica. Scritti su fascismo, antifascismo e continuità dello Stato* {On the origins of the Republic. Essays on fascism antifascism and the continuity of the state}. Turin: Bollati Boringhieri Editore.

Pellegrino, Bruno and Luigi Zingales. 2017. Diagnosing the Italian disease. *VoxEU*. 28 November. Available at www.voxeu.org/article/diagnosing-italian-disease#:~:text=Italy%20stands%20out%20among%20developed,abruptly%20stopped%20growing%20around%201995.

Pellegrino, Bruno and Luigi Zingales 2019. Diagnosing the Italian disease. *NBER Working Paper*, no. 23964, October 2017, revised May 2019.

Perotti, Roberto. 2016. *Status Quo. Perché in Italia è così difficile cambiare le cose (e come cominciare a farlo)* {Status quo. Why is it so difficult to change things in Italy (and how to start doing it)}. Milan: Feltrinelli.

Persson, Torsten and Guido Tabellini. 2005. *The Economic Effects of Constitutions*. Cambridge, MA: MIT Press.

PEW Research Center. 2021. *Public Trust in Government: 1958–2021*. Available at https://www.pewresearch.org/politics/2021/05/17/public-trust-in-government-1958-2021/.

Phelps, Edmund. 2002. *Enterprise and Inclusion in Italy*. Norwell, MA: Kluwer Academic Publishers.

Phelps, Edmund. 2015. *Mass Flourishing*. Princeton, NJ: Princeton University Press.

Phelps, Edmund, Raicho Bojilov, Hian Teck Hoon, and Gylfi Zoega. 2020. *Dynamism*. Cambridge, MA: Harvard University Press.

Pirrone, Salvatore and Paolo Sestito. 2006. *Disoccupati in Italia* {Unemployed in Italy}. Bologna: Il Mulino.

Pisani-Ferry, Jean. 2018. The upheaval Italy needs. *Social Europe*. 2 May.

Pombeni, Paolo. 2015. Closing the Account with the Past. Clemency Measures: Amnesties and Reprieves (1946–1953). In *Pombeni (ed), The Historiography of Transition: Critical Phases in the Development of Modernity (1494–1973)*. London: Routledge.

Prodi, Romano. 2021. *Strana vita, la mia* {My strange life}. Milan: Solferino.

Prosperetti, Giulio. 2019. *Ripensiamo lo stato sociale* {Rethinking the welfare state}. Milan: Wolters Kluwer-Cedam.

Puleo, Renata. 2020. *L'etica della Fondazione Agnelli e di Eduscopio in piena pandemia*. 23 November. Available at www.roars.it/.

Putnam, D. Robert. 1993. *Making Democracy Work, Civil Traditions in Modern Italy*. Princeton, NJ: Princeton University Press.

Putnam, D. Robert. 1995. Bowling alone: America's declining social capital. *Journal of Democracy* 6(1): 65–78.

Putnam, D. Robert and F. John Helliwell. 1995. Social capital and economic growth in Italy. *Eastern Economic Journal* 21: 295–307.

Pyke Frank, Giacomo Becattini, and Werner Sengenberger (eds). 1990. *Industrial Districts and Inter-Firm Co-operation in Italy*. Geneva: International Institute for Labour Studies.

Quintieri, Beniamino (ed.). 2006. *I distretti industriali dal locale al globale* {Industrial districts from local to global}. Soveria Mannelli (Catanzaro): Rubbettino Editore.

QS. 2021. *Quacquarelli Symonds World University Rankings*. Available at www.topuniversities.com/.

Ravazzoni, Roberto. 2010. *Liberare la Concorrenza. Lo stato dell'arte delle liberalizzazioni nel terziario in Italia* {Free the competition. The state of the art of liberalization in the service sector in Italy}. Milan: EGEA Bocconi University Press.

Regione Emilia-Romagna. 2019. Commissione speciale di ricerca e di studio sulle cooperative cosiddette spurie o fittizie. Relazione Conclusiva {Special study commission on spurious or fictitious cooperatives. *Final Report*}. Available at http://www.manuelarontini.it/false-cooperative-come-stanarle-dalla-regione-arriva-una-serie-di-indicatori/.

Reichlin, Pietro. 2018. Vecchi vizi dietro il vento del cambiamento {Old vices behind the appearance of change}. *Il Sole 24 Ore*. 4 October.

Reporters Without Borders. 2021. *World Free Press Index*. Available at https://rsf.org/en.

Rizzica, Lucia, and Marco Tonello. 2015. Exposure to Media and Corruption, *Bank of Italy. Working Papers*, no. 1043, November.

Rodrick, Dani. 2014. The past, present, and future of economic growth. *Challenge* 57(3): 5–39.

Roe, J. Mark. 2000. Political preconditions to separating ownership from control. *Columbia Law School, Working Paper*, no. 155, 21 January.

Roe, J. Mark. 2003. Political determinants of corporate governance. Harvard Law School. *Discussion Paper*, no. 451. Available at papers.ssrn.com/sol3/papers.cfm?abstract_id=472366.

Roemer, E. John. 1998. *Equality of Opportunity*. Cambridge, MA: Harvard University Press.

Rossi, Salvatore. 2006. *La regina e il cavallo. quattro mosse contro il declino* {The queen and the horse. four moves against decline}. Bari: Laterza.

Rossi, Salvatore. 2009. *Controtempo. L'Italia nella Crisi mondiale* {Countertime. Italy in the World Crisis}. Bari: Laterza.

Rossi, Salvatore. 2020. *La politica economica italiana dal 1968 a oggi* {Italian economic policy from 1968 to today}. Bari: Laterza. [1st edn: 1998].

Rothstein, Bo. 2011. *Quality of Government. Corruption, Social Trust, and Inequality in International Prospective*. Chicago, IL: University of Chicago Press.

Rotondi, Zeno (ed.). 2013. *Filiere produttive e nuova globalizzazione* {Supply chains and new globalisation}. Bari: Laterza.

Sadun, Arrigo (ed.). 2011. *Italy in the International Economy since the Second World War*. Soveria Mannelli (Catanzaro): Rubbettino.

Sallusti, Alessandro and Luca Palamara. 2021. *Il sistema. Potere, politica, affari: storia segreta della magistratura italiana* {The system. Power, politics, business: The secret story of Italian judiciary}. Milan: Rizzoli.

Saltari, Enrico and Giuseppe Travaglini. 2006. *Le radici del declino economico. Occupazione e produttività in Italia nell'ultimo decennio* {The roots of economic decline. Employment and productivity in Italy in the last decade}. Novara: De Agostini.

Salvati, Michele and Norberto Dilmore. 2021. *Liberalismo inclusivo: Un futuro auspicabile per il nostro angolo di mondo* {Inclusive liberalism: A desirable future for our corner of the world}. Milan: Feltrinelli.

Salvemini, Gaetano. 1955. *Scritti sulla Questione Meridionale, 1896–1955* {Writings on the Southern Question, 1896–1955}. Turin: Einaudi.

Sandel, J. Michael. 2020. *The Tyranny of Merit: What's Become of the Common Good?* London: Penguin Books.

Santambrogio, Marco. 2021. *Il complotto contro il merito* {The plot against merit}. Bari: Laterza.

Sapir, André. 2018. High public debt in euro area contries: Belgium and Italy. *Bruegel Policy Contribution*, no. 15, September. Available at https://www.bruegel.org/wp-content/uploads/2018/09/PC-15_20183.pdf.

Saraceno, Pasquale. 1980. *La questione meridionale nella ricostruzione post bellica, 1943–1950* {The southern question in post-war reconstruction}. Milan: Giuffrè.

Sartori, Giovanni. 2015. *La corsa verso il nulla* {Running towards nothing}. Milan: Mondadori.

Schivardi, Fabiano and Roberto Torrini. 2011. Cambiamenti strutturali e capitale umano nel sistema produttivo italiano {Structural changes and human capital in the Italian productive system}. *Bank of Italy. Occasional Papers*, no. 108, November.

Schizzerotto, Antonio. 2011. Social stratification. In *International Encyclopaedia of Political Science*, September, 8: 2443–2448. Los Angeles, CA: SAGE Publications.

Schizzerotto, Antonio and Ivano Bison. 1996. Mobilità occupazionale fra generazioni e mobilità di carriera {Occupational mobility across generations and career mobility}. In Giampaolo Galli (ed.) *La mobilità della società italiana* {Mobility of Italian society}. Rome: SIPI.

Scotti, Vincenzo and Sergio Zoppi. 2020. *Governare l'Italia. Da Cavour a De Gasperi a Conte oggi. A settant'anni dalla nascita della Cassa per il Mezzogiorno* {Governing Italy. From Cavour to De Gasperi and Conte. Seventy years after the start of Cassa del Mezzogiorno}. Rome: Eurlink.

Sestito, Paolo. 2002. *Il mercato del lavoro in Italia. Com'è. Come sta cambiando* {The labour market in Italy. How it is and how it is developing}. Bari: Laterza.

Sestito, Paolo, 2014. *La scuola imperfetta. Idee per spezzare un circolo vizioso* {The imperfect school. Ideas to break a vicious circle}. Bologna: Il Mulino.

Sestito, Paolo and Roberto Torrini. 2020. *Molto rumore per nulla: l'Italia, tra riforme abortite e ristagno economico* {Much ado about nothing: italy between unsuccessful reforms and economic stagnation}. Kindle Edition.

Sestito, Paolo and Eliana Viviano. 2018. Jobs Act: Reform in the context of the Italian labour market. *Economic Policy* 33(93): 101–130.

Signorini, L. Federico and Ignazio Visco. 1997. *L'Economia Italiana* {The Italian economy}. Bologna: il Mulino.

Silva, Francesco (ed.). 2012. *Storia dell'IRI* {History of IRI}. Bari: Laterza Editore.

Simoni, Marco. 2012. *Senza Alibi. Perché il capitalismo italiano non cresce più* {Without Alibi. Why Italian capitalism is no longer growing}. Venice: Marsilio.

Sinn, Hans-Werner, Christian Holzner, Wolfgang Meister, Wolfgang Ochel, and Martin Werding. 2006. *Redesigning the Welfare State*. Cheltenham: Edward Elgar Publishing.

Smith, Adam. 1776. *Inquiry into the Nature and Causes of the Wealth of Nations*. London: W. Strahan and T. Cadell.

Spaventa, Luigi. 2014. *Contro gli opposti pessimismi, per uscire dal declino e dalla crisi* {Against the opposite pessimisms, to escape decline and crisis}. Rome: Castelvecchi, Lit Edizioni.

Summers, Lawrence. 2020. Accepting the Reality of Secular Stagnation. March. *IMF, Finance and Development*. Available at www.imf.org/external/pubs/ft/fandd/2020/03/larry-summers-on-secular-stagnation.htm.

Svimez. 2021. *Rapporto annuale* {Annual report}. Bologna: Il Mulino.

Sylos Labini, Paolo. 2015 [1974]. *Saggio sulle classi sociali* {Essay on social classes} [new 2015 edn]. Bari: Laterza.

Tabellini, Guido. 2008. *L'Italia in Gabbia. Il volto politico della crisi economica* {Italy in the cage. The political face of the economic crisis}. Milan: EGEA Bocconi University Press.

Tanzi, Vito. 2007. *Argentina, an Economic Chronicle. How One of the Richest Countries in the World Lost Its Wealth*. Bethesda: MD: Jorge Pinto Books.

THE. 2021. *Times Higher Education World University Rankings*. Available at https://www.timeshighereducation.com/.

Toniolo, Gianni (ed.). 2013a. *L'Italia e l'economia mondiale dall'Unità a oggi* {Italy and the world economy from Unification to today}. Collana Storica della Banca d'Italia. Venice: Marsilio editore.

Toniolo, Gianni (ed.). 2013b. *Oxford Handbook of the Italian Economy since Unification*. Oxford: Oxford University Press.

Toniolo, Gianni. 2013c. An overview of Italy's economic growth. In Gianni Toniolo (ed.) *Oxford Handbook of the Italian Economy since Unification*, pp. 3–36. Oxford: Oxford University Press.

Toniolo, Gianni, and Vincenzo Visco (eds). 2004. *Il declino economico dell'Italia, cause e rimedi* {The economic decline of Italy, causes and remedies}. Milan: Mondadori.

Torrini, Roberto. 2005. Cross-country differences in self-employment rates: the role of institutions. *Labour Economics* 12: 661–68.

Transparency International. 2021. *Global Corruption Barometer: European Union 2021*. Available at https://www.transparency.org/en/publications/gcb-european-union-2021.

Traù, Fabrizio. 2000. *La questione dimensionale nell'industria italiana* {The dimensional issue in Italian industry}. Bologna: il Mulino.

Traù, Fabrizio. 2003. *Structural Macroeconomic Change and the Size Pattern of Manufacturing Firms*. Palgrave Macmillan.

Villari, Rosario. 1981. *Il Sud nella storia d'Italia* {The South in the history of Italy}. Bari: Laterza.

Visco, Ignazio. 2009. *Investire in conoscenza* {Investing in knowledge}. Bologna: il Mulino.

Visco, Ignazio. 2010. Speech at the Bank of Italy Conference on "Il Mezzogiorno e la politica economica dell'Italia" {The Mezzogiorno and the economic policy of Italy}. Bank of Italy, June.

Visco, Ignazio. 2015. *Perché i tempi stanno cambiando* {Why times are changing}. Bologna: il Mulino.

Visco, Ignazio. 2018. *Anni difficili. Dalla crisi finanziaria alle nuove sfide per l'economia* {Difficult years. From the financial crisis to the new challenges for the economy}. Bologna: il Mulino.

Visco, Vincenzo. 2017. *Colpevoli evasioni* {Guilty evasions}. Milan: Università Bocconi Editore.

Weil, N. David. 2012. *Economic Growth* (International edn). Boston, MA: Pearson, Addison-Wesley.

Williamson, E. Oliver. 2000. The new institutional economics: Taking stock, looking ahead. *Journal of Economic Literature* 38(3): 595–613.

WilmerHale Report. 2021. *Investigation Findings and Report to the Board of Executive Directors.* 15 September. Available at https://www.worldbank.org/en/news/statement/2021/09/16/world-bank-group-to-discontinue-doing-business-report.

Wolf, Martin. 2014. Reform alone is no solution for the eurozone. *The Financial Times.* 21 October.

Woolcock, Michael and Deepa Narayan. 2000. *Social Capital: Implications for Development Theory, Research, and Policy.* Washington, DC: World Bank Group.

Wooldridge, Adrian. 2021. *The Aristocracy of Talent.* London: Penguin Books.

World Bank. 2020. *Doing Business.* Available at https://openknowledge.worldbank.org/bitstream/handle/10986/32436/9781464814402.pdf.

World Intellectual Property Organization. 2020. *Global Innovation Index.* Available at www.globalinnovationindex.org/Home.

World Justice Project. 2021. Available at www.worldjusticeproject.org/.

Zamagni, Vera. 2018. *The Italian Economy.* Newcastle upon Tyne: Agenda Publishing.

Zarnowitz, Victor. 1992. *Business Cycles, Theory, History, Indicators, and Forecasting.* Chicago, IL: University of Chicago Press.

Zingales, Luigi. 2012. *Manifesto capitalista, Una rivoluzione liberale contro un'economia corrotta* {Original English Title: Capitalism for the people}. Milan: Rizzoli.

Index